TRANSPLANT

The Give and Take of
Tissue Transplantation

FRANCIS D. MOORE, M.D.

Moseley Professor of Surgery, Harvard Medical School
Surgeon-in-Chief, Peter Bent Brigham Hospital
Boston, Massachusetts

SIMON AND SCHUSTER | NEW YORK

6956
march '72

To
C.D.M. AND P.W.M.

A Note of Acknowledgment

The preparation of this book was but a minor task compared with the scientific effort of the research. My first indebtedness is therefore to those doctors at this hospital, and the surgeons of our staff, who have performed this work. Dr. Joseph E. Murray has been in charge of the major components of the surgical work in this field, in both research and clinical care, for the past fifteen years. Dr. John P. Merrill and Dr. J. Hartwell Harrison, taking responsibility for medical care and kidney-donor management, respectively, have made an unmeasurable contribution in guidance of broad policy and in the difficult details. To Dr. George W. Thorn, Hersey Professor and Physician-in-Chief, goes the gratitude of all of us concerned with this work because of his long interest in renal failure, his perfection of the artificial kidney which has made the care of these patients possible, and for his enthusiastic support of the transplant program. The work of Dr. John R. Brooks, Dr. Charles B. Carpenter, Jr., Dr. J. M. Corson, Dr. Nathan P. Couch, Dr. Warren Guild, Dr. Edward B. Hager, Dr. C. J. Hampers, Dr. Dwight E. Harken, Dr. David M. Hume, Dr. Donald D. Matson, Dr. Ben Miller, Dr. Alfred P. Morgan, Dr. Somers H. Sturgis, Dr. Carl W. Walter, and Dr. Richard E. Wilson is of far greater importance than one might judge from their occasional mention in the text.

In the past five years, Dr. Alan G. Birtch has taken over the study of liver transplantation and the production of antilymphocyte globulin in the Peter Bent Brigham Hospital. Dr. Charles B. Carpenter, Jr., has become the principal immunologist in our transplant group, and both of them have assisted us in composing the chapters dealing with modern immunology and liver transplantation in this edition.

Dr. Gustav J. Dammin, Friedmann Professor of Pathology and Pathologist-in-Chief, has provided the continuous microscopic control (by direct examination of transplanted tissues) that has been essential to success. The use of whole body irradiation for transplantation, as described in the text, was managed by Dr. James B. Dealy, Jr., then Radiologist-in-Chief at this hospital.

Dr. William Curran, Harvard's medicolegal expert, has provided guidance in the legal aspects of transplantation.

I would like to acknowledge the work of those many doctors from other hospitals and laboratories who have helped in the gathering of these data, supplying notes, letters, photographs, or anecdotes to round out the story. These include Dr. Charles A. Hufnagel, who has told his story of the first transplant; Dr. Joseph Ferrebee, who has described some of the work at Cooperstown; Dr. James Priestley, who helped us identify the important role of Dr. C. S. Williamson of the Mayo Clinic; Dr. Emile Holman, who has written us of his early work on skin grafting; Dr. Linder of Heidelberg and Dr. Fuchsig of Vienna, who helped us track down the first kidney transplanter—Dr. Ullmann; Dr. Michael Woodruff of Edinburgh, who has told his story of acquired tolerance in children; Dr. Danforth, who has written about those tolerant chickens; Dr. James V. Scola of Springfield, who has written of his unique operation; Dr. Jacques Poisson, who has written of the French experiences; and particularly Dr. Willem Kolff of Cleveland, who has helped us tell an accurate story of the early days of the artificial kidney in Nazi-occupied Holland. In this second edition we have included personal notes on many other topics. Dr. Paul Terasaki of the University of California at Los Angeles has written of his early work in tissue typing; Dr. Jean Hamburger of Paris of the early French experience; Dr. Norman Shumway of Stanford University, Dr. Denton Cooley of Baylor University, and Dr. Christiaan Barnard of the Groote Schur Hospital in Cape Town have all written interesting notes for this text, about their experiences in cardiac transplantation.

Sir Peter Medawar has provided several reminiscences of his early work. It is sad to record his recent illness, but a pleasure to attest to his recovery and his attention to the details as noted in a recent letter: "I am progressing, as you surmise, though naturally not as fast as I should like. The healing of nerve as also of bone are an absolute disgrace and really require more intensive study than they have received so far. . . ."

Next I should like to thank those who have helped me with the literary task. Mr. David McCord, poet, historian, and Brigham Trustee, has read much of the text and helped me tighten up my use of the language as well as proposing the original title, *Give and Take*. Dr. Merrill, Dr. Thorn, Dr. Murray, Dr. Harrison, Dr. Birtch, Dr. Dammin, Dr. Wilson, and Dr. Carpenter have reviewed much of the text. Dr. Albert H. Coons has given us an interesting account of the development of immunofluorescence. Miss Mildred Codding has drawn several illustrations, later joined in this work by Miss Tehrie Holden. Miss Joan Voorhees and Miss Margaret Ball have supervised many of the laboratory studies undertaken in this field. Miss Doris Lewis and Mrs. Donald Height have contributed their administrative and editorial skills to the text.

I should like also to acknowledge my debt to Mr. F. S. Deland, Jr., counsel for the Walnut Medical Charitable Trust which is devoted to assisting young people in the study of science and assisting scientists to disseminate their findings to the public. Any earnings arising from this book will be devoted to the work of this Trust. Many have asked how they might contribute. Contributions may be addressed to the Walnut Medical Charitable Trust, c/o F. S. Deland, Jr., 225 Franklin Street, Boston, Massachusetts. Such contributions are deductible from income for purposes of federal tax.

The major support of this research has come from many different agencies over the past twenty years. Particularly I should like to mention the endowment funds of Harvard University and the Peter Bent Brigham Hospital. The Avalon Foundation, the John A. Hartford Foundation, and several federal agencies have consistently helped and supported us through research grants and contracts. Notable amongst these are the Atomic Energy Commission, the United States Army, and the National Institutes of Health.

Finally, I should like to express my gratitude to my family, who have been so patient throughout this effort and of so much assistance in details. Mrs. Moore has edited the entire text; Mr. Peter B. Moore, Mrs. Sarah Moore Warren, and Mr. Francis D. Moore, Jr., have reviewed the text from the point of view of the molecular biologist, the college student in the liberal arts, and the premedical undergraduate, respectively. If the book is interesting to young people not personally concerned with medical research, we can thank these younger colleagues on the project.

Contents

List of Illustrations

For certain of the figures, permission for publication was kindly given by authors and publishers as follows:

Figure   2   Dr. Burnet and Vanderbilt University Press
        3   Dr. Danforth and the Journal of Experimental Zoology
        4   Dr. Billingham and the publishers of Nature
        6   Editor, Journal of Experimental Medicine
        7   Dr. Simonsen and Munksgaard, A.S.
        8   Dr. Kolff and J. & A. Churchill
        9   Dealy, 1960
    10, 11   Schwartz, Eisner, and Dameshek and Journal of Clinical Investigation
       12   Dr. Calne and the editor of Lancet
       14   Putnam, Science
       15   Green, N. M., "Electron Microscopy of the Immunoglobulins," and Academic Press
       17   Humphrey and Dourmashkin, "The Lesions in Cell Membranes Caused by Complement," Academic Press, 1969
18, 19, 20   Dr. Gustav J. Dammin, Dr. Edward S. Reynolds, Dr. Eleanora G. Galvanek
       21   Juul-Jensen, "Criteria of Brain Death," Aardus, Denmark, Munksgaard, 1970

Preface

My argument, therefore, runs as follows: we need a wide-spread understanding of science in this country, for only thus can science be assimilated into our secular cultural pattern. When that has been achieved, we shall be one step nearer the goal which we now desire so earnestly: a unified, coherent culture suitable for our American democracy in this new age of machines and experts.

—CONANT, J. B., "On Understanding Science;
An Historical Approach."
THE TERRY LECTURES, YALE UNIVERSITY.

In 1963 I gathered together a story of the origins of transplantation under the title of *Give and Take*. I wanted to record this bit of contemporary scientific history while it was still fresh and growing. The book was written especially for students of the history of science, for patients who might be considering a transplant, for persons closely concerned with transplantation for professional reasons, or for an interested public.

In the eight years since that time, the world of transplantation has been explored, exploited, and populated by thousands of patients. The public, the press, and students especially interested in science have seen organ grafting move from a rare curiosity to the center of the medical stage. Transplantation of the heart exposed for a larger public many matters formerly discussed only among physicians. Other topics have grown in importance, such as the ethics of therapeutic innovation (applying new and unknown procedures to sick people), tissue matching and histocompatibility testing, the definition of brain death, the uniform anatomical gift acts, the acceptability of life with a transplant (as contrasted with home dialysis).

21

Each of these has become a special study in itself. Transplantations of the liver, pancreas, and lung have now been sufficiently attempted in man so that preliminary judgments can be made about the promise and the problems of each. Clearly the record needs updating.

Through all this has been woven the thread of clinical medicine and surgery, the compassionate care of critically ill patients—both rich and poor. This is never obvious to the onlooker who sees only glittering hard science in the stainless steel framework of the complicated modern hospital with its intensive care wards, dialysis units, and complex machinery. But the patient is an individual, suffering from severe disease, and it is to his merciful treatment that the entire effort is devoted.

This effort is costly; the economics of transplantation, one of the most expensive forms of clinical* care ever made available to the sick, now are in need of some discussion. Dividends of well-being for individual patients are the only justification for the investment of social resources in the care of human illness. Are these dividends coming in?

For many who learned of this field by the publicity resulting from cardiac grafts, heart transplants are the only transplant operation. After the initial excitement, public response to these operations has been negative and critical. If heart grafting can be faulted, it is on the score of "too much and too soon." The operation was often undertaken by doctors not sufficiently familiar with the intricacies of transplant immunology and surgical transplantation. Perhaps this was unavoidable, as specialized cardiac surgical techniques were complex yet essential to success. The years of cardiac transplantation coincided exactly with the development of antilymphocyte sera and histocompatibility testing, and our evaluation must be made against this broader background of change in transplant science.

During the past eight years the success and scope of kidney transplantation have increased immensely. It is now an operation carried out in virtually every country of the world. This wide application has brought in its wake some new problems unforeseen in 1963. The immunologic aspects of cancer, for example, have come into sharp focus through the development of tumors in patients immunosuppressed for kidney transplantation. At the same time the increased selectivity of donor procurement based on

---

* *Clinical,* from the Greek *klinikos,* literally "to recline as in a bed." This word has many meanings, all relating to the practical application of knowledge to human patients. By evolution of its meaning, the word "clinic" has come to mean any kind of institution in which patients are taken care of, whether in bed or walking about; the term "clinical" might also be paraphrased as "practical, of practical utility."

tissue grouping has rendered an acceptable match much less likely for any random donor-recipient pair. We realize now that a national tissue procurement program is needed, and there is increased urgency for methods of organ storage.

In 1963 this book could have been the story of scientific adventures in one or two laboratories, and clinical trials in only a very few hospitals. The study of transplantation as commenced in this department of Harvard Medical School twenty years ago reflected much of the story of tissue transplantation until about 1962. Of course, we were not alone in this work; we have tried to give full credit to all the other scientists, physicians, surgeons, laboratories, and hospitals concerned with the development of tissue transplantation; we apologize for any inadvertent omissions.

Now, in addition to the few departments active in the United States prior to 1963, there are at least seventy-five major departments of medicine, surgery, and immunology working full time on tissue transplantation. They are closely knit by a communications network consisting not only of the scientific journals but of personal friendships, travel, visits, and innumerable scientific meetings. Important new series of successful kidney transplantations have been reported from Australia, New Zealand, central and eastern Europe, South America, and South Africa.

The stimulus to prepare this new record of transplant history came from many sources, not the least of which was the reception accorded the 1963 *Give and Take*. It was evidently read and enjoyed by many patients and their families and by students who enjoyed learning how modern science really grows, undistorted by Hollywood spectaculars, television scenarios, or bitter controversy. The book was also used by journalists and legislators who need a conscientious document of the dates, names, places, and events in transplant history. In this new 1971 version, we have updated *Give and Take* for the same wide audience, filling in the appropriate background for a branch of human learning that must continue to command liberal public support. The first seven chapters are updated but otherwise hardly altered; the last half of the book is new.

FRANCIS D. MOORE, M.D.

Brookline, Massachusetts
June, 1971

TRANSPLANT

The Give and Take of
Tissue Transplantation

1

GRAFTS THAT LIVE AND BREATHE

The Central Problem

I will praise thee; for I am fearfully and wonderfully made.
—PSALMS 139

ORGANIZED LABOR; CELLS OF THE ORGANISM

A cell is an energy-converting power plant that burns fuel—sugar or fat absorbed from the diet—to do work. Cellular work may exert its force in muscular contraction, as in the pumping of the heart, or it may expend its energy in manufacturing, as the adrenal gland converts cholesterol into steroid hormones.* The work of cells may also be in the transmission of special impulses, as in the brain and spinal cord; cells may be involved in making digestive juices, as in the pancreas, or in absorbing foodstuffs, as in the intestine, or in altering these food-stuffs to make compounds useful to other tissues, work done in the liver.

In contrast to such variety in productive enterprise, the exhaust systems of most body cells are much the same. Each cell discharges

---

* *Hormone,* from the Greek, "to excite"; hormones are chemical messengers which excite a response in other tissues.

waste products into the rivers of body fluid that finally empty outward via the liver and the kidney. All cells also give out carbon dioxide for exhaust via the lungs. This is the end product of burning fuel—the oxidation of sugar. Other specialized by-products of cellular metabolism* are exhausted into the body fluids for excretion. Urea, for example, is a compound made in body cells to take care of waste nitrogen. It is excreted in the urine. Some of the other chemical by-products are toxic or poisonous, and are managed by the liver, which chops them up into smaller pieces for discard in the urine, or excretes them in larger molecular fragments through the bile.

Although each cell of the body is a complete factory in itself, detailed organization of cells in the organs of the body is highly variable. These details make a lot of difference in transplantation operations. In some organs and tissues there are sheets of cells, each one essentially the same, and all working from the same blood supply with little evidence of organization among them. In other organs, although each cell is a complete unit in itself, the cells are arranged in special anatomical alignments and in tiny local structures that have great significance. There is a sensible order of supply and production. The arrangement of the cells in the kidney, for example, is very precise. The many different kinds of cells in the renal tubule† are arranged to perform their functions in sequence like an assembly line, using energy to process the fluid of the urine as it comes down the tubule and before it leaves the body. These cells allow some wastes to pass out into the urine. They recall other substances that are needed and should not be lost. The renal tubular cells are thus a very efficient system for the reclamation of waste.

The differences among cellular arrangements become important in considering the tissues whose blood vessels must be joined together directly to do a transplant operation—in contrast with tissues that can be divided into small bits or pieces and transplanted freely without

---

* *Metabolism*, literally "changing"; the chemical activity of body cells in changing the nature of compounds they burn or process, for example, changing cholesterol in food into a highly special steroid hormone to stimulate other cells of the body.

† *Renal*, pertaining to the "ren" or kidney. *Tubule*, a tiny tube conducting fluid filtered from the blood and to be processed into urine.

joining the blood vessels. Organs with special orders of supply and internal organizations of cellular arrangements (such as kidney or liver) require the major blood vessels intact for successful transplantation. Tissues that have their cells in even sheets (such as parathyroid or adrenal) are those that can be transplanted without their blood vessels. In either event, it is the transplantation of *working* cells, using oxygen, that is important. These cellular organs, after transplantation, must go ahead with their work no matter how they are transplanted. They are grafts that "live and breathe," using oxygen in tissue respiration and obtaining useful energy from body fuels for cellular work.

The Size of Things

The extremely small size of most cells, and of everything in them, must be appreciated at the outset. The letter "o," as printed here, has a hole that is approximately 1 millimeter in diameter. (This is abbreviated as 1 mm and is one tenth of a centimeter, or 1 mm=0.1 cm.)

For most doctors accustomed to looking at things through the microscope, a common reference for size is the width of the human red blood cell. This is readily recognizable because it is shaped like a coin or discus, and it is 7 microns across. One micron (1.0μ) is $1/1000$ of a millimeter, or $1 \mu = 0.001$ mm. If a line of these red blood cells were arranged side by side, like coins in a collection, or a row of checkers awaiting play on a checkerboard, there would be room for about 150 of them across this round hole of the letter "o."

Body cells are about the same size as the red blood cell, though some are somewhat larger. The functioning cells of the liver and kidney are 10 to 25 micra across. Some of the white cells in the blood, such as the small lymphocytes* that actively reject transplants, are slightly smaller, approximately 3.5 micra in diameter. About 100 to 200 body cells of these various types would fit side by side in the middle of the printed letter "o."

---

* *Lymphocytes,* the suffix "cyte" (from the Greek *kytos* or "hollow vessel") means "cell." A lymphocyte is, therefore, a cell from the lymphatic system. These are cells concerned with antibodies and rejection of grafts, as will later become clear. The same suffix is used to denote white cells or "leukocytes," red cells or "erythrocytes," and other cells both in the blood and in organs.

With the aid of the electron microscope, cell structures are visible at huge magnification. There is room in one lens-view for only a portion of the cell's edge and what is inside it, including the nucleus—the control center—and the chromosomes,* which contain nucleic acids that control the genetic† qualities of the offspring. At a magnification of 100,000 times, the electron microscopist can identify certain small strands as molecules of deoxyribonucleic acid, or DNA, the genetic material of the cell that carries the message determining the hereditary nature of the offspring. These molecules are quite long (as long as 3 micra and longer), but they are very narrow, about 20 Ångstroms wide. An Ångstrom is a unit for measuring very small distances; there are 10,000 Ångstroms in a micron, or $1 \text{ Å} = 0.0001 \mu$. Thus, the hole of the printed letter "o" is 10,000,000 Ångstroms wide; in this hole there would be room, side by side, for 500,000 molecules of DNA.

Weights and concentrations are equally small, as applied to the chemical reactions and drugs that act within the cellular factories and interfere with their production lines. For example, actinomycin, a drug that interferes with the action of DNA, is used at a dose of approximately 0.16 milligram (abbreviated as mg) for a full-sized adult person. If this drug were distributed evenly throughout all the water in the human body, there would then be 0.16 mg in 40 liters (about 10 gallons) of water, or a concentration of about 0.004 mg per liter. This concentration would be equivalent to taking the tiniest grain of salt that one can see with the naked eye, dividing it into a hundred pieces, and diluting one of these fragments in a quart of water.

Small as these cells are, together they form a large group, the "body cell mass" of the body. The total mass, which includes many billions of cells of all different types, shapes, and sizes, weighs about 55 pounds in an adult person.‡ The structures with which we are

---

* *Chromosome,* literally "colored segment"; darkly stained material in the nucleus that doubles when the cell divides and carries with it the nucleic acids which control the genetic properties of the offspring.

† *Genetic,* literally "pertaining to the genes"; the genes are portions of those nucleic acids that determine the form of the offspring. The word "genetic" has therefore come to refer to the property of transmission of parental characteristics to offspring.

‡ The rest of the body consists of the *connective tissues,* the *skeleton,* and *body fluids* outside of cells.

concerned in this book, such as kidney, liver, spleen, adrenal, and pituitary, are each composed of a large number of cells which make up the cellular tissues that breathe by using oxygen and convert foodstuff-energy into work or new chemicals. Grafts of these tissues require highly specific conditions in order to live and breathe, and do their work. They cannot tolerate extremism, and if they die, are not readily replaced. They are in sharp contrast to those grafts that can do their work as inert supporting structures.

ENGINE AND CHASSIS

Supporting the cellular tissues are the extracellular substances of the body, the tissues that lie *between* the cells. These are the structural components and the rivers of body fluid. They support the cells and move the products around, bringing in supplies and taking out wastes. They are epitomized by solids such as bones and by fluids such as blood plasma,* but also include the walls of arteries and veins, and the cornea, or glassy front of the eye, as well as tendons and fascia.† These structural components are much more easily grafted than the cells that live and breathe. The structural parts can be grafted between individuals without the use of special protective measures. These structures do not require cellular life in order to function, even though active living cells have made the structural components to begin with. Some kind of factory must make the concrete with which a road is built, but after the road has been laid the factory can go out of business, and the road still remains useful; the extracellular substances do not require continuing energy from food or fuel in order to function.

Bone grafts achieve their purpose of supporting the body and even inducing the formation of new bone after the bone graft itself is dead. Human artery grafts can be successfully transplanted between individuals without showing any signs of life whatsoever in the grafted tissue. These structural grafts can be taken from the human body some hours after death, in contrast to the few precious minutes tolerated in removing a cellular organ from the body for transplantation. And they

---

* *Plasma,* the fluid portion of blood in which the red blood cells are floating.
† *Fascia,* literally "bands"; the fibrous bands that hold the muscles together.

do not require the delicate control of temperature, oxygen tension, carbon dioxide removal, and acid-base balance necessary for the organ grafts that live and breathe. Indeed, arteries can be used for grafting after sterilization by exposure to an electron beam that would kill all the cells in a kidney or liver graft.

There is one other type of graft to be mentioned, which may become important. This is the graft taken from a living being of one species, such as a cat, and put into another, such as a dog. These grafts between species arouse an intense rejection response. Usually they have been studied as grafts between unrelated species. The picture may be a little different if they are a closely related species, such as a coyote to a wolf, a chicken to a turkey, or between primates. Primates are the order of species that include man, the anthropoid apes, and monkeys.

Finally, there are grafts taken from one place on the body and fastened somewhere else on the same patient—such as grafts of skin taken from the leg to cover a burn on the arm. Such grafts are easy to do and tell us a lot about the grafting process because they take well and make such a contrast to grafts between individuals.

Transplant Definitions

The prefix "homo" comes from the Greek *homos*, which means "one and the same," not to be confused with the word "homo" found in the species *Homo sapiens*, in which "homo" means "man." Thus, a "homotransplant" is a transplant between two individuals of one and the same species, regardless of whether or not they are men.

It was from the definition of the prefix "homo" that the term "homograft" or "homotransplant" developed, meaning a transplantation from another individual of the same species. This term has now, however, been superseded by the term "allograft" or "allotransplant," or more strictly "allogeneic transplant," "allo" deriving from the Greek prefix *allos*, or "other," indicating a graft from another person (of the same species). This is implied in the term "allogeneic," which means another animal of another genetic background, but from the same species. "Allograft" and "homograft" are synonymous.

The definitions are as follows:

Allografts or allotransplants (synonyms: allogeneic grafts, allo-transplants, homografts, homotransplants, homologous transplants) are transplantations between two individuals of the same species, the typical transplantation of an organ or tissue from man to man or between two of the same kind of animals such as two dogs or two mice. The great bulk of transplantation research has been devoted to the perfection of allografts. The word "allograft" or "allotransplanta-tion" will be used throughout this book except where the older term, "homotransplant" or "homograft," has been used in a letter or a comment that we quote directly.

Isografts (synonym: isogeneic grafts) are grafts between identical twins or grafts between animals so highly inbred that their genetic material is virtually identical, and they are referred to as highly inbred strains.

Autografts (synonym: autotransplants) are grafts consisting of tissue moved about within the same animal or within the same patient —as, for example, a skin graft taken from the thigh and placed on a burn. Another example is an experimental skin graft moved around from place to place on one animal to contrast its behavior with an allograft placed on that animal from another animal donor.

Xenografts (synonyms: xenotransplants, heterografts, hetero-transplants) are grafts between two animals of different species—a rat to a mouse, or baboon to man. These grafts have been tried experi-mentally over many years, and now have been attempted clinically in a few cases.

HOOKING UP TO THE POWER SUPPLY

Some allografts of organs or tissues can be divided into small bits or pieces and placed loosely in the new host, in a "bed" in which blood vessels are abundant. These cells then proceed to pick up their power source locally, as a new blood supply. They do not require a compli-cated anatomical organization. Small grafts of pituitary gland, adrenal gland, parathyroid gland, and thyroid gland have been done in this way.

In sharp contrast are those whole organs in which the cells have to be arranged in a special order; one cannot simply chop them up and distribute them around. These are the grafts of whole organs which require the joining of blood vessels for their function, such as kidney and liver.

When an artery, or a vein, is joined directly to another, its joining is called an "anastomosis" (Fig. 1).* Anastomotic connections of arteries and veins, as well as other channels in the body—such as the ureter (the tube draining from the kidney), or the bile ducts (the small ducts draining bile from the liver)—are necessary for the allografting of whole organs.

As one watches a surgeon joining two blood vessels end-to-end, using very fine thread and making a very accurate suture, the method seems quite evident and obvious. For many years the joining of blood vessels seemed to be an impossible surgical mystery. Then, around the turn of the century, following the leadership of Dr. Alexis Carrel, surgeons learned to do this in a very simple way, with a needle and thread. The artery is held with a special clamp to keep the blood from leaking out, and three guide sutures are put in place. Using special small needles and thread, the two vessels are then anastomosed, by suturing them end-to-end.

The essence of this procedure is minute accuracy and delicate care in the use of the instruments and the needles. It is really very simple, as Dr. Carrel said in his original description, which for the first time showed the surgical world how to do this:

La méthode, que je vais décrire, est très simple. Elle convient également aux artères et aux veines, aux vaisseaux de gros ou de petit calibre. Elle respecte l'intégrité de la tunique endothéliale. L'anastomose présente une étanchéité absolue, et ne provoque aucune diminution du calibre du vaisseau. Elle permet de réaliser aussi facilement une réunion termino-latérale, qu'une réunion termino-terminale. Son exécution est facile.

Aucune des méthodes actuellement employées, ne présente tous ces avantages. Cette supériorité est due à l'emploi *d'aiguilles extrêmement*

---

* *Anastomosis*, literally "joining mouth to mouth," from the Greek *ana*, which means "to," and *stoma*, which means "mouth"; usually used to mean the joining of two round hollow structures such as arteries or veins.

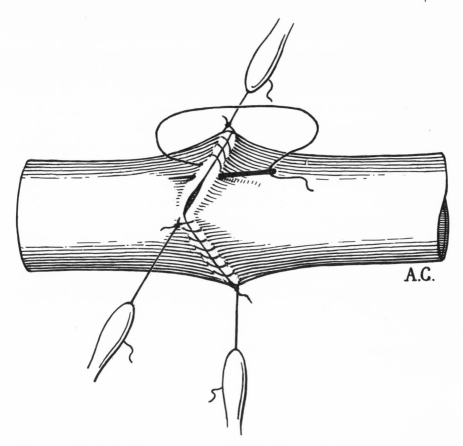

FIGURE 1.   Joining blood vessels by suture-anastomosis. Adapted from the line drawing by Alexis Carrel published in *Lyon Medical* in 1902. The walls of the two blood vessels (here drawn as about 5 mm in diameter) are held together by three holding sutures. Another is then used to sew over-and-over, using very fine needles ("aiguilles extrêmement fines"). This method of suture anastomosis, demonstrated initially by Carrel, is still used throughout surgery, particularly in the transplantation of organs.

fines, et à une manœuvre qui permet la *dilatation du vaisseau* au moment de la suture et prévient le rétrécissement.*

---

* Carrel advised using "very thin thread of linen used in making the laces of Valenciennes."

Note that Dr. Carrel, almost seventy years ago, emphasized that the needles (*aiguilles*) must be extremely fine and delicate. At the present time it is possible to purchase very perfect tiny sutures made of plastic or silk, with the needles joined directly to the end of the thread so that there is not even a rough place where the thread joins the needle. Several companies make these highly specialized little sutures, which have been such a boon to surgery in general and to transplantation in particular. For very tiny blood vessels, it is possible to do the whole anastomosis under a microscope. Blood vessels as small as 1 mm in diameter (a little smaller than a pencil lead) can be sutured under direct vision. The renal artery in man is a large vessel, 7 to 10 mm in diameter.

About 1950, the Institute for Surgical Instruments in Moscow developed a suturing machine which depended upon the introduction of tiny staples of microscopic size into the walls of the blood vessels. This ingenious instrument has now been used in many laboratories and hospitals. It has certain advantages over the suturing method of Dr. Carrel, but it is a rather bulky piece of machinery to introduce into a small operative incision. One often hears the careless statement that "using this new suture machine, anastomoses of blood vessels can be done in a few seconds that ordinarily would take 20 minutes." This statement neglects the fact that it takes many minutes to prepare the vessels to fit over the metal cuffs of the machine. It is true that once all this work is done, then indeed the crushing together of the staples takes but a moment. At the present time the easiest and quickest way to join blood vessels deep in a surgical incision is by the simplest kind of end-to-end suture by hand, essentially the way Dr. Carrel did it.

TURNING ON THE POWER

After the surgeon has completed the vascular* anastomoses of artery and vein, and whatever other structures or ducts are necessary to transplant an organ, he removes the protecting clamps and lets the blood course through the organ. But even this is not enough, for this

---

* *Vascular*, pertaining to the blood vessels. A vascular anastomosis is the joining together of blood vessels.

blood must be as close to normal as possible. The blood must be perfect in its composition because the cells of the transplanted organ are
highly fastidious, requiring a special kind of fluid environment to live
and breathe and work.

First and foremost, cells require very large amounts of oxygen in
the blood. The oxygen is carried in the bright red hemoglobin* pigment of the red blood cells, and there must be plenty of these, well
ventilated as they pass through healthy lungs. Similarly, the exhaust
products, many of which are highly acid, must be removed briskly so
that the normal mild alkalinity of the blood is maintained. The acid-
base normality of arterial blood at a pH† of 7.42 cannot stray far from
the mark if the graft is to start work in its new site. The total solute
strength of the blood (the number of molecules in solution), and of
the surrounding extracellular fluids, must be close to its normal value.
The concentration of sugar must be just right, so that the cells will
have fuel to burn. All of these delicate biological balances, and many
others, must be maintained within narrow limits of tolerance if the
organ is to survive.

Often the graft's own function is part of the normalizing procedure. This is true, for example, both in the kidney and liver, which will
not start work unless bathed in normal body fluids; but their own
continued function is in turn required to maintain the normality of
those same body fluids.

The patient's other vital organs, which supply nourishment, hormones, blood flow, and riddance of waste, must all be functioning
properly if the transplanted organ is to recommence its activities as
soon as possible.

Finally, the whole operation must be conducted without the
probability of eventual bacterial infection. Freedom from bacterial
contamination, known as asepsis,‡ must be carefully guarded in any
operation—especially in transplantation whereby the same treatment
that lets the new host accept the graft also makes him vulnerable to

---

* *Hemoglobin,* the globin (protein) of blood (hemo-); the red pigment found in the red
blood cells which contains iron and carries oxygen.

† *pH,* a measure of the acidity or hydrogen ion concentration. Normal human arterial
blood has a pH of 7.42.

‡ *Asepsis,* without sepsis (infection).

bacterial infection. Transplantation is frequently an operation that involves two patients—the donor and the recipient. Hazards of surgical infection are doubled. There may be as many as fifteen or twenty doctors and nurses concerned with such a complicated operation. The achievement and maintenance of an adequately sterile environment is difficult, yet without it the success of the operation is threatened.

With the blood vessels joined, the power supply led into the organ, the blood and body fluids normal, and with no bacteria present, one might confidently hope that a new allograft would function effectively.

And Then . . . Wreckage

Unfortunately, such polite acceptance of the new allograft from one unrelated person to another has rarely been achieved, never without special treatment, and never at all until the spring of 1962.

Instead, as the pink and living organ rests in its new place, destruction gradually occurs. At first, things go very well. Blood flow is good; cellular function begins, and the outlook is deceptively optimistic. In a day or two function begins to wane slightly, and the graft begins to swell. Within a week one can see under the microscope that the cellular factories are surrounded by millions of invading lymphocytes that appear to be destructive to the cells. The cells swell, and then lose their normal structure, and finally die. This invading army surrounds, engulfs, and overruns the beautifully organized cellular tissues which have been transplanted. The patient now begins to run a fever, and shows a markedly elevated count of white cells in the blood, as if he were fighting off some infection such as appendicitis, even though in this instance no bacteria are involved.

In a few more days, cellular function in the graft ceases altogether. Even though the blood supply is maintained and the organ still shows some semblances of life, its normal function has been completely destroyed. If left in place, the rejected graft shrinks to a useless lump or scar if life can continue without it. A bit of skin, an endocrine gland, or even a kidney can shrivel up rather harmlessly before it is removed. Because the heart and the liver are unpaired organs for which no satisfactory machine substitute is yet available, and without whose function life cannot go on, the rejection process kills the host before tissue destruction becomes final.

This wreckage is a process known as "rejection," by which the body throws off an allograft. The avoidance of rejection is the story of tissue transplantation.

A First Attempt in Man

With the end of World War II, the disruption of peacetime laboratories and medical research was ended. Certain surgical advances were now firmly established, some of them hastened by the war itself. This was particularly true of vascular surgery, the repair of injured blood vessels, and the use of whole blood transfusions in very large volume, as well as the use of antibiotics to combat infection. In addition, the events of World War II had led to the description, for the first time, of a particular type of acute renal failure known as "acute tubular necrosis."* This disease, first described by Dr. Bywaters in England, was called the "crush syndrome" and was seen in patients who had been buried for a time under falling masonry in the London blitz. When the patients were dug out of the rubble, they developed shock† and failure of kidney function. Patients of this type were now recognized because they could be kept alive by blood transfusions long enough to display this difficulty with their kidneys. Previously, in former wars or accidents, they died from the shock of the original crushing injury itself.

In the late 1940's, it occurred to many people that the transplantation of tissues deserved renewed and energetic investigation. Even at the start of this era there were many patients (as there were to be many others later) whose urgent plight placed doctors under severe and unrelenting pressure to move ahead and attempt transplantation, however prematurely. An early experience with kidney transplantation in the treatment of acute tubular necrosis, now seemingly an event of ancient history, serves therefore to end this first chapter.

---

* *Acute renal failure,* the cessation, in a short time, of the output of urine from the kidneys; the word *necrosis* literally means "the death of tissue"; *acute tubular necrosis* is, therefore, the acute death of tubular tissue cells in the kidney.

† *Shock,* low blood pressure and flow, often leading to death, seen after severe injury and blood loss.

The surgeon here was Dr. Hufnagel, later to become Professor of Surgery at Georgetown University in Washington. At that time he was one of the surgeons at the Brigham Hospital, working on new heart valves and new ways of operating on diseased blood vessels.

The case was that of a young woman, who, while pregnant, had developed an infection in the uterus followed by severe shock. She then developed anuria,* most likely a special form of acute tubular necrosis, but it was not clear whether this acute tubular necrosis was due to the shock resulting from the infection in her uterus, or due to a transfusion which the patient had been given and which might have been outdated or incompatible blood.

She became severely ill, and after about ten days without making any urine, she went into a deep coma. Death seemed imminent. Dr. Thorn asked Dr. Hufnagel if he would try grafting on a kidney. Let Dr. Hufnagel tell the story:

. . . When I was the Cabot Fellow in 1947 (working in the Surgical Research labs at Harvard) I spent considerable time working with transplantation of the kidney and had also developed a technique for rapid freezing of blood vessels. I had a considerable group of animals with transplantations of the kidney, and at the same time we were working with adrenal transplantation. From time to time, we had been on the lookout for a patient in whom a kidney transplant might be needed, as an urgent and desperate measure to save her life.

In this case everyone was quite sure that the patient was not going to open up with urine output, and she was almost dead. Dr. Ernest Landsteiner was the Urologic Resident at the time. After a series of consultations it was finally agreed that the patient should have a transplant from a cadaver to see if she could be tided over this problem long enough to get well.

Accordingly we solicited the help of Dr. David Hume who went hunting for a prospective donor. We were fortunate in being able to obtain a cadaver kidney later that same day. The kidney was removed under aseptic conditions and taken immediately to the patient.

Because the patient's condition appeared extremely critical, there was some administrative objection to bringing the patient to the operating room. In the dark of the night—about midnight—when the kidney had been obtained immediately after the death of the donor, our little group (Land-

---

* *Anuria*, without urine.

steiner, Hume, and myself) proceeded to one of the end rooms on the second floor, and by the light of two small gooseneck student lamps prepared to do the transplant.

The brachial artery and a large vein in the antecubital fossa* were isolated. The anastomosis was accomplished very rapidly in spite of the unusual conditions in which we were working. The kidney itself with a short segment of the remaining ureter was wrapped in sterile sponges and covered with sterile rubber sheeting, leaving only the tip of the ureter exposed. An attempt to bury the kidney beneath the skin was made, but because of the position of the vessels, a considerable part of the kidney was still uncovered. The entire area was kept warm with the use of the same gooseneck lamps. Immediately the kidney began to secrete urine.

Needless to say, we hovered closely about for a considerable number of hours. As usual, however, at the Brigham in those days, as the light of morning dawned, our duties called us to more routine and mundane things. The kidney continued to excrete urine, and by noon of the next day, the patient herself began to show marked improvement. She began to become more alert and by the following day was entirely clear in her mind. The day after the transplant the ureter began to show signs of swelling, and a portion of it was removed to allow for better drainage of the urine. By the following day the kidney was showing evidence of decreasing output, and because of the great improvement in the patient, it was elected to remove it. I am not quite sure as to the exact time sequence, but two or three days after the removal of the kidney, the patient began to enter a diuretic phase† and her subsequent recovery was relatively uneventful.

It was only shortly after this that the enthusiasm for plastic materials and the knowledge of the surface properties of plastics made possible the development of a more efficient artificial kidney so that the use of short-term transplants was not pursued with any vigor, even though we continued to try to solve the problem of the long-term homotransplantation. In those days it was very difficult to engender any clinical enthusiasm for transplantation because the opposition to trials in this direction was very great. It certainly is much easier today. . . .

The three young surgeons involved in the case were Dr. Landsteiner, the urologist, Dr. Hufnagel, the vascular surgeon, and Dr. Hume, just commencing his research interest in the transplant field. This same combination of three skills was to remain the surgical triad

---

* *Brachial artery,* the artery of the arm near the elbow; *antecubital fossa,* the area in front of the elbow.

† *Diuretic phase,* phase of making more urine (diuresis).

in the transplant problem for many years to come. Two of these young men were to continue, very much concerned with surgical research, while the third was to become one of the leading urologists of New England. One of the three, Dr. Hume, was to devote most of his professional career to the problem of tissue transplantation. He began the first major series of human kidney allotransplantations within a few years and later, as Professor of Surgery at the Medical College of Virginia in Richmond, became director of one of the most active and productive transplant units in the world.

2

INDIVIDUALITY
AROUSES ANTAGONISM

The Hostile Host

. . . Skin for skin, yea, all that a man hath, will he give for his life.

—JOB 2:4

DR. HOLMAN AND SOME BITS OF SKIN

Many early experiments in grafting tissue from one animal to another demonstrated the fact, now so familiar, that one living being will not accept cellular tissue from another, as an allograft, without a battle. The new host is a hostile one; he regards the strange tissue as foreign. Although rejection had often been seen in the laboratory, there were many unanswered questions: What is the nature of this rejection process? Is it something new and different in all biology, or is it simply a new aspect of a familiar biologic reaction? Is this rejection process subject to scientific analysis and biologic understanding?

A few early experimenters failed entirely to discern the hostility of the individual toward grafted tissue, and for many years (even as recently as the middle 1920's) some doctors still thought that skin could be traded freely from one person to another. Others saw the rejection process but regarded it as strange and mystical, having nothing to do with any other, more familiar, phenomenon in the animal world.

Many scientists discerned that the rejection process was not unique. This chapter and the next will be concerned with those evidences showing that the rejection of grafted tissue is neither unique nor mystical, but indeed is a familiar process—the process of immunity.* This discovery has played the most essential role in our learning how to overcome rejection and make transplantation possible.

Among the early experiments was one carried out by Dr. Holman, later to become Professor of Surgery at the Stanford University Medical School in California. He did these experiments in 1923 and 1924 when he was a young surgical resident, working first under Dr. Halsted and then at the Brigham under Dr. Cushing. He had just arrived in Boston, having completed his studies at the Johns Hopkins Medical School in Baltimore. Among other things he did there (which he was anxious now to report) were some studies on skin grafting. His clear and simple observations demonstrated not only the uniqueness of the individual, but also the phenomenon of increased immunity to a second grafting which was later to be named by Professor Medawar the "second set phenomenon." The study of this, in detail, was to lay the foundation for our present knowledge of transplantation immunity.

Dr. Holman's original observations were based on the study of a five-year-old child. They were remarkable findings because they carried such a simple message, still important almost fifty years later. The child's leg had been badly mangled, and when the raw surfaces were ready for skin grafting, Dr. Holman considered grafting some skin from the child's mother. The mother's blood was crossmatched with that of the child, and they were found to be of compatible groups. Therefore, according to Dr. Holman,

. . . 151 small deep pinch grafts† were removed from the mother's thigh and applied to the inner and anterior granulating surface of the denuded leg.

---

* *Immunity,* the power to resist infection or invasion of bacteria or foreign matter. The word literally means "freedom from burden."

† *Pinch grafts,* small pieces of skin about ⅛ of an inch across taken for grafting—"as big as a pinch."

. . . Seven days later, 168 additional pinch grafts were removed from the mother's thigh and applied to the balance of the denuded surface of the child's leg. Within three days all of the grafts showed signs of taking, and the entire wound was in excellent condition. . . . About two weeks following the second skin graft, it was first noted that a rather widespread exfoliative dermatitis* had developed over the entire body, and marked desiccation of the skin was taking place on the scalp, face, arms, and legs. . . . About this time it occurred to me that the general dermatitis was most probably a phenomenon of anaphylaxis† or protein intoxication, and a manifestation of sensitiveness to the foreign protein of the mother. As the original small pinch grafts from the mother were still present, it was decided that these should be removed. On December 23, therefore, 3½ months after the first appearance of the dermatitis, all of the original grafts were curetted away. Within ten days there was a tremendous improvement in the general condition of the patient, and the exfoliative dermatitis rapidly disappeared.

Dr. Holman had thus discovered a patient who was sensitized by his mother's skin, so as to produce an inflammation of his own skin. This is a phenomenon that today might be referred to as an "autoimmune" disease. With these experiences in mind, Dr. Holman then undertook the following studies in a 28-month-old child with extensive burns of face and body which ultimately required skin grafting:

On April 3, donor J. W. contributed 9 homografts; and donor E. H. contributed 12 homografts.

On April 21, when all homografts of J. W. and E. H. were thriving and spreading nicely, a third donor, M. F., contributed a group of 9 homografts.

On April 25, donor E. H. contributed a *second* group of homografts.

On May 2, the homografts from J. W. and the first homografts of E. H. showed signs of beginning regression. Moreover, the second homografts from E. H. applied on April 25 were being rejected. . . . During this evidence of developing rejection of all homografts from J. W. and E. H., the homografts of a third donor, M. F., were thriving and spreading. However, about May 14 they, too, began to melt away and eventually disappeared completely.

These observations prompted Dr. Holman to deduce that

---

* *Exfoliative dermatitis*, a severe inflammation of the skin with itching and peeling.
† *Anaphylaxis*, heightened immunity.

. . . the agency which caused the first homografts to disappear had no effect on the viability of the grafts from the third donor, and that the destroying agency is specific for each set of grafts. It seemed plausible to suppose, therefore, that each group of grafts develops its own antibody which is responsible for the subsequent disappearance of the new epidermis.

Reminiscing in 1963 about his work done nearly forty years before, Dr. Holman wrote in a letter: "What an opportunity we missed by not pursuing this further!"

Antigens, Antibodies, and Immunity

In a world teeming with dangerous bacteria, survival depends on the prompt recognition of foreign protein* within the body and its prompt isolation or destruction. The individual must not only recognize those proteins of other living organisms (such as bacteria) as being strange to him, but also have a way of making warlike contact with them, binding them up or destroying them somehow so that they can be discarded. Many foreign proteins of viruses or bacteria are associated with invasive infection and serious disease. This property of recognizing strange protein as foreign and potentially dangerous is important in combating infections from bacteria and viruses, and the power to recognize and destroy such proteins is known as immunity. The ability to develop immunity is common to all higher forms of life. It is a highly organized defense system, exhibited in all the vertebrates, such as birds and mammals, and very highly developed in the mammals and primates.

In man immunologic development is so close to perfect that the many viruses, bacteria, and parasites with which he might become infected are warded off effectively and daily. The defects in the system show up only with the occasional serious infection, occurring a few times during a lifetime of exposure. A mild infection occurring for the

---

* *Proteins* (from the Greek, "primary, of first importance") are the large molecules that comprise the bulk of the material in a living cell. Most proteins are very highly specialized and accomplish a specific purpose in the organism. Normally the proteins within the body are entirely those manufactured within the cells of the body itself. Bacteria contain other proteins manufactured within themselves, and unique to each species of bacteria.

first time arouses an immunity that throws it off; if it occurs a second time, there is a heightened immune response to this second challenge, and frequently no disease at all develops. An example is the lifetime immunity to such diseases as measles once they have occurred in childhood. The historic epidemics and plagues which have changed history often resulted from the new exposure of a whole population to some bacterium or virus to which it had not previously been exposed. Such people were very susceptible, and did not have a heightened immunologic response; the first infection was very severe and resulted in fatality. Thousands of American Indians died of measles, while the settlers barely suffered!

Healthy human beings have a remarkable ability to throw off bacterial and viral diseases to which they have previously been exposed and to which they have developed immunity. The immune process "remembers" the previous exposure, and this is one of its most remarkable attributes. This memory of immunity finds a close parallel in the transplant field, as in the "second set" response to a skin allograft described by Dr. Holman and studied so carefully by Dr. Medawar twenty years later.

The immune process has two leading components: the antigen and the antibody. The term "antigen" literally means "the thing that generates antagonism"; it is the substance—usually a protein—that excites an immune response. When the antigen gains entry into the body it arouses an immune response that consists in calling forth its specific antagonists, the antibodies.

An antibody is also a protein, usually one known as a globulin. It is manufactured in special tissues devoted to the development of the immune process. The antibody, with the help of another substance named "complement," then binds with, precipitates, or inactivates the invading protein antigen and readies it for removal.

A state of immunity is thus a condition in which antibodies are present to fight off a specific antigen. Many diseases make themselves felt with fever and illness because the patient is sensitive to the state of warfare between antigens and antibodies. When the antibodies win, the disease resolves, and all is well. A typical example is the crisis of lobar pneumonia in which a very ill patient suddenly, over the course of a few hours, resolves the process. Fever falls, he sweats profusely and becomes almost well. By contrast, in very severe infections the antigens win this encounter, bacteria overwhelm the defenses, and death results.

There is a third contrasting condition—the condition of immunologic "tolerance" in which the host permits the antigen to dwell in the body unmolested. The antigen remains, antibodies do not confront it, and no disease results. For example, there are viruses normally present in the human being which do not cause any disease at all.

Between 1925 and 1945, it gradually became evident that transplanted tissue must contain antigens which arouse an immune response in the new host, and that the antibodies of this new host then throw off the graft as rejection.

Viewed in this framework of antigens, antibodies, and the immune process, it appears that successful allotransplantation of cellular tissues might be achieved in one of three ways:

1. By placing the tissue in a privileged position so that the antibodies (carried by the blood) cannot get at it.
2. By changing the tissue itself so that it is no longer antigenic.
3. By changing the new host so that he cannot or does not make antibodies.

Attempts have been made toward all three of these ways of making transplants "take." Apparently the most successful method is the third. Suppression of the production of antibodies is called "immunosuppression." It has been accomplished both with drugs and by irradiation. An animal or a patient that has had his immune responses lowered by immunosuppression is much more vulnerable to infection. His guard has been lowered. Not only can a transplant be accepted, but bacteria are more apt to invade. If it were possible to suppress the immune response to transplanted tissues without damaging the patient's immunity to bacterial disease, then a *specific immunosuppression* would have been achieved, making the transplantation possible without exacting too high a price from the patient. This highly unlikely feat has been the objective of much research. To accomplish it the biologist must know precisely how the body achieves immunity in the first place.

Clones and Clonal Selection:
The Theories of Burnet

A biologic riddle of outstanding importance in all of the transplant problem relates to the precise mechanism by which a foreign protein antigen elicits a response in those cellular tissues responsible for making antibodies, and known collectively as the reticuloendothelial system. Sir Macfarlane Burnet of Melbourne, Australia, has concerned himself with this problem for many years. Burnet's writings express a biologic simplicity and a conceptual clarity that have given them a special place in immunology, most particularly in the transplant field.

The immunity-producing cells of the reticuloendothelial system include the lymphocytes, the other white cells (known as leukocytes), and other cells found in the blood (such as plasma cells) and also in the spleen, lymph nodes, bone marrow, and elsewhere. It is characteristic of the highly immune state that these tissues become enlarged. A patient who has been fighting off attacks of malaria for many years has a very large spleen. Patients who are combating viral infections in the intestine have very large lymph nodes in the abdomen.

By corollary, the state of immunosuppression is one in which these organs and tissues are smaller and less effective. The count of white blood cells goes down; the lymph nodes shrink. This is the picture produced by whole body irradiation or by immunosuppressive drugs if the doses are large enough.

Precisely how do these cells and tissues act? How do they respond to this foreign protein when it arrives on the scene? As Professor Burnet points out, any theory of immunology must be able to explain at least three special aspects of the immune phenomenon, all three of which are important in the transplantation of tissue. These three special aspects of immunology are *recognition, tolerance,* and *memory:*

1. How does the immune system *recognize* its own proteins as harmless and "self"—how does one explain the nonantigenicity of body components?
2. How can we explain that sequence of events by which an animal may be induced to *tolerate* the presence in itself of

tissues, viruses, or organisms of another source—how to explain induced tolerance?

3. Finally, how does one explain that special and seemingly unique property by which days, weeks, months, or even years after the first exposure to an antigen, a host organism reacts very much more strongly to the second exposure, recognizing its former unfriendly contact—how does one explain immunologic *memory?*

Professor Burnet was dissatisfied with the concept current in the 1940's that one's own proteins had a "self-marker" hitched to them—a sort of biologic driver's license that permitted them to circulate around in the body unassaulted by plasma cells and lymphocytes. He classified this "self-marker theory" as "semimystical in character and generally unattractive." In its place he proposed what he called the *clonal selection** theory of immunity (Fig. 2). This theory, whatever its ultimate place in biology, has the virtue of simplicity, and provides an explanation for many of the phenomena seen in the allotransplantation of tissues. The advent of modern molecular immunology, as described in Chapter 9, lets us witness some of the detailed molecular events of the immune process; Burnet's theory of clonal selection still covers many of the cellular phenomena seen in allotransplant rejection.

According to Professor Burnet's concept, the embryo in its mother's uterus (the tiny infant long before birth), has many millions of clones or colonies of these cells, all of them able to react against proteins by making antibodies. When the cells are very young, the presence of an appropriate antigen kills those clones that react against it. They are young and vulnerable. As the organism matures, there comes a "critical point" when, instead of being killed by contact with a protein antigen, the clone begins to react more strongly and produces considerable antibody.

Thus, by the time the infant is born, the clones of antibody-

---

* The word *clone* comes from the Greek root for "twig or branch." Here it refers to the group of descendants, or colony of cells, that result from the division of a single cell and subsequent cell multiplication in the antibody-producing cells of the reticuloendothelial system. The term "clonal selection," therefore, refers to a process by which certain clones are selected by the body to remain and make antibodies in later years.

A representation of the process of immunologic maturation

Phase of differentiation or randomization

Embryonic   Stabilization of patterns

Development of tolerance by elimination of reacting
clones

←Critical point of Medawar

Birth or hatching→

Maturation

Postnatal

Liberation of natural antibodies and potentality of antibody production

Development

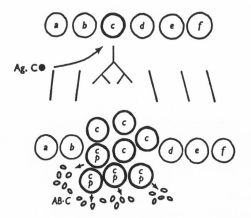

FIGURE 2.   The clonal selection theory of Burnet (from Burnet, 1959). Diagram
of the sequences of maturation of the cells that make antibodies. This shows the
"critical point of Medawar," which Burnet had predicted on the basis of his
previous discoveries. Medawar had shown that this was the point prior to which
it was possible to produce actively acquired tolerance.

Below is shown Burnet's own hand-drawn illustration of his clonal selection
theory. The clone, or colony, represented by cell C is the one selected by the
matching antigen (Ag C.) to make antibodies. It reproduces rapidly and makes
many new cells, some of which make and release antibody (AB.C).

producing cells in his body which might react against his own circulating "self" proteins have been killed off in their immature phase. Only those clones of cells that can react against *foreign* protein are left alive—"clonal selection." If, during the state of intrauterine ignorance, before birth, strange protein is introduced (as in Dr. Medawar's later experiments, and in the studies of chickens and cattle described further on), then the clones that might react against this foreign protein are destroyed. Therefore, at a later time in life, when that protein is again introduced (even though originally foreign), it is "recognized as self." The experimenter has played a trick on nature by finding a precise moment when foreign protein can gain acceptance by the "select" group of living clones. The theory predicted correctly this experimental result—namely, that foreign protein introduced before birth would, for many years, be accommodated or tolerated as harmless and recognized as "self" by the mature organism.

Sir Macfarlane closes his book on the clonal selection theory with the words, ". . . and it is an article of my scientific faith that there is intrinsic virtue in simplicity, if it aids understanding without doing violence to the facts of observation and experiment." Very early in Burnet's concepts of tolerance, he had predicted that protein exposed to a young embryo at a proper stage would later be recognized as friendly, and accepted without a battle. The experiments of Dr. Billingham, working with Dr. Brent and Dr. Medawar in London, confirmed this prediction in 1953, making it one of the important achievements of modern transplantation research.

3

TOLERANCE: NATURAL AND ACQUIRED

Nature Permits the Impermissible

What a chimera, then, is man! What a novelty . . . !

—PASCAL, *Pensées*

ON CATTLE AND CHIMERAS

In ancient mythology the chimera was a formidable female with a lion's head, a goat's body, and a dragon's tail. The Greek root for this word connotes the concept of a very young goat; even in mythology, youthfulness had something to do with chimerism.

Whatever this mythologic beast did, and whatever its age, the term chimera has been borrowed from mythology by transplant immunology to signify *any organism including within it diverse living tissues of two or more genetic origins, without immunologic reaction between them.* Thus, a person who carries some foreign blood cells (from another person of a different blood type) circulating in him without any transfusion reaction is a chimera; a person who has a kidney transplanted from someone else (other than an identical twin), but without demonstrating any adverse or immunologic reaction to it, is likewise a chimera. In 1945 the realization arose that chimerism bore a strong relation to transplantation; any person with a successful allotransplant of any tissue or organ would be a chimera if there were no continuing immune rejection process. Attention therefore shifted from the laboratory to the cow pasture, because chimerism exists naturally, though rarely, in cattle.

Dr. Owen, a teacher of veterinary science at the University of Wisconsin, was the first to prove that two genetic types could live together in the same organism without any signs of antagonism or disease. He showed this to be true in cattle twins. Dr. Owen knew that cattle twinning was unusual, and that identical twins in cattle almost never occurred. He likewise was aware of the previous studies of Dr. Lillie, who in 1916 had reported that in bovine twins of opposite sexes there was often a union of the circulatory systems between the two placentas* in the uterus of the mother cow. The female twin was then born with abnormal sterility, a lack of ability to reproduce, and was termed by farmers and veterinarians a "freemartin."

Dr. Owen reported in 1945 that in some cattle twins each member of the pair carried blood cells of two different types. He concluded that at some stage prior to birth, with the circulation of the two placentas intertwined, the twins seeded down each other's bone marrow with primitive cells from which blood cells would grow. This cross-colonization of the bone marrow prior to birth permitted the two different blood types to live together without any rejection battle. Evidently the two genetic types of blood cells got used to each other at an early age and became mutually "tolerant."

A few years later, Dr. Dunsford and his group in Sheffield took up the thread of this idea, and through a remarkable chain of circumstances discovered a pair of human twins that showed many of these same phenomena. Stimulated by Dr. Owen's report, they had been looking for some human twins who might show two different blood cell types circulating simultaneously in the bloodstream without disease or reaction. "Chance favors the prepared mind," and Dr. Dunsford was both prepared and favored when the blood bank laboratory reported to him the case of a woman, aged 25, whose blood was very difficult to "type." She had donated some blood, and the technicians

---

* *Placenta*, the organ carrying blood from the mother to the infant; expelled following birth as the "afterbirth."

did not know what type it was because some of the cells they saw under the microscope were type A and others were type O. Learning of this, Dr. Dunsford saw the resemblance to the situation described by Dr. Owen in cattle.

He called up this blood donor, a certain Mrs. McK., and asked her to come to the hospital. On her arrival, there occurred a critical moment in the history of transplantation. Without knowing anything further about Mrs. McK. or her family, Dr. Dunsford asked her if she had a twin. Later he wrote: "Mrs. McK., somewhat surprised, answered that her twin brother had died 25 years previously at the age of 3 months."

Here was a scientist presented with an unexpected observation—blood cell chimerism—and immediately making the proper interpretation: Mrs. McK. must have had a twin. The circulation in their mother's uterus must have been crossed very early (before Burnet's "critical point"), so that cells were exchanged between them. They could carry each other's blood groups throughout life without having a blood reaction. But then, as Dr. Dunsford said, no comparison was perfect. Although Mrs. McK. had traded blood with a twin brother, she indeed was not a "freemartin," because she already had a child. The similarity to twinning in cattle went just so far and no farther!*

Finally, Dr. Woodruff and Dr. Lennox, working in Scotland, finished off this scientific sequence that began with the description of natural chimeras in cattle by performing the perfect experiment in man.

They discovered another pair of twins similar to those described by Dr. Dunsford six years previously. They found twins, one male and one female, of whom the male carried 86 percent red blood cells type A and 14 percent type O, and the female carried 99 percent type O cells and 1 percent type A. This indicated that the twins had shared the blood supply in their mother's uterus, and were similar to the bovine twins studied first by Dr. Owen, and later observed in the case of Mrs. McK.

---

* These studies of Owen and of Dunsford relate to nonidentical, or fraternal, twins; two different blood cell types can, therefore, be identified as circulating together. Such are not found in identical twins, wherein complete genetic identity exists of all the tissues, including blood cells, as described in Chapter 5.

Drs. Woodruff and Lennox traded skin grafts between these twins. The skin from the brother that was placed on the sister's arm was accepted perfectly well and remained indefinitely unchanged. Some critic might have objected that this skin actually was just regrown from the girl twin. Therefore, these scientists took a little sample of that skin and by "nuclear sexing"—a procedure of examining the characteristic shape of the nucleus under the microscope—they showed that this skin graft on the girl twin indeed was from a man. Thus they had carried out in man precisely the experiment that the work of Dr. Owen had predicted would be possible.

The significance of these studies lay in the demonstration of ways in which nature had overcome the transplant barrier. Nature had surmounted the barrier by mixing blood types before birth. This produced natural tolerance. Could such a tolerance ever be produced intentionally or experimentally? Could it ever be made to last throughout life? Chickens answered the first question, and mice the second.

DR. LONGMIRE'S CHICKENS

In 1950, Drs. Cannon and Longmire, working in the Surgical Research Laboratories at the University of California at Los Angeles, followed up the experimentation in newly hatched chicks. They had learned of work carried out twenty-one years previously, and reported in 1929 by Dr. Danforth and Dr. Foster, on skin grafts in chicks.

Drs. Danforth and Foster had, like Dr. Owen with his calves, been studying veterinary science (though members of the Department of Anatomy at Stanford) and were interested in the extent of species differences between various breeds of chickens, such as the Rhode Island Red and the Plymouth Rock. To study this question they exchanged skin grafts between chicks on the day that they were hatched. The skin grafts took quite well, and it was concluded that the constitutional makeup of various kinds of chickens was quite close and was "such as to admit exchange of skin" (Fig. 3). Had they operated a few days later, they might have discovered that success was not due to any special properties of chicken breeds, but to their operating when the chicks were newly hatched.

Drs. Cannon and Longmire took up this work because they

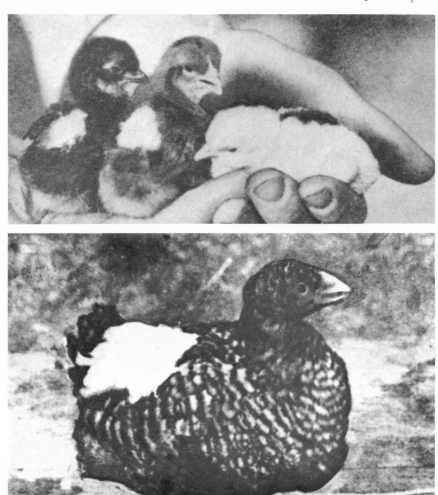

FIGURE 3. Tolerant chickens. From Danforth and Foster (1929). The chicks (above), when newly hatched, traded skin between the Plymouth Rock (light) and the Rhode Island Red (dark). The skin grafts took perfectly and are here shown growing in their new hosts a week or so later. Danforth and Foster considered this as due to some constitutional similarity between the two breeds of chickens. Cannon and Longmire, in 1950, showed that it was due to the operation having been done when the chickens were newly hatched. Billingham, Brent, and Medawar found in these experiments a reason to study immunology in the newborn, and in mice even prior to birth. From their experiments finally came the discovery of actively acquired tolerance.

Below is shown a chicken months later, carrying the adopted skin and feathers, demonstrating the prolonged "take" of the neonatal grafts.

were intrigued with the findings reported by Danforth and Foster— that the newly hatched chicks would exchange grafts. To make the demonstration even more dramatic, Cannon and Longmire turned the transplanted chick skin around backward before placing it in its new position on its new host. The result was that some of the red hens not only had white feathers, but these feathers grew pointing in the wrong direction!

Now, using this model, Cannon and Longmire took the additional step that Danforth and Foster had omitted. They waited until the chickens were over 3 days old, and then showed that the take of skin grafts from other chicks was reduced to only 1 percent. At 14 days of age, there were no lasting allografts whatever. Once the chick was old enough, constitutional dissimilarity was just as overbearing as in any other species; it was the newly hatched state that gave the chicks the special ability to tolerate each other's skin.

Drs. Cannon and Longmire's experiment took advantage of *natural tolerance* in the newborn chick to make skin grafts take. They did not produce a new, lasting, and intentional tolerance, an *actively acquired tolerance*, lasting for many weeks or months. The artificial production of this latter state, similar to natural chimerism in cattle, remained for Professor Medawar and his colleagues; and their work began, as had Dr. Holman's, with skin grafts on a burned patient.

THE "SECOND SET" OF PROFESSOR MEDAWAR AND ACTIVELY ACQUIRED TOLERANCE

In World War II, as in previous wars for many centuries, there had been renewed interest and rapid development in surgical methods for the treatment of wounds, fractures, and burns. In 1942 and 1943, Dr. Gibson and Mr. Medawar, of Mr. Clark's Surgical Unit and the Department of Pathology at the Glasgow Royal Infirmary, undertook a study of the fate of skin allografts used in the treatment of burns. Dr. Gibson was in charge of this plastic surgical work and Mr. Medawar was a lecturer in zoology at Oxford University. Their study was commissioned by the British government and was an outgrowth of wartime interest in methods of skin grafting, so much needed for the treatment of burns suffered not only by the troops but also by the civilian population assaulted by bombing raids.

The two men first made careful observations of a burned patient in whom pinch grafts had been placed in an attempt to cover the burn. This was precisely the setting in which Dr. Holman had made his observations in 1923. In this particular instance, in Glasgow, the pinch grafts came both from the patient (autografts) and from other people (allografts).

The authors concluded, as Dr. Holman had, that homografts were not a practical method of covering burn defects. But they discovered a great deal more on the way. They observed the hastened rejection of grafts put on a second time from the same donor, and they stated:

The second set of homografts did not undergo the same cycle of growth and regression as the first: dissolution was far advanced by the eighth day after transplantation. The degenerative changes that affected the first set of homografts appear simultaneously in their immediate contemporaries of the second set.

In this quotation is found the first use of the term "second set" grafts, a term that was to be widely used to describe the immunologic phenomenon of "memory" in allografting, and that later became the basis for studying allotransplant immunology in detail.

Most important, however, was the final conclusion of Gibson and Medawar, as follows:

The time relations of the process, the absence of a local cellular reaction, and the accelerated rejection of the second set of homografts suggest that the destruction of the foreign epidermis was brought about by a mechanism of active immunization.

Stimulated by these results of careful observation in man, Medawar carried forward the investigation after he returned to his department in Oxford. His research, still supported by the War Wounds Committee of the Medical Research Council, consisted in setting up an "animal model" in which these initial observations could be made repeatedly and under ideally controlled conditions. He used skin grafts on rabbits, and by 1944 could establish statistical norms for the length of survival of autografts and allografts and statistical prediction for the accelerated rejection of "second set" allografts, and could make microscopic pictures showing the phenomena of transplant immunology for the first time in great detail. Again, he concluded: "The mechanism by which foreign skin is eliminated belongs to the general category of actively acquired immune reactions."

In the following year, Dr. Medawar undertook the experiment of placing skin from a third rabbit onto the first recipient. He found that the heightened and accelerated response or "second set rejection" is individual-specific and is not shared by skin from an indifferent or third donor.

As Dr. Medawar proceeded with the problem, he became interested in recipients of younger and younger ages. He moved back to the newborn, and then to the animal prior to birth. Finally, in 1953, Drs. Billingham, Brent, and Medawar published their work, "Actively Acquired Tolerance of Foreign Cells," describing for the first time a situation in which later allografts could be induced to "take" and exist for the life of the recipient. Confirming many of the theories of Professor Burnet, they stated:

The effect of this first presentation of foreign tissue in adult life is to confer "immunity," that is, to increase the host's resistance to grafts which may be transplanted on some later occasion from the same donor or from some other member of the donor's strain. But if the first presentation of foreign cells takes place in foetal* life, it has just the opposite effect: resistance to a graft transplanted on some later occasion, so far from being heightened, is abolished or at least reduced. Over some period of its early life, therefore, the pattern of the host's response to foreign tissue cells is turned completely upside down. In mice, it will be seen, this inversion takes place in the neighborhood of birth.

Thus, by the injection of tissue or graft into the very young animal, tolerance could be acquired. This, known as "actively acquired tolerance," stands today as the only clear and simple method by which allograft acceptance may be produced without crippling or damaging the other immune processes of the recipient.

---

* *Foetal (fetal) life,* during the life of the embryo (fetus) before birth.

Their experiment should be viewed in detail because it shows how such major biologic conclusions are drawn from a simple experiment, each detail of which seems minor but is actually of the greatest importance (Fig. 4).

In the experiment to be described, a CBA* female in the 15th–16th day of pregnancy by a CBA male was anesthetized with Nembutal and its body wall exposed by a median ventral incision of the skin. The skin was mobilized but not reflected and particular care was taken not to damage the mammary vessels. By manipulation of the abdomen with damped gauzes six fetuses were brought into view through the body wall. Each was injected intra-embryonically with 0.01 ml of a suspension of adult tissue cells of A-line mice through a very fine hypodermic needle passed successively through the body wall, uterine wall, and fetal membrane. After injection of the fetuses, the skin was closed with interrupted sutures.

Five healthy and normal-looking young were born four days later; of the sixth fetus, there was no trace. Eight weeks after their birth, when the lightest weighed 21 grams, each member of the litter was challenged with a skin graft from an adult A-line donor. The first inspection of the grafts was carried out eleven days later; that is, at the median survival age of A-line skin grafts transplanted to normal CBA hosts. The grafts on two of the five mice were in an advanced stage of breakdown; the grafts on the other three (one male and two females) resembled all the grafts in every respect except their donor-specific albinism. Each of these three grafts became perfectly incorporated into its host skin and grew a white hair pelt of normal density and stoutness. Fifty days later one of the three mice received a second A-line graft from a new donor and this graft also settled down without the least symptom of an immunological reaction.

This first demonstration of "actively acquired tolerance" was spectacular. Mice were running around in Dr. Medawar's laboratory carrying fur on them of a different color from a different strain, and carrying it throughout their life without fuss, bother, or illness.

"Actively acquired tolerance" as developed by Drs. Billingham, Brent, and Medawar would not be practical under most human circumstances because it would require the identification, prior to the birth of an individual, of a potential donor for some organ needed

---

* CBA and A-line, two highly inbred strains of laboratory mice often used in transplantation research.

No. 4379   October 3, 1953   NATURE

'ACTIVELY ACQUIRED TOLERANCE' OF FOREIGN CELLS

By Dr. R. E. BILLINGHAM*, L. BRENT and Prof. P. B. MEDAWAR, F.R.S.

Department of Zoology, University College, University of London

THE experiments to be described in this article provide a solution—at present only a 'laboratory' solution—of the problem of how to make tissue homografts immunologically acceptable to hosts which would normally react against them. The principle underlying the experiments may be expressed in the following terms : that mammals and birds never develop, or develop to only a limited degree, the power to react immunologically against foreign homologous tissue cells to which they have been exposed sufficiently early in foetal life. If, for example, a foetal mouse of one inbred strain (say, CBA) is inoculated *in utero* with a suspension of living cells from an adult mouse of another strain (say, A), then, when it grows up, the CBA mouse will be found to be partly or completely tolerant of skin grafts transplanted from any mouse belonging to the strain of the original donor.

This phenomenon is the exact inverse of 'actively acquired immunity', and we therefore propose to describe it as 'actively acquired tolerance'. The distinction between the two phenomena may be made evident in the following way. If a normal adult CBA mouse is inoculated with living cells or grafted with skin from an A-line donor, the grafted tissue is destroyed within twelve days (see below). The effect of this first presentation of foreign tissue in adult life is to confer 'immunity', that is, to increase the host's resistance to grafts which may be transplanted on some later occasion from the same donor or from some other member of the donor's strain. But if the first presentation of foreign cells takes place in foetal life, it has just the opposite effect : resistance to a graft transplanted on some later occasion, so far from being heightened, is abolished or at least reduced. Over some period of its early life, therefore, the pattern of the host's response to foreign tissue cells is turned completely upside down. In mice, it will be seen, this inversion takes place in the neighbourhood of birth, for there is a certain 'null' period thereabouts when the inoculation of foreign tissue confers neither tolerance nor heightened resistance—when, in fact, a 'test graft' transplanted in adult life to ascertain the host's degree of immunity is found to survive for the same length of time as if the host had received no treatment at all.

Earlier Work

The literature of experimental embryology is rich in evidence that embryos are fully tolerant of grafts of foreign tissues. It is less well known (though no less firmly established) that embryonic cells transplanted into embryos of different genetic constitutions may survive into adult life, although their hosts would almost certainly have rejected them if transplantation had been delayed until after birth. The transplantation of embryonic melanoblasts[1] provides the most conspicuous evidence of this phenomenon—not because melanoblasts are peculiar in their immunological properties, but simply because their genetic origins are at once betrayed by the

* British Empire Cancer Campaign Research Fellow.

pigmentation of the cells into which they ultimately develop. Unfortunately, experiments with embryonic melanoblasts, having been done with quite different purposes in mind, do not make it possible to decide whether survival into adult life is due to an antigenic adaptation of embryonic cells which have been obliged to complete their development in genetically foreign soil, or whether it is due to a suppression or 'paralysis'[2] of the host's immunological response.

An exactly comparable phenomenon has been described by Owen[3], who found that the majority of dizygotic cattle twins are born with, and long retain, red blood cells of dizygotic origin : each calf contains a proportion of red cells belonging genetically to itself, mixed with red cells belonging to the zygote lineage of its twin. There is no reason to doubt that this is because the cattle twins, being synchorial, exchange blood in foetal life through the anastomoses of their placental vessels. (This is not a peculiarity of cattle, for a human twin with red cells of dizygotic origin has lately been described[4].) Inasmuch as the provenance of the red cells was revealed by their reactions with specific agglutinins, it is most unlikely that the survival of foreign erythrocyte-forming cells into adult life was made possible by any kind of antigenic adaptation. Moreover, we have found that the majority of cattle twins at birth and for long after are fully tolerant of grafts of each other's skin[5]. Being freshly transplanted, these grafts can have had no opportunity to 'adapt' themselves antigenically to foreign hosts, but they survived nevertheless.

The experiments of Cannon and Longmire[6] have a direct bearing on the phenomenon of actively acquired tolerance. About 5–10 per cent of skin grafts exchanged between pairs of newly hatched chicks of different breeds are tolerated and survive into adult life ; but the percentage of successes falls rapidly as the age at which the chicks are operated increases, and reaches zero by the end of the second week. These results will be referred to later.

Experiments with Mice

A single experiment will be described in moderate detail : the recipients were mice of CBA strain, the donors of A strain. The data for transplantations between normal mice of these strains are as follows. The median survival time of A-line skin grafts transplanted to normal CBA adults (regardless of differences of sex, or of age within the interval 6 weeks–6 months) is 11.0 ± 0.3 days[7]. In reacting against such a graft, the host enters a state of heightened resistance ; a second graft transplanted up to sixty days after the transplantation of the first survives for less than six days, and immunity is still strong, though it has weakened perceptibly, after four months. Heightened resistance may be passively transferred to a normal CBA adult by the intraperitoneal implantation of pieces of lymph node excised from a CBA adult which has been actively immunized against A-line skin[8].

In the experiment to be described (Exp. 73), a CBA female in the 15–16th day of pregnancy by a

FIGURE 4.   Actively acquired tolerance. Title page from the paper by Billingham, Brent, and Medawar in *Nature* for October 3, 1953. Here was reported for the first time a permanent breakdown of the transplant barrier permitting successful homotransplants of skin. This was produced by inoculation of cells into a mouse prior to birth. The cells were taken from another strain which thereafter could be a skin donor for the rest of the animal's life.

many years later; and then the injection into the embryo in its mother's womb of a preparatory protein substance from this future donor. Hardly a feasible scheme in anybody's world! And yet the demonstration that by this method, in the animal, the seeming insoluble barrier to allografting could be permanently and completely overcome constituted a clear message to biologists that in this little known field of transplant immunology, effective solutions could be found. The demonstration that the transplant barrier could be breached provided an inspiration for many scientists who shifted the focus of their work to this field. For physicians and surgeons, the hope was rekindled that a solution might be found for the allotransplantation of new organs to sick patients. It was evident that successful transplantation could be performed only when a protective reaction was breached or abated. Previous advances in medicine and surgery had resulted by preventing or overcoming a disease process through assistance given to natural processes. Here was a new field where success could be reached only by overcoming a natural process—the immune response to foreign tissue. Ordinarily this immune response to alien protein is essential for life. The solution offered by these scientists was hardly one adaptable to clinical medicine.

Indeed, it was in precisely these terms that Dr. Billingham and his co-workers viewed their experiments:

The experiments to be described in this article provide a solution—at present only a "laboratory" solution—of the problem of how to make tissue homografts immunologically acceptable to hosts which would normally react against them. The principle underlying the experiments may be expressed in the following terms: that mammals and birds never develop, or develop only to a limited degree, the power to react immunologically against foreign homologous tissue cells to which they have been exposed sufficiently early in foetal life. If, for example, a foetal mouse of one inbred strain (say, CBA) is inoculated *in utero* with a suspension of living cells from an adult mouse of another strain (say, A), then, when it grows up, the CBA mouse will be found to be partly or completely tolerant of skin grafts transplanted from any mouse belonging to the strain of the original donor. This phenomenon is the exact inverse of the "actively acquired immunity" and we therefore propose to describe it as "actively acquired tolerance."

Dr. Medawar's subsequent papers and reports added further fuel to the fire. In March 1960 he delivered the Dunham Lectures at Harvard. The largest teaching amphitheater at the Medical School was filled beyond capacity, and other amphitheaters equipped with loudspeakers were needed to take the overflow. The intensity of scientific interest in a rapidly growing field is something few can appreciate unless they have witnessed it. In December of the same year, Medawar and Burnet were awarded the Nobel Prize for this work.

CAN A NEWBORN CHILD BECOME TOLERANT OF HIS FATHER?

Dr. Billingham and his collaborators modestly remarked that actively acquired tolerance as they produced it would scarcely be useful in man. Professor Woodruff wondered if in some species the favorable period for production of actively acquired tolerance might not occur after birth, as well as before, and he wondered if it were something that could be produced in man.

Woodruff and Simpson, therefore, studied this phenomenon in the rat, and showed that in rats immediately *after* birth one could produce the same sort of actively acquired tolerance as was produced by Billingham, Brent, and Medawar in mice *prior* to birth. Woodruff showed that if one waited two weeks, a lesser degree of tolerance was produced in the rat, and if one waited four weeks, there was no effect at all.

Of further interest was that Woodruff and Simpson then studied the extent of this tolerance, and showed that in the "tolerant rat," a second skin graft taken from the same donor would sometimes be rejected while the first skin graft still remained in place.* This is one example of a general phenomenon that Professor Woodruff has named "adaptation." The term signifies a change in the graft itself or in the relationship between the graft and the recipient as a result of which the graft becomes less liable to rejection as time passes. It is possible that several different mechanisms may be involved in such an adaptation, particularly protective antibody-coating of the lining of the blood

---

* This interesting observation was a foretaste of the finding later to be reported by Dr. Joseph Murray that dogs carrying a kidney from one donor will sometimes reject a second graft taken from the same donor.

vessels. Until the precise mechanisms are clarified, it is best to use the term "adaptation" in a purely descriptive or operational sense to mean the process whereby a graft gradually becomes accepted.

Professor Woodruff and his colleagues took the findings of Billingham, Brent, and Medawar one step farther. Having shown that actively acquired tolerance could be produced in the rat after birth, they then sought to discover whether anything like this could be produced in man. For this experiment Professor Woodruff made some white blood cell suspensions from the fathers of newborn male children. The parents had given permission to have the infants injected with a tiny droplet of the white blood cell suspension. Then, when the babies were six months old, a small skin graft was taken from the father and placed upon the child's arm.

Professor Woodruff reported that this skin survived longer than would otherwise be expected. This suggested to him that a state of partial tolerance had been built up by the procedure of injection from the father at the time of birth. Woodruff did not carry these experiments any further because they seemed potentially dangerous to the child. Serious "graft versus host" reactions ("runt disease") were being reported for the first time in the literature, and he thought it was dangerous to expose the children to such a possibility, however remote. Writing of this work in a recent letter, Woodruff stated:

We did not pursue attempts to induce tolerance in human infants at birth when the dangers of runt disease became apparent, but quite a number of people have since looked to see whether infants who have received exchange transfusions subsequently showed tolerance to skin from the original blood donor, and they have in fact demonstrated this on a number of occasions.

The actively acquired tolerance discovered by Drs. Billingham, Brent, and Medawar was thus produced in man (at least in some small measure), demonstrating, if nothing else, that man was no exception to the general laws of transplantation immunology!

4

THE UNBREACHED BARRIER

Kidney Transplantation
Without Immunosuppression

The lyf so short, the craft so long to lerne
—CHAUCER, *Parlement of Foules*

VIENNA AT THE TURN OF THE CENTURY

Now our story turns from sophisticated transplant immunology to the story of surgical kidney grafting; and with this change we move from the intensive study of skin grafts, acquired tolerance, chicken feathers, and cattle chimerism to much more clumsy attempts at achieving the complicated graft of a fully vascularized* whole organ. Because of its simple blood supply and its obvious function, together with its possessing an opposite number—a paired organ—the kidney has occupied the attention of transplant scientists from the very beginning.

Twenty years before Dr. Holman's study of skin grafting, and forty years before the casualties of World War II led Professor Medawar to study skin grafts, a Viennese journal published the first recorded article in medical history on the subject of kidney transplantation (Fig. 5). The author was a Dr. Ullmann. In the issue of the

---

* *Vascularized*, carrying its full supply of blood vessels with it and connected by anastomosis to the new host.

Programm

der am

Freitag, den 24. Januar 1902, 7 Uhr Abends,

unter dem Vorsitze des Herrn Prof. Breus

stattfindenden

Sitzung der k. k. Gesellschaft der Aerzte in Wien.

1. Dr. Hugo Frey: Zwei Fälle intracranieller Complicationen bei Ohreneiterungen. (Demonstration).

2. Dr. Otto Grosser: Ueber arterio - venöse Anastomosen beim Menschen.

Vorträge haben angemeldet die Herren: Hofrath Prof. Weichselbaum, Prof. Benedikt, Dr. Gustav Kaiser, Docent Dr. S. Fränkel. Dr. S. Jellinek, Docent Dr. K. Ullmann, Prof. Englisch. Dr. A. Jolles. Dr. H. Teleky und Prof. Zuckerkandl.

Bergmeister, Paltauf.

*

Die p. t. Mitglieder werden hiemit eingeladen, den Jahresbeitrag pro 1902 statutenmässig bis 1. März 1902 einzuzahlen.

Die nach diesem Termine noch offenen Beiträge werden mittelst Postauftrages zuzüglich der hiedurch erwachsenen Kosten zum Incasso gelangen.

Das Präsidium.

Wiener klinische Wochenschrift

unter ständiger Mitwirkung der Herren Professoren Drs.

G. Braun, O. Chiari, Rudolf Chrobak, V. R. v. Ebner, A. Freih. v. Eiselsberg, S. Exner, M. Gruber, A. Kolisko, Rich. Freih. v. Krafft-Ebing, I. Neumann, H. Obersteiner, R. Paltauf, Adam Politzer, F. Schauta, J. Schnabel, C. Toldt, A. v. Vogl, J. v. Wagner, Emil Zuckerkandl.

Begründet von weil. Hofrath Prof. H. v. Bamberger.

Herausgegeben von

Ernst Fuchs, Karl Gussenbauer, Ernst Ludwig, Edmund Neusser, L. R. v. Schrötter und Anton Weichselbaum.

Organ der k. k. Gesellschaft der Aerzte in Wien.

Redigirt von Dr. Alexander Fraenkel.

Verlag von Wilhelm Braumüller, k. u. k. Hof- und Universitäts-Buchhändler, VIII/1, Wickenburggasse 13.

Die „Wiener klinische Wochenschrift" erscheint jeden Donnerstag im Umfange von mindestens zwei Bogen Grossquart.

Zuschriften für die Redaction sind zu richten an Dr. Alexander Fraenkel, IX/3, Maximilianplatz, Günthergasse 1. Bestellungen und Geldsendungen an die Verlagshandlung.

Redaction:
Telephon Nr. 16.283.

Abonnementspreis jährlich 20 K — 20 Mark. Abonnements- und Inseraten-Aufträge für das Inund Ausland werden von allen Buchhandlungen und Postämtern, sowie auch von der Verlagshandlung übernommen. — Abonnements, deren Abbestellung nicht erfolgt ist, gelten als angenommen. — Inserate werden mit 60 h à 50 Pf. pro zweigespaltene Nonpareillezeile berechnet. Grössere Aufträge nach Uebereinkommen.

Verlagshandlung:
Telephon Nr. 6094.

XV. Jahrgang. **Wien, 13. März 1902.** **Nr. 11.**

Experimentelle Nierentransplantation.

Vorläufige Mittheilung.[1]

Von Dr. Emerich Ullmann, Privatdocenten für Chirurgie in Wien.

Meine Herren! Gelegentlich meiner Versuche über Darmtransplantation, über welche ich voriges Jahr dieser Gesellschaft zu berichten die Ehre hatte, dachte ich daran, ob es nicht möglich wäre, auch die Niere zu transplantiren. Die ersten diesbezüglichen Versuche misslangen aus dem Grunde, weil ich als Versuchsthier das Schwein wählte, dessen Venen ausserordentlich zart und zerreisslich sind. Erst als ich die Transplantationen an Hunden ausgeführt habe, gelangen sie vollständig. Ich will vorweg betonen. dass es sich bei meinen Versuchen

und als solchen wählte ich erst die Inguinalgegend, später auf Herrn Hofrath Exner's Empfehlung den Hals, weil an der letzteren Stelle die Thiere sich nicht lecken können und eine Verunreinigung am ehesten vermieden werden kann — wird durch einen Schnitt Arterie und Vene, am Halse also Carotis und Vena jugularis auf eine weite Strecke hin freigelegt; dieselben werden peripheriewärts ligirt und centralwärts mit je einem armirten Schieber — armirt, damit keine Verletzung der Gefässe entsteht — versehen. Nun werden die Gefässe durchschnitten und sowohl Carotis als Jugularis zur Gefässvereinigung, wie sie von Payr angegeben wurde, vorbereitet. Die Gefässe werden durch kleine Magnesiumröhren, die nur auf die Weise herstellen liess, dass die eine Hälfte der Röhren glatt ist, die andere Hälfte zwei

FIGURE 5. The first kidney transplanter. Announcement and title page from the work of Ullmann. Above is shown the announcement of the meeting to be held on the twenty-fourth of January, 1902, in Vienna. Dr. Ullmann was not given wide publicity, and his initials were incorrect. Below is shown his paper. It must have made quite an impression at the meeting because it is now given the lead position in the publication.

This is scientific reporting of the era fifty years before Billingham, Brent, and Medawar (Figure 4). "Nierentransplantation" is kidney transplantation.

previous week, there is a statement of the meeting to be held the following week. Dr. Ullmann is billed as discussing his work. His presentation was entitled "Nierentransplantation" or "Transplantation of the Kidney." In this brief report, Dr. Ullmann refers to previous work he had done on transplantation of the intestine and other organs. He describes in detail the transplantation of a dog's kidney from its normal position into the neck of the same animal, requiring anastomosis of the renal artery to the carotid artery.* In a subsequent note in the same journal, he reported transplanting a kidney from one dog into another, and later the kidney from a dog into a goat. He emphasizes his having carried out his kidney transplantation by direct vascular anastomosis, and he states: "It had not been deemed possible heretofore to transplant so large an organ as the kidney; nevertheless, it has been done and the vitality of the transplanted kidney has been retained along with its physiological function."

He then forecasts his future experiments, including his plan to make an animal preparation in which both of the animal's own kidneys are removed:

Further experiments will show whether kidneys can be transplanted from one dog to another, whether the kidney of one species of animal can be transplanted into another species and still retain its physiological function, and even whether (though it scarcely seems possible) transplanted kidneys can take over the burden of the entire blood-purifying process, i.e., whether the animal will remain alive if its own kidneys are removed and the transplanted ones are the only ones to function.

Several months later the local surgical society met again (June 27, 1902), and there was further discussion by Dr. Ullmann as follows:

I was unsuccessful at first in transplanting a kidney from one species of animal to another, but I am able to demonstrate to you today, before this distinguished audience, a goat into whose neck region the kidney of a dog has been transplanted. You can see that the kidney is functioning completely normally and that urine is flowing in drops from the end of the protruding ureter. I must frankly admit that the success of this experiment surprised even myself. Although it has been known for a time that an

---

* *Renal artery,* the main artery to the kidney; *carotid artery,* the main artery leading from the chest through the neck and to the head.

excised kidney, when perfused with foreign blood, soon resumes secretion, I did not really believe that this would be the case in a living animal; this opinion was shared by all the experts.

During the discussion period, Professor von Eiselsberg asked what had become of the dog which Dr. Ullmann had shown them previously. Dr. Ullmann replied that microscopic examination of the implanted kidney had not yet been performed.

Actually, no microscopic section or renal functional data are shown, and the additional report adds little knowledge, save to indicate that, indeed, the kidneys could be transplanted and the blood would flow through the newly transplanted organ, and urine flow from the ureter—at least long enough to fetch the animal over to the meeting for demonstration.

It is quite interesting that this first report of kidney transplantation involved an autograft, then an allograft, and finally a xenograft (dog to goat). Dr. Ullmann makes no particular point of any difference on this score, but did demonstrate the xenotransplant to the audience. This apparently terminated Dr. Ullmann's scientific work.*

Whatever the reason for Dr. Ullmann's abandonment of his transplant studies, their significance is unquestioned if for no other reason than that they influenced Dr. Carrel as he embarked on this work. Dr. Carrel refers to these studies of Dr. Ullmann in his very earliest papers.

A FRENCHMAN IN CHICAGO AND NEW YORK

Born in France in 1873, Dr. Carrel (whose sutures were described in Chapter 1) became a world figure of remarkable stature in surgery even though he spent most of his life removed from the daily chores of patient care. In 1900, he graduated in medicine at Lyons and began his laboratory studies there. In 1904, he came to Chicago, where, at the University, he carried out his first work on kidney transplantation.

---

* Born in Hungary in 1861, Dr. Ullmann graduated at Vienna in 1884 and had written extensively on surgical subjects, ranging from liver resection to gynecology, for twenty years. He was made professor in 1919, but soon gave up academic work and died in 1937. He never described any further experiments in transplantation.

In 1906, the Rockefeller Institute called him to New York. He carried his work further there, describing the techniques of transplantation, vascular suture, and blood transfusion and was the first scientist in America to receive the Nobel Prize. When war came, Dr. Carrel returned to France to carry out his studies on wound healing, with du Nouy. He was the collaborator in development of a chlorinated solution used to irrigate infected war wounds. This was known as Carrel-Dakin solution, and is still used in many hospitals. In 1919, he came back to the Rockefeller Institute and returned to his prime interest, the cultivation and perfusion of organs and tissues *in vitro.** Charles Lindbergh became a collaborator of Dr. Carrel's in 1928–1929, in developing a special kind of blood pump. About ten years later Dr. Carrel published his book, *The Culture of Organs.*

From Dr. Carrel's work came much knowledge of blood transfusion and blood vessel anastomoses, and many concepts that have led to the invention of pump oxygenators and extracorporeal circulation† as currently used in cardiac surgery. It is of historic interest that Dr. Carrel's earliest work both in France and in the United States was devoted to the subject of kidney transplantation.

Dr. Carrel's first American work was carried out in the Hull Physiologic Laboratory at the University of Chicago. The first publication was by Dr. Carrel and Dr. Guthrie, in *Science* in 1905, in which they described the transplantation of a kidney from the flank into the neck of the same dog. They showed that the operation could indeed be done, and that the kidney then proceeded to work satisfactorily. The following year, the same collaborators began an experiment which was to be a prototype of hundreds or thousands performed since, in the study of kidney transplantation. This publication was entitled "Successful Transplantation of Both Kidneys from a Dog into a Bitch with Removal of Both Normal Kidneys from the Latter." It was also in the form of a brief letter to the editors of *Science.* The authors told of a

---

* *In vitro,* literally "in glass"; an experiment carried out in a laboratory container or device; as opposed to *in vivo,* an experiment carried out in the normal living animal.

† *Pump oxygenator,* a machine to pump the blood and oxygenate it, in essence an artificial heart-lung; *extracorporeal circulation,* a term referring to the situation of a patient whose blood is flowing through a pump oxygenator and thus being circulated outside the body.

THE UNBREACHED BARRIER | 71

true allotransplant, done by direct anastomosis of the aorta and the vena cava (the large blood vessels below the heart, which supply blood to the kidneys). The significant fact was that both normal kidneys were removed from the bitch, so that her survival depended wholly upon the function of the transplants. This is the "kidney transplantation after bilateral nephrectomy"* referred to so many times in later chapters. They reported that by the eighth day the animal was up and about, doing quite well.

Dr. Carrell continued this work after he returned to the Rockefeller Institute two years later (in 1908), describing an extensive study of this subject. This was his major publication on the subject of transplantation. Amusingly enough, there is noted here a tendency to premature publication evidently observed among the great as well as among the near-great! Now, in 1908, he reveals for the first time that the dog, which he reported in 1906 as jumping up and running around on the eighth posttransplant day, had on the ninth day vomited, been operated upon, and died. One cannot help but note that the article initially describing the work was entitled "Successful Transplantation . . ." (although there must have been ample time to perform a follow-up during the proofreading process). A more charitable view would hold that it was a successful transplant, if even for only a short time. It functioned, put out urine, and maintained life in a bilaterally nephrectomized animal.

In any event, Dr. Carrel and his co-workers then changed their studies from the dog to the cat, and carried out a very large number of operations (Fig. 6). In the cat, the kidneys were transplanted *en masse*, meaning that both kidneys were removed at once with the major vessels above and below them (the aorta and vena cava), and put into the normal position in the new host. This operation, of course, required removal of both kidneys in the recipient.

Dr. Carrel was now able to discuss the character of the urine, the anatomical results, and the microscopic examination. He was delighted with the progress of his animals, and in some he had survivals at least

---

* *Bilateral nephrectomy;* the suffix "ectomy" means "removal of." Therefore, "bilateral nephrectomy" is the removal of the kidney on both sides (i.e., the removal of both kidneys).

Cat 6 looking at a piece of meat. Photograph taken on the twenty-first day after the operation.

FIGURE 6. One of Dr. Carrel's kidney-transplanted cats, 21 days after Carrel had carried out a bilateral kidney transplantation. The animal is apparently healthy enough to view a piece of meat with some interest, as indicated in the legend. Many of Carrel's publications contain wistful and humorous comments on the fine state of health and activity of his animals.

up to the sixteenth postoperative day: ". . . the cat is put into another room and spends all day climbing on and jumping off the furniture." He concludes that "It is possible to re-establish efficiently the function of transplanted kidneys." At the same time it was evident that he was beginning to focus on the problem that was to concern him most, and yet remain unsolved—namely, the problem of whether the kidney transplanted from one cat to another had any different fate from that moved around within the same cat.

Dr. Carrel gave very considerable credit to Dr. Murphy of Chicago for early studies on the method of blood vessel anastomosis. But Dr. Carrel hastened to point out that his own method of "circular suture" was far superior. Also at this time, Dr. Carrel tells the story of removing an artery from one animal and keeping it in a chilled salt solution for a few days, and then putting it into another animal and observing that it functioned quite well as an artery. This experiment was a foretaste of work to be done forty years later on preservation of the human aorta for replacement in diseases of the aorta.

Finally, in 1910, Dr. Carrel brought together his thoughts on kidney transplantation, and here he focused clearly on the central problem of the contrast between allografts and autografts. He wrote:

Should an organ, extirpated from an animal and replanted into its owner by a certain technique, continue to functionate normally, and should it cease to functionate when transplanted into another animal by the same technique, the physiological disturbance could not be considered as brought about by the surgical factors. The changes undergone by the organ would be due to the influence of the host, that is, the biological factors.

Dr. Carrel never did discover these "biological factors" or answer the question he himself posed: Was an allograft any different from an autograft? In the end, the answer to this question came from the study of skin rather than kidney.

It was not for another thirteen years (with the interruptions of World War I) that further progress was described in experimental kidney transplantation with the work of Dr. Williamson, at the Mayo Clinic Foundation in Rochester, Minnesota.

DR. WILLIAMSON AT THE BROTHERS MAYO

In 1923, Dr. Williamson reported an observation that in retrospect seems so obvious as scarcely to require comment. But to Dr. Williamson and his contemporaries it was an entirely new and clear observation, and yet quite puzzling. It was the very observation that Dr. Carrel had sought: a kidney transplanted from one animal to another showed an entirely different reaction from one moved about from one place to another in the same animal. Dr. Williamson was viewing in the much more complicated setting of a transplanted kidney what Dr. Holman that same year was witnessing in Baltimore in his skin grafts on the burned child. So far as we know, neither knew of the other's work.

After describing the events in the autotransplant (done within the same animal) in which the kidney maintains its normal function for weeks or months, he wrote:

The homotransplants present an entirely different result . . . very little difference between the urine from autotransplants and homotransplants can be noted, but this similarity of function is of relatively short duration. We have found that the average duration of function following a transplant of this type is four days.

Dr. Williamson was building on Dr. Carrel's work and was reasoning in much the same way. He states:

In the past this failure (of homotransplants) has largely been attributed to external conditions, such as thrombosis of the blood supply, obstruction to the ureter, and infection. But the fact that the autotransplant survives in spite of these factors seems largely to disprove the so-called mechanical theory of failure. . . . It seems to us that, underlying these failures is some fundamental biological principle which we have not yet been able to identify. It is unfortunate that the lower animals, such as the dog, do not possess a blood grouping like that of man. In the future it may be possible to work out a satisfactory way of determining the reaction of the recipient's blood serum or tissues to those of the donor, and the reverse; perhaps in this way we can obtain more light on this as yet relatively dark side of biology. . . . As yet we do not feel justified in attempting to explain definitely any of the observations that we have made in this preliminary report.

Dr. Williamson showed admirable scientific reticence in not going beyond his data to explain the findings!

Dr. Williamson's work is also more "modern" than Dr. Carrel's in its scientific appearances, because he analyzed the urine for its chemical constituents, and injected test substances into the blood to see how the kidneys would excrete them. Dr. Williamson was understanding clearly, for the first time, the rejection of a kidney. He continued working on this subject for several years, and finally in 1926 he published excellent microscopic photographs showing the reaction of rejection in a kidney allotransplant.

Dr. Williamson then left Rochester and the Mayo Clinic to become Head of the Department of Surgery at the University of Arkansas. In 1928, he opened practice in Green Bay, Wisconsin. He died in 1952.

At the time of Dr. Williamson's work, only a few years had passed since the description of blood groups had made blood transfusions safe, although many severe reactions still occurred. Dr. Williamson noticed that there were chance similarities between animals that sometimes permitted an allotransplanted kidney to survive long beyond its proper life expectancy. He wrote: "Were it possible to classify the experimental animals by blood grouping, it should be fairly easy to establish the truth or falseness of this supposition, provided tissue grouping corresponds to blood grouping, a fact not as yet established."

The interest that both Dr. Williamson and Dr. Holman had shown in transplant blood grouping was most appropriate, and ahead of its time. During the intervening years, this basic relationship was often neglected, and transplants across blood group incompatibility were repeatedly and unsuccessfully attempted. About 1960, it again became clear, as these early workers had predicted, that blood group compatibility was of major concern in the allografting of tissues and organs. Finally, in 1963, their ideas of tissue typing and tissue grouping, with histocompatibility crossmatching, began to be realized. They have now become the basis for the matching of donors and recipients.

The book on kidney transplantation remained essentially closed for another twenty-year period and another world war. Then, in the postwar world of 1945–1950, it was opened again by new assaults on the problem in London, Copenhagen, and Boston.

Kidney Transplants in London and Copenhagen: The State of the Art in 1953

If 1902 must be listed as a banner year, when the first kidney transplantation was done in a laboratory, then the year 1953 is another important milestone. It marked the completion and bringing together of modern allograft immunology with the surgical approach to kidney transplantation in animals and in man.

In 1953, Drs. Billingham, Brent, and Medawar described "actively acquired tolerance," as mentioned in Chapter 3. Likewise in 1953, the experimental allotransplantation of kidneys in nephrectomized dogs became a standard laboratory model. And at the same time the first systematic human studies of kidney transplantation in sick patients were in full swing.

It is historically appropriate that all of these things should have come together in 1953, just one year before the first identical twins presented themselves for transplantation; all were necessary steps to be taken before the first transplantation of a kidney between two living human beings could be successful. In considering the events of this notable year, let us look first at the status of experimental kidney transplantation, fifty years after Dr. Ullman and thirty years after Dr. Williamson.

Two of the important pioneers in experimental kidney transplantation began their work shortly after World War II. These two were Dr. Dempster at the Hammersmith Hospital in London and Dr. Simonsen of the Laboratory for Rheumatic Research and the Surgical Department of the Finsen Institute in Copenhagen. Of the two men, Dr. Dempster was more concerned with surgical problems and the microscopic picture, while Dr. Simonsen was more inclined toward immunologic investigation, particularly the study of "autoimmune" diseases.*

Dr. Simonsen's initial work was concerned with the factors involved in what he called "biologic incompatibility in kidney transplantation in dogs." He was interested not only in kidney allotransplantation but in the possibility that antikidney antibodies might be responsible for some kidney diseases in man. He considered that the results in his dogs with transplanted kidneys were due to an immune rejection response, and thought that everything he observed was accountable within the framework of Dr. Medawar's work on skin grafts in mice. (See Figure 7.) He clearly described the hastened rejection response when a kidney was transplanted a second time from the same donor:

The results of these experiments are hardly explicable other than by acquired antibody formation in the recipient against individual-specific

---

* *Autoimmune,* immunity against "self-tissues"; an aberration of the Burnet hypothesis; the suspected cause of several obscure diseases.

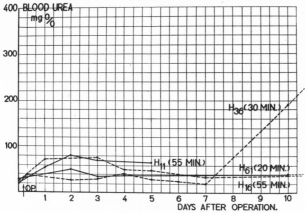

BLOOD UREA CURVES FROM DOGS WITH
1 AUTOTRANSPLANT (THE OTHER KIDNEY REMOVED)

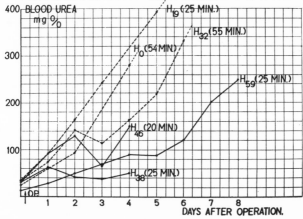

BLOOD UREA CURVES FROM DOGS WITH
1 HOMOTRANSPLANT (OWN KIDNEYS REMOVED)

FIGURE 7. Differences between an allograft and an autograft (from Simonsen, 1953). Here, for the first time, were shown the biochemical differences between a kidney moved around in the same animal (autograft above) and one moved from one animal to another (allograft below). In both sets of experiments the other kidney was removed; the function of the transplant is therefore critical for survival and determines the biochemical reactions in the animal. These charts show the values for blood urea after the grafting. Each line represents the time course of one experiment. It will be noticed by the low values for urea that the autografted kidneys (above) functioned well for many days.

Below are shown the contrasting changes in blood urea after allotransplantation. It will be noticed that, as the kidney is rejected, the blood urea rises sharply because the kidney is not excreting wastes properly. The times indicated after each curve are those of the ischemic interval—i.e., the length of time the kidney lacked blood supply during the course of transplantation.

antigens in the transplant. The observations have particularly been compared with and discussed in relation to similar findings by Medawar *et al.* in skin grafting experiments on rabbits.

His comments about the "second set" response in kidney are as follows:

When the primary transplant was removed after three–four days and replaced by the other kidney from the same donor, the secondary transplant disintegrated at a faster rate than the primary one, both from a functional and morphological point of view. . . . When the first stage transplant was removed three–four days after the operation and replaced by a kidney from *another* donor, this secondary transplant was not damaged more than the first stage transplant.

In addition, Dr. Simonsen began to work repeatedly on a dog experiment in which both of the animal's own kidneys were removed and a single transplanted kidney was in place. Now, as with some of Dr. Carrel's cats, the continued good health and survival of the animal depended on continued function in the graft. This was a critical experiment and was soon to become a model in many laboratories.

Dr. Dempster's work in London followed a rather similar course. He had two animals who survived ten days wholly on the function of the transplant and concluded that the "second set" response led to a different kind of rejection process. He also made injection studies of the renal artery, and was of the opinion that vascular spasm of the arteries was important in kidney rejection. In addition, he did some early studies using whole body irradiation,* both to irradiate the host for immunosuppression and to irradiate the transplanted kidney. Neither one yielded good results in these early reports.

Both Dr. Simonsen and Dr. Dempster were working with healthy animals. Neither one made an effort to produce chronic disease of the kidneys in their dogs prior to transplant, and thus one could not conclude much about the fate of a transplant in a sick patient. Both of them were doing scientific work in the laboratory from which human

---

* *Whole body irradiation,* exposure of the whole body to high-energy irradiation (x-rays, for example).

application in the hospital might at any time result. For such to be applied to man, marked advances were required in the clinical management of late kidney failure and uremia.* New methods of treatment were needed, other than transplantation, to help the patient weather the crisis before and after the transplant operation. For this, an artificial kidney was necessary.

The Artificial Kidney and Dr. Kolff of Holland

There are three kinds of diseases which account for the majority of fatal kidney failure in young people in this country today.† One, known as "Bright's disease," has the more formidable scientific name of glomerulonephritis, indicating that there is inflammation (-itis) of the kidney (nephron) arising in the little cups that filter the blood, known as the glomeruli.‡ Next in frequency is chronic pyelonephritis, meaning that the inflammation of the kidney (nephritis) begins in the kidney drainage system (kidney pelvis or pyelo). The third common group of diseases is that which includes congenital abnormalities, meaning that the patient was born with them. These include single kidneys, malformations of the kidneys, kidneys with cysts in them, and kidneys that are fused or joined in an abnormal and unsatisfactory way ("horseshoe kidney").

As these chronic kidney diseases progress, waste products accumulate in the blood. Patients suffering from chronic kidney failure and uremia display a pale, washed-out, yellow-pasty look; they lose appetite and weight; they cannot excrete water and salt properly, so they develop puffiness about the ankles (edema), fluid in the abdomen (ascites), and have an overwatered state referred to since the days of

---

* *Uremia,* the presence in the blood of chemical substances normally found in the urine; generally used to denote the state of sickness associated with kidney failure, and the inability to excrete body wastes.

† In older patients, *nephrosclerosis,* or hardening of the arteries in the kidney, produces the majority of cases of kidney failure; this is but one part of the generalized degenerative vascular disease known as *arteriosclerosis,* or hardening of the arteries, and it does not lend itself well to transplantation for that reason.

‡ *Glomeruli,* literally "little ball-shaped structures"; the filter cups of blood vessels in the kidney.

Mr. Pepys' diary as the "dropsy." Treatment was always medicinal, and rarely lasting or effective.

As early as 1914, it occurred to several people that the filtering function of the kidney might be reproduced mechanically. Each nephron, or kidney unit, has a little filter in the upper end, the glomerulus; millions of these present in the kidney filter out a fluid known as "glomerular filtrate," which then is processed (as described in Chapter 1) by the renal tubular cells.

It was an appealing idea to carry out this filtering process (the blood-washing part of the kidney's function) by passing the blood through some kind of filtering membrane. Several tried, but with little success. Thirty-five years before the successful development of such a device, Dr. Abel, Dr. Rowntree, and Dr. Turner of Johns Hopkins had seen the possibilities of the method, and in 1914 reported that diffusible substances could be removed from the blood of living animals by "dialysis," or washing the blood against a membrane with salt water on the other side. During this dialysis, waste products can pass through the membrane and be washed away with the drain water if they are small molecules that easily pass through the tiny holes in the membrane. The successful dialysis of diffusible substances through such membranes made it clear that an artificial kidney might be developed eventually.

In the middle 1930's others took up this work. Dr. McEwen, working at the Presbyterian Hospital in Chicago, was one of the first to cherish this idea; he tried to do this by making filter membranes out of a plastic solution called "celloidin"; the membranes were not much good, and the blood clotted too soon. *

At about that time two widely separate things happened, seemingly unrelated, which made the development of an artificial kidney possible. First was the isolation and preparation of a chemical substance that prevents the blood from clotting, known as heparin. Second was the commercial manufacture of long cellophane tubings. The tubes were initially made for sausage casing, and from this humble

---

* In 1964 Dr. McEwen, now a chemist at the University of California, wrote that his experiments were submitted for publication to what he called the *Journal of Negative Results!* Little came of the work although the concept was clear.

origin the artificial kidney was developed. Blood was conducted through the long cellophane tubings, and heparin was used to prevent clotting. The whole structure was then placed in a bath of sterile salt solution and it was possible thus to dialyze the blood, washing out the waste products accumulated in kidney failure and uremia.

This idea was first brought to practical fruition by Dr. Kolff of Holland. He performed his work during the war in occupied Holland, under the eyes of the Nazis who were totally ignorant of its significance. Dr. Kolff's first description of this in English was published in the Scandinavian literature, in 1944. Because of wartime blockade on scientific communication, the Scandinavian literature was not widely read in this country, and it was not until after the war that word of this development spread to students in this country. In 1946 Dr. Kolff described his work, in Dutch, under the title, "De Kunstmatige Nier" (the artificial kidney). Within a few months an abridged English translation appeared under the title, "New Ways of Treating Uremia; the Artificial Kidney, Peritoneal Lavage, Intestinal Lavage"; Dr. Kolff thus gave his discovery to the world, and other investigators could now take up the work.

In a recent letter, Dr. Kolff has written about some of these early events. Their critical role in the history of transplantation, as well as their performance in a Nazi-occupied country, makes them especially significant.

As the youngest volunteer assistant in the department of medicine at the University of Groningen in the Netherlands I had the care of four beds, or rather of the patients in them. One of my first patients was a young man suffering from chronic nephritis and slowly dying of renal failure. He was hypertensive, had headaches, became blind, and was vomiting every day. His old mother was the wife of a poor farmer, her back bent by hard work, dressed in her traditional Sunday black dress, but with a very pretty white lace cap. I had to tell her that her only son was going to die, and I felt very helpless. Gradually the idea grew in me that if we could only remove 20 grams of urea and other retention products per day, we might relieve this man's nausea, and that if we did this from day to day life might still be possible. This was in 1938, and soon afterwards, I met Dr. R. Brinkman, Professor of Biochemistry, who showed me the wonders of cellophane. Brinkman used cellophane to concentrate blood plasma, to determine osmotic pressures, and he himself had built several dialyzers. There were only a few papers published about hemodialysis. . . . in order to determine how much cellophane I would need to make an artificial kidney, I took a piece of cellophane tubing, commercially available as sausage casing. A piece 45 cm [about 20 inches] long was filled with only 25 cc of blood. I fixed this on a small board and rocked it in a saline bath. I had added 400 mg percent of urea to the blood and found that after one-half hour of dialysis all the urea had passed out of the blood.

I had built several apparatuses, and I had to pay for these machines myself; none was well enough constructed to be applicable clinically.

On the 10th of May, 1940, the German Armies invaded the Netherlands. My wife and I happened to be in the City of Hague. . . . Four days later from the upper floor of the hospital we saw a large mushroom cloud rise over the City of Rotterdam, which had been set alight by the incendiary bombs of the German Luftwaffe.

Dr. Kolff then diverted his attention to setting up a blood bank; this experience in the handling of blood was later to be of great help to him, but for political reasons he moved to the small city of Kampen situated where the River Yssel runs into the Zuider Zee. Here he enlisted the help of local industry left inactive by war, and he finished making his first artificial kidney. His first patient was treated with the artificial kidney on March 17, 1943. At about that same time, on the other side of the North Sea, Dr. Gibson and Dr. Medawar in Glasgow were looking closely at skin grafts on a burned patient; when these two observations were finally brought together, kidney transplantation was made possible. Dr. Kolff continues:

From March 17, 1943, until July 27, 1944, 15 patients were treated. Of these 15 patients only one survived. . . . I sometimes wonder what would have happened to this project if I had done it, not in the Netherlands, but in some location in the United States, and if having treated 15 patients in one and one-half years I could not have claimed a single therapeutic triumph!

Dr. Kolff then had several more artificial kidneys made, and he gave them to various hospitals in Britain, Canada, and America (Fig. 8). He states that "the last one disappeared to Poland, behind the Iron Curtain, and was never heard from since." Because all of these have disappeared, he had none with him when he came to America and he wrote:

Figure 8.   Dr. Kolff's artificial kidneys. This photograph, from Dr. Kolff's original publication, was taken in Holland during the second World War and shows the first few artificial kidneys that Dr. Kolff had developed from biologic concept to engineering reality. At the close of the war these kidneys, generously provided by Dr. Kolff, were sent to various centers in Europe and America, so that others could study and perfect further this important device that was to make it safe for patients to be cared for before transplantation.

Each of these machines, about the size of a baby carriage, was needed to replace the work of a kidney which can easily fit in the palm of a man's hand. The mechanical ingenuity of man, with all his engineering know-how, can never pack into such a small space the apparatus, chemical or mechanical efficiency that nature puts into small packages. The first artificial hearts, for example, were very large machines, and the first artificial lung was about the size of a grand piano.

When I visited Boston in 1947 I had given away all the kidneys I had and all I could do was to present blueprints to Dr. Carl Walter who then built the Peter Bent Brigham version of the rotating kidney. The Harvard group with John P. Merrill probably did more for the further propagation of dialysis than any other group.

On Dr. Kolff's visit to America, and when Dr. Thorn learned of this device, its significance immediately became apparent. Dr. Thorn had long been interested in kidney disease during his years at Johns Hopkins. After coming to Boston, he continued with this traditional interest of the Brigham Hospital. At the time of the war, Dr. Thorn perceived that in acute renal failure (such as the crush syndrome) the kidney would heal if the patient could be kept alive long enough. As Dr. Thorn now recalls that period he writes:

Thus the stage was set when we read of Dr. Kolff's early experience with the artificial kidney which he had constructed in Holland during the German occupation. Dr. Kolff made a visit to the United States and we invited him to the Brigham where he discussed with us his results and the practical problems leading to the construction of a suitable dialysis unit. He encountered marked febrile reactions in several of his patients. Dr. Carl Walter agreed to help with the engineering aspects and I asked Dr. John Merrill if he would be willing to take over this area for us. John and Carl worked together with the help of the engineering group on the Cape, and were able to come up with a greatly improved Brigham model of the Kolff kidney. Then began the long series of studies and experiments in the indications and contraindications for the use of this instrument. The development of the artificial kidney was an integral part of a long-range program leading to the transplantation of kidneys for irreversible renal failure or malignant hypertension.

The group that Dr. Thorn gathered for this task was a special one. Each man could lend special talents to the further perfection of the artificial kidney. One, Dr. Merrill, was completing his residency at the time, and took up the study of renal failure and the artificial kidney, later to involve him so deeply in the development of transplantation. Another, Dr. Walter, was a surgeon with long experience and knowledge in the development of special instruments, new devices, operating room sterilizers, and surgical equipment. Two others, Dr. Callahan and Dr. Smith, were young men collaborating in both mechanical development and clinical use. This team of five men, working at the Brigham Hospital in 1948 and 1949, developed the artificial kidney to a practical reality. This device was known as the Kolff-Brigham kidney, and it came into extensive use after their first report in 1950. Dr. Thorn and his team told how to make and assemble the kidney, how to put it together, how to make antiwetting surfaces that kept the blood from clotting, how to make rotating couplings that would keep the blood from being churned too much, and how to keep it sterile. They reported 33 dialysis procedures in 26 patients, all with excellent chemical and clinical results.

Many patients now began to arrive at the hospital for the treatment of chronic kidney failure; they were given an entirely different kind of treatment from that ever given before. If kidney failure was *acute*, then a blood dialysis on the artificial kidney two or three times in the course of a week or two might keep the patient healthy and alive long enough to let his kidneys heal. Many such cases were now documented, especially in those suffering from acute tubular necrosis and the crush syndrome, much like the girl operated upon three years previously by Drs. Hufnagel, Hume, and Landsteiner (p. 40). A year or two later this same artificial kidney was used in military casualties of the Korean War to treat acute kidney failure in wounded American soldiers.

The patient with *chronic* kidney failure presented a totally different problem. If there was no likelihood that his own kidneys would heal, then the artificial kidney became merely an instrument for the merciless prolongation of a hopeless life. In such a case, it could not tide the patient over until he could get well himself, for the simple reason that in chronic kidney disease the kidneys themselves are destroyed. The artificial kidney was at the same time an instrument that cured patients, and a Pandora's box that opened up new and difficult problems. A patient with chronic kidney failure might be kept alive for weeks, months, or years, but he had little to look forward to if his own kidneys could not be replaced. For physicians who had struggled for many years with chronic kidney disease and its resultant high blood pressure, one of the most attractive distant prospects was that of total removal of the two diseased kidneys that caused high blood pressure and often cost the patient his life. If both kidneys were to be removed, at least one new kidney had to be put in place! By 1950, the artificial kidney could readily be used; blood transfusion, antibiotics, and the general forward movement of medical science made new and more extensive surgical operations much safer and more feasible. Under such circumstances kidney transplantation deserved an entirely new look.

The first patient to be treated with the artificial kidney at the Brigham Hospital as part of a kidney transplantation was Mr. F. A. (PBBH 8V438). At the age of 37, this boiler repairman had been referred to the Brigham Hospital from the Springfield Hospital because of progressive kidney failure. His disease had commenced 17 years before when he developed acute glomerulonephritis after a severe streptococcus* sore throat.

Although the patient's disease had progressed slowly for many years, he finally developed a rapidly climbing blood urea and every other evidence of severe kidney failure. At the Springfield Hospital, he was cared for by medicinal means, which improved his condition temporarily. He was then transferred to the Brigham Hospital for dialysis on the artificial kidney, and over a period of about ten days he was dialyzed on the artificial kidney several times, which reversed his uremic state almost to normal.

The patient was returned to the Springfield Hospital in March 1951, under the care of Dr. Scola. To Dr. Scola must go the credit for doing the first transplant in a patient treated on the artificial kidney. He discovered that there was a patient nearby suffering from cancer of the ureter. A perfectly normal kidney had to be removed in order to get rid of the lower end of the ureter. This kidney, removed for the treatment of ureteral cancer, was transplanted into Mr. F. A. The transplant was done in a unique way, by joining the renal artery to the splenic artery after removal of the spleen.

In a recent letter Dr. Scola writes of this operation:

The donor was a 49 year old man who had to lose a good kidney due to

---

* *Streptococcus,* the round organism (coccus) growing in chains (strepto); a very dangerous bacterium that often causes sore throats and, thereafter, acute glomerulonephritis. Now a rarity because of penicillin treatment.

a tumor of the lower left ureter and his blood crossmatched with that of the recipient.

In considering the problems that might be encountered at operation, one strong possibility was that the recipient's renal artery may be narrowed (not infrequent in severe kidney disease) or may be multiple and small and not match the donor's vessels. Therefore, I was prepared to remove the spleen and swing the splenic artery down to the renal area. This is exactly what happened at operation on March 31, 1951, because the recipient's renal artery was atrophic. When I discovered this I entered the peritoneal cavity and easily brought the splenic artery retroperitoneally to the left renal fossa. The donor's renal artery was injected with heparin just prior to clamping (another team operated on the donor). After the anastomosis was completed, the recipient's renal artery was injected with heparin.

The transplanted kidney was without blood supply for 70 minutes.

This remarkable and highly original operation was weathered nicely. The patient did well for a few days, though he did not make a great deal of urine, and never sufficient to maintain normal life.

After the operation, the patient was sent back to the Brigham Hospital. He gradually rejected the kidney, developed more marked renal failure, became unresponsive to dialysis on the artificial kidney, and finally died about five weeks after the operation on May 7, 1951. At the autopsy, the kidney was found to be surrounded by infection and to show all the changes that we now associate with rejection.

Dr. Hume of Boston:
The Transplant Series Begins

By 1951, Dr. Thorn and Dr. Merrill had accumulated a large experience in treatments done on the artificial kidney. Increasingly, they saw patients for whom the artificial kidney offered little hope. Kidney transplantation was needed, and it was time for a renewed trial. It fell upon the shoulders of Dr. Hume, who had, with Dr. Hufnagel and Dr. Landsteiner, done that operation four years before, to take the responsibility for the first of these surgical transplants in the first major undertaking of its type; Dr. Miller was to take responsibility for some of the early phases of organization and correlation of medical data in this enterprise.

Dr. Hume was a native of Muskegon, Michigan, a graduate of

Harvard College with a B.S. degree, and of the University of Chicago Medical School. He had come to the Brigham Hospital as a surgical intern in 1943 and, with time out for service in the Navy, had carried forward his clinical and experimental work in the finest tradition of surgical science. Up to this time, most of Dr. Hume's experimental work had dealt with the control of the pituitary gland. Transplantation had played but a minor part in his interests and publications. He had completed his senior surgical residency in 1951, and as a skilled junior member of the staff with a strong interest in investigation, he was the ideal person to take over this enterprise.

Using the artificial kidney to tide the patient over preoperative and postoperative intervals, kidney transplantation was now to be given a trial in patients in whom there was no outlook for long-term survival except by repeated dialysis treatments on the artificial kidney. These were to be human allotransplants of kidney placed in the upper thigh. The operation could be carried out without prolonged general anesthesia. Although the position of the kidney in the thigh had many anatomical disadvantages, it was a sound procedure for this first series, since it gave the operating team maximum opportunity to control and observe the behavior of the transplant. Furthermore, if the transplanted kidney was harming the patient, it could easily be removed. Its anatomical changes could be sampled for microscopic examination with little discomfort to the patient.

The donors of these kidneys were to be either the bodies of recently deceased individuals or young people who had to lose a kidney anyway during treatment for a condition known as "hydrocephalus."* In this first series of transplantations, no kidneys were removed from healthy people who would not otherwise have had to lose one.

Just as in any new scientific undertaking, the final result here was

---

* *Hydrocephalus*, "water on the brain." It is a swelling of the head due to an accumulation of too much fluid in the ventricles of the brain, usually as result of a congenital abnormality in the drainage system of the brain. This can be treated by conducting this fluid through a small plastic tube out through one of the ureters so it is lost through the bladder along with the urine (Matson, 1949). The operation brings relief to hydrocephalic children and permits them to lead normal lives. In the course of this operation, the kidney itself must be sacrificed, and such kidneys often were the ones used for the early thigh transplants. Dr. Matson, neurosurgeon of the Brigham Hospital, made such kidneys available for transplantation by careful timing of his operation with the projected transplant.

not clearly seen at the outset. It was hoped that the transplanted kidneys might function longer than was previously reported in animals, or that the general advances in surgery, medicine, and biology would permit some unexpected success in transplantation. There was every reason to expect something new when all the techniques of modern medicine and surgery were applied. This expectation alone justified the undertaking, and the first patient was operated upon by Dr. Hume on April 23, 1951, about three weeks after Dr. Scola operated upon his patient in Springfield.

The results in the first few patients were very disappointing. Long-term survival was not attained. The new kidney itself was a "graft that lived and breathed." It took up oxygen, expended energy, and made good urine. The patient's biochemical disorder of uremia was reversed to normal. But then rejection occurred. The only new observation was that in chronically ill patients rejection was slower than in a healthy dog. Evidently the sick patient could not summon antibodies to reject the new kidney as rapidly as a normal animal.

But, despite disappointments, Dr. Thorn, Dr. Merrill, Dr. Hume, and their team persisted. In 1953, there occurred an event in their little group of patients which pointed up the fact that in science, as indeed in all other fields of human endeavor, a start must be made if anything at all is to be achieved. The special event here was the remarkable case of Dr. W.

THE CASE OF DR. W.

Now the patient was a doctor, a 26-year-old physician (Dr. G. W., PBBH 7E503), who was admitted to the hospital on October 17, 1953, suffering from chronic glomerulonephritis. His illness had commenced when he was only 12. He had had a severe cold which was followed by a streptococcus infection. In a few days, blood and abnormal protein had appeared in his urine.

About 12 years later, he was found to have elevated blood pressure and swelling of his ankles at night. He began to develop severe headaches and difficulties with his vision, and a rapidly increasing blood pressure. He was transferred to the hospital for consideration of a kidney transplantation.

On admission, Dr. W. was pale, and had marked accumulations of edema fluid. The chemical findings were those of advanced kidney failure.

On February 11, 1953, a kidney transplantation was performed, in which the new kidney was placed in his right thigh after two preliminary operations designed to make a little skin pocket to cover the kidney adequately. This kidney had been removed immediately from a patient who had died during an operation on the heart. The blood types were compatible, and the kidney was placed in a bag made of thin polyethylene film. The hope thereby was to prevent the antigens from the kidney from reaching the antibody-producing cells of the patient. The total ischemic interval* was 180 minutes. The initial postoperative course was very stormy, and the patient showed a marked tendency to bleed abnormally. He required many blood transfusions. The transplant made no urine, and a large blood clot formed around the kidney. The polyethylene bag was found to be torn, and by the nineteenth day after the transplantation the blood urea level had risen to ten times normal. Things looked very dark, and the course did not seem much better than those of any of the previous patients.

Then, on the nineteenth day, the picture changed. The kidney began to "open up," producing increasing amounts of urine until, around the twenty-fifth day, it was making 400 ml of urine every day. This situation improved steadily until the thirty-seventh day, when the kidney put out 1000 ml of clear urine in one day, and the output then ranged from 1000 to 3000 ml daily for almost six months.

This series of events was unprecedented. The patient had weathered every conceivable mishap and complication including infection, bleeding, and total kidney failure. But finally his wounds healed, and the kidney started to perform very well. The patient got out of bed and began to walk around; his appetite returned and he gained weight; his blood urea values returned toward normal, and his blood counts came back up to normal. He was discharged on the eighty-first day after transplantation—the first patient in history to be discharged out of the hospital living solely on the function of a kidney taken from another person.

---

* *Ischemic interval,* interval without blood flow.

Dr. W. then returned to the hospital every two or three weeks for checkups to be sure everything was all right. Careful observations were made on the function of this kidney, and they disclosed a very healthy kidney. By the one hundred-third day after the transplantation, the patient's blood chemical values were completely normal. The only difficulty was a continued elevation in blood pressure, for which he was placed on a number of drugs intended to bring his blood pressure down. This treatment was unsuccessful. Five months and 25 days after the transplantation, the patient died rather suddenly from a recurrence of renal failure with severe high blood pressure. Although the kidney output of urine had ceased toward the end, the patient died as much from heart failure as from kidney failure. At no time had it been considered possible to remove his own two diseased kidneys. But this very frustration made it doubly clear that bilateral nephrectomy must become a part of any successful renal transplantation done in the future as treatment for chronic glomerulonephritis with its attendant high blood pressure.

The kidney graft after death showed that its arteries had developed arteriosclerosis (hardening of the arteries due to the deposit of fatty substances in the wall) as a result of the severe high pressure of the blood coursing through it. There was little evidence of rejection; rather, the patient succumbed to the widespread indirect effects of his kidney disease and high blood pressure. Reviewing the course of this particular patient, favorable factors included the compatibility of the blood groups, the short ischemic interval, and the skill developed by Dr. Hume in doing the operation and by the whole team of doctors in taking superb care of the patient. The explanation of precisely why this patient lived 175 days with good kidney function while none of the others had shown anything approximating such a good result must remain a mystery. The polyethylene bag might have helped somewhat, but it was torn. Most students of transplantation would probably offer only the explanation that there is the occasional long-term stray success in transplantation without immunosuppression, both in animals and in man. Some of nature's creatures are more closely related to each other than might appear on the surface—a sort of random tissue-resemblance. In this instance some sort of close antigenic or genetic relationship must be postulated between a young woman dying during a heart operation and a physician-patient dying of kidney failure. In terms of histocompatibility matching, not used extensively for another fifteen years, its seems likely that the donor and the recipient of this transplanted kidney shared many antigens even though they were unrelated. This was a chance occurrence expected in about 4.0 percent of random pairings. This is frequent enough to account for the rare spectacular success of allografts between unrelated persons or experimental animals, using minimal or zero immunosuppression as was the case here.

The Barrier in Retrospect

Initially, there were nine patients operated upon by Dr. Hume in collaboration with Dr. Merrill and Dr. Thorn. This was the first series of allotransplantations in unmodified* patients, using unprotected kidneys. In 1953 Dr. Hume returned to the Navy for his second tour of active duty. In 1956 he was called to the Medical College of Virginia as Professor and Head of the Department of Surgery. In Richmond he carried forth his work on kidney transplantation with characteristic vigor and effectiveness.

In Boston, he was succeeded in this work by Dr. Murray. Dr. Murray, a graduate of Holy Cross College and Harvard Medical School, had in 1949 completed his surgical residency at the Brigham. His special study of plastic surgery at the New York Hospital was completed in 1951. Since 1951 he had been working in the laboratory, specifically determining the best way to do a kidney graft. By 1954 he was satisfied that the best way to do kidney grafts was to place the kidney in the abdomen, behind the peritoneal membrane, with the ureter draining directly into the bladder. Although some workers had suspected that even autografted kidneys did not function in a completely normal way, Dr. Murray had demonstrated conclusively that they did.

Taking up Dr. Hume's work, Dr. Murray performed six additional operations of the same general type. Thus, there was a total of fifteen

---

* The term *unmodified* has come to refer to a patient who as a recipient of a transplant has had no superimposed attempt at immunosuppression by any method.

individuals who were the first to have kidney allotransplantation without any help from drugs or irradiation.

No patient had been given truly prolonged relief. In none was a success to be claimed, even in the case of Dr. W. In several the initial function of the kidney was very poor for technical reasons. In none was the kidney cooled prior to transplant. In all cases the finest possible care was given, and elegant chemical and microscopic studies were carried out so that the student of this subject could learn and move forward on the basis of this experience.

As the eventful year of 1953 drew to its close, and with it this series of transplantations, a number of very important lessons had been learned that were rapidly to be translated into the more hopeful experiences soon to be encountered. These were lessons learned, not only from the animal experiments of Dr. Simonsen and Dr. Dempster, and the beginning program of animal work in the Harvard laboratories, but also from the initial experiences in man. In all of these cases, both in dogs and in man, the kidney transplantation was exposed to the processes of "nature in the raw." There were no artificial attempts by drugs or iradiation to modify the immunity of the patient. This was transplantation *without* immunosuppression. The lessons learned from it could be enumerated as follows:

1. A transplanted human kidney could, in a few days, bring back to normal the disordered biochemical and clinical status of the uremic patient suffering from chronic renal failure.

2. The blood vessel and ureteral anastomoses had to be performed with great care just as they did in the animal; the ureteral anastomosis to the skin was unsatisfactory and favored the development of infection. Placing the kidney inside the abdomen, joining it to the vessels of the pelvis, and suturing the ureter to the bladder had been shown by Dr. Murray in the laboratory to be far preferable.

3. The uninhibited rejection response in a patient with chronic uremia was slower than in the healthy dog.

4. Thanks to the studies of Dr. Dammin and his Department of Pathology, the histologic[*] sequences of human transplantation

---

[*] *Histologic*, from the Greek *histos* for loom or warp, refers to the detailed pattern of cells and fabric of tissues as seen under the microscope.

were now seen and described for the first time under the micro-scope. They were much the same in man as in the animal. An invading army of lymphocytes and plasma cells from the reticuloendothelial system swarmed into the kidney and de-stroyed the tubular parts of each nephron, leaving the glom-eruli free. Finally the entire kidney was overwhelmed, reducing its function to zero.

5. In occasional unrelated individuals, one might find unexpected compatibility similar to that of Dr. W.

6. Although the biochemical and clinical disorders of uremia and chronic renal failure were reversed by the transplant, blood pressure might remain high; removal of the diseased kidneys was going to be necessary.

Thus ended the story of kidney allotransplantation without im-munosuppression. To critics—and there were many at the time—it appeared to be a sorry tale bringing little hope for the future. But to those closer to the work, and in light of later events, it was an im-mensely important experience. Its accomplishment was an essential surgical and immunologic preliminary to the entirely unexpected turn of events that soon was to follow.

5

MOST KIDNEYS ARE PAIRED; MOST PEOPLE ARE NOT

The Identical Twin Episode

Be not slow to visit the sick.

—BOOK OF ECCLESIASTICUS

TWINNING, PAIRING, AND GRAFTING

While many mammals are fortunate enough to bear their families all at once in litters, most human beings must content themselves with children born one at a time. Human mothers have twins but once in every 90 pregnancies. Most of these twins do not resemble each other, they are brotherly or "fraternal" twins. They arise because two of the mother's ova, or eggs from her ovary, have arrived in the uterus simultaneously. There, they have been fertilized by two of the many millions of the father's sperm cells which have been deposited there. One such twin may be red-haired and the other a brunette; one a boy, and the other a girl. One may be tall and the other short; one a mathematician and the other a poet. These fraternal twins are called "dizygotic"* twins because they come from two ova. Most certainly they are not identical.

---

* *Dizygotic,* arising from two zygotes or sets of genetic materials; as opposed to monozygotic or identical twins arising from but one ovum.

95

But one pair of each three sets of twins arises because of a remarkable circumstance: the duplication of cellular tissues resulting from the father's fertilization of only a single ovum in the mother. They arise only once in every 270 pregnancies. It is estimated that in a population of 200,000,000 people, there are between 600,000 and 750,000 pairs of these identical or "monozygotic" twins.

In the autumn of 1954, the problem of allografting was on dead center. The anatomic and physiologic sequences of rejection were clearly defined, but there seemed little hope of solution. Suddenly, a remarkable opportunity arose—an opportunity to return to normal life for many years a dying patient who, by the transplantation of a cellular organ from another living person, was to be given good health. This circumstance arose because of illness in one individual of a pair of identical twins. The graft was therefore an isograft rather than an allograft. Its success was evident to all, and had an immediate and far-reaching effect on the entire transplant research effort, both in this country and abroad. By the same token, we were for the first time presented with the doctors' dilemma—distributing a rich supply of healthy tissue between two individuals, assisting one by giving him a transplant and injuring the other by taking a kidney. The question of the distribution of scarce anatomical resources, and its ethical implications, was clearly perceived in 1954 although it did not attract wide public attention or stimulate the passage of new legislation for another decade.

The effects of the identical twin experience on transplant research were as stimulating as the work of Drs. Billingham, Brent, and Medawar. Coming only a year after their laboratory report, the twin transplants served notice to the medical world that a new field of surgical care and immunologic study was at hand.

The remarkable identity of an identical twin pair has long been the subject of song and story. Identical twins are so much alike that minute variations in the form of the hands or the folds of the ear, minor abnormalities in the color of the eyes, and minor and subtle blood-group properties are all shared exactly alike in the two. The single ovum of the mother has had but one lot of nucleic acid. To this has been added an exactly equal amount, contained in the chromosomes from the father's sperm. These genetic chemicals have then been shared precisely between two offspring rather than among the cells of one. The two children therefore resemble each other like two cells within a single individual, and they resemble each other much more exactly than any parent ever resembles a child.

From the earliest consideration of any kind of tissue graft or transplant, it has been suspected that tissue could be exchanged readily between identical twins. This concept, that the genetic similarity between identical twins was so great that their tissues could be traded freely, antedates the modern era of transplant research by centuries. There are many references to grafts between identical twins in the medical literature. In one, reported from Germany in 1927, skin was traded between identical twins to help reconstruct congenital deformities of the hand which were the same in both. In other instances, and more frequently than in any other application, the healthy twin has donated skin to help the closure of a burn defect in the other. In one report, from a small town in Colorado (Blandford and Garcia, 1953), the extent of this skin graft was very great; so great, in fact, that the *donor* had to receive a blood transfusion!

Dr. Brown, a plastic surgeon in St. Louis, reported the case of a child who needed skin to cover a burn. He put on some skin allografts from the mother. These were rejected in due course, as one would expect from Dr. Holman's study. In this same report (1937) Dr. Brown stated that for many years he had been looking for a pair of identical twins to see if they could trade skin; finally he found one. Both members were healthy. They consented to have small skin grafts traded to see if they would take satisfactorily. This was done, and the skin was exchanged without any evidence of rejection whatsoever.

Other than the skin, there are but few tissues or organs which an identical twin might be able to give to his sick brother. Of these, the kidney is foremost because it is paired.

Considering that one of every 270 pregnancies results in the birth of identical twins, and that the vast majority of kidneys are paired organs, it would be inevitable that one day a disease or injury to the kidneys of an identical twin would raise the possibility of donation of a kidney from the healthy twin for a transplantation. It would also be likely that this donation could be accomplished more successfuly in a hospital where the work of the doctors and their clinical departments was already focused on kidney disease, the treatment of uremia, and the use of the artificial kidney.

Thus it was that in the autumn of 1954 this precise circumstance came to light in a way which was highly favorable for its recognition and success.

THE CASE OF MR. R. H.

The first such patient, Mr. R. H. (PBBH 9G7820), had evidently been quite healthy until he was 22 years old, though he had contracted scarlet fever when he was only 5. Scarlet fever is a streptococcus infection rarely seen nowadays because of the use of penicillin. At the time of this patient's youth (about 1937), streptococcus infections were still a serious problem, and they were frequently followed by acute kidney disease of the glomerulonephritis type. Scarlet fever was probably the initiating factor in Mr. R. H.'s chronic kidney failure.

While in military service, Mr. R. H. had begun to notice some puffiness in his feet and legs. The medical officers who examined him discovered what had not been evident on his induction physical examination—namely, that his blood pressure was elevated. Within a few days he was found to have some abnormalities of urine, and finally he developed an elevation of urea in the blood. It became evident that he was suffering from chronic renal failure, which was quite rapidly progressive in its severity.

During 1952 and 1953, the patient was admitted for further diagnosis and treatment on several occasions, at the Boston Public Health Service Hospital. It became increasingly clear that his chronic nephritis was severe and that the outlook for survival was very poor. Neither he nor any of those immediately in charge of his case had any reason to know or suspect that these were the same years when the animal experiments of Dr. Simonsen and Dr. Dempster showed that kidneys transplanted with blood vessel anastomoses could work quite successfully, and likewise the years when Dr. Hume was showing that in man the same short-term function could be accomplished. The practical step of kidney transplantation was becoming a reality while Mr. R. H. was becoming progressively sicker; only the immunologic barrier to allotransplantation remained an unsurmounted obstacle.

In the fall of 1954, Dr. Miller of the United States Public Health Service telephoned Dr. Merrill at the Brigham Hospital to suggest that there might be an opportunity here for transplantation of a kidney from one person to another because his patient, Mr. R. H., had a twin brother. On the recommendation of Dr. Miller, the patient was then transferred to the Peter Bent Brigham Hospital on October 26, 1954. Here was a physician, experienced in the care of patients with chronic kidney disease, who could see the immense possibility opened up by the presence of an identical twin, even though he himself never had occasion to do research in this particular field of study. Upon transfer, the patient was admitted to the Kidney Study Unit, where many patients in chronic kidney failure were cared for daily. When necessary, these patients could be dialyzed on the artificial kidney, and this dialysis was needed for Mr. R. H.

Along with this work, extensive study was undertaken to determine whether or not the twin brother was actually an identical twin. The brothers looked quite similar, but were not exactly the same height; all of the blood groups (both major and minor) were identical; the obstetrician reported that they were born with but a single placenta; there was a tiny birthmark on the ear which was identical in both of them. Still and all, identity of twinning should be established beyond doubt, if possible.

Four years before, in England, a problem of family identity had arisen involving three five-year-old boys: there was a possibility that as infants they had been incorrectly identified in the newborn nursery. Two of them were thought to be identical twins, and skin graft trades among the children were performed to decide the matter. It was assumed that in identical twins skin grafts would take perfectly, while in other relationships they would not. As a result of this three-way skin trade, two of the children were restored to their rightful parents.* In this case of misidentity, the assumption that identical twins could trade skin freely was actually used as a means of establishing identity.

The same concept was now transferred to the brothers H. Skin

---

* This was the work of the dean of British plastic surgeons, Sir Archibald McIndoe, who worked at the hospital in East Grinstead during the war. A transplant research fund has since been established in his memory which made it possible to bring Dr. Simonsen from Copenhagen to this center for the study of transplantation.

grafts were traded. These skin grafts, each about the size of a postage stamp, were placed on the arms of the two men. After many weeks there was no evidence whatsoever of graft rejection in either case, and this was confirmed by microscopic examination of biopsies from each skin graft.

Now was a time for decision in the dilemma that soon was to become so urgent and frequent. Was it right and proper to sacrifice a normal kidney from a healthy person, to rescue another who was ill?

A prime consideration here was the status of the urinary tract in a healthy brother. If he had any abnormality of either kidney, then clearly neither should be removed no matter how great the need of the other twin. Careful diagnostic study undertaken by Dr. Harrison, urologic surgeon to the hospital, and long experienced in surgery of the kidney, failed to disclose any defect. If a twin had contracted acute glomerulonephritis from a streptococcal infection in childhood, was there not a likelihood that the healthy twin might later fall prey to the same disease? This question could not be answered with certainty, though statistical studies of this type of kidney disease in twins had failed to disclose any increased tendency on the part of the other twin to contract the disease (Addis, 1948).

There was no question about the desire of the healthy donor to help his brother. Identical twins, brought up together, and long devoted to each other, have an unusual emotional stake in each other's illness. This fraternal devotion was later to become important in medicolegal decisions.

About the twentieth of December, 1954, a final meeting of surgeons, physicians, and immunologists was held to make the final decision about Mr. R. H. Should the transplantation be carried out? Where should the kidney be put—in the thigh or in the abdomen? How should the ureter be drained to the outside? All of the experiences of the laboratory and of the previous allotransplants were called into play. It is particularly important that Dr. Murray's laboratory experience with kidneys placed in the abdomen of dogs gave everyone the courage to go ahead with the decision to place the kidney in the abdomen with direct anastomosis of the ureter to the bladder.

All sensed that a remarkable opportunity had been offered at the right moment and (hopefully) to the right group of doctors; the decision was unanimous to go ahead.

On December 23, 1954, the operation was performed. Dr. Harrison removed the left kidney from the healthy donor. This kidney was then taken directly into the next operating room where Dr. Murray was performing the operation on the recipient, and had dissected out the blood vessels in the pelvis of the sick twin. It was the conviction of all concerned with this transplant that the kidney should be placed here, near where it belonged in the retroperitoneal area of the abdominal cavity. In identical twins, in whom the immunologic barrier was presumed to be absent, the best position for the kidney would be near its normal position, protected from injury by the bony pelvis and with its ureter running directly into the bladder. As soon as Dr. Murray received the kidney he joined the artery and vein to the blood vessels of the patient.

The length of time between the removal of an organ and its implantation in its new site is called the "ischemic" period. Actually the important period of time is that between the final clamping or division of the main renal artery in the donor and the opening up of all the blood vessels anastomoses in the recipient. It will later become evident that not only this interval but likewise the temperature of the kidney during this time is critical for its subsequent survival. In this first experience with a successful kidney transplant, the ischemic period was a little less than one and a half hours, and no attempt was made to cool the kidney.

As soon as the new kidney was in place, with the blood vessels open, and even before Dr. Murray and Dr. Harrison had sewn the ureter to the bladder, drops of crystal-clear normal urine could be seen coming from the divided end of the ureter. The two diseased kidneys were not removed.

After the operation the sick man recovered rapidly. Before the operation his heart had been enlarged, and there was fluid in his lungs. Within a few weeks the heart had decreased in size, the fluid in the lungs cleared, and clinical progress was good with return of appetite, strength, and vigor. The piling up of waste products in the blood, so noticeable by elevation of the blood urea, soon returned to normal.

The urine volumes were normal. Within a month the patient was on the road to convalescence.

His elevated blood pressure did not return to normal as rapidly as had been hoped. There is strong evidence that diseased kidneys, whose function is abnormal and whose blood supply may be restricted, make a substance known as "renin"* which elevates the blood pressure. As long as the two diseased kidneys were still in place it seemed that the blood pressure would not return to normal. Therefore, these two diseased kidneys, which were now making no urine at all, were removed. By the sixth postoperative month, all of the surgical operations were over, and convalescence was complete.

The patient was finally discharged from the hospital, fully recovered. The patient could return to work. He soon was married (to the nurse who cared for him in the hospital) and raising a family.

PERSPECTIVES FROM THE TWINS

After a year had gone by, and their patient was still in good health, the transplantation group felt justified in reporting this event to the medical public. Their report ends with three questions:

Why one identical twin and not the other should develop glomerulonephritis, and whether the kidney of the unaffected twin transplanted into the diseased recipient will be susceptible to further attacks is a question still to be answered. Unanswered also is the question as to whether the transplanted kidney in its unusual position with a short and abnormally innervated ureter will escape eventual infection.

All three of these questions have been of critical importance in kidney transplantation; but long before the article was published or the questions posed, this experience in identical twins was known by word of mouth to interested physicians and surgeons throughout the world.

To many doctors, learning of this experience, it seemed to be a medical freak. Many coincidences were necessary. Not only must the

---

* *Renin* (the "kidney substance") is changed to *angiotensin,* literally "a substance that produces pressure in blood vessels," a hormone that causes high blood pressure or hypertension.

twins be identical, but they must be of a reasonably youthful age, one of them in the end stages of renal failure. To cap all the other coincidences, the sick twin must then be in the hands of a physician who will consider a transplant and seek the necessary consultations. Despite this impressive series of requirements, the experience of Mr. R. H. was soon matched, and while still the first, he was no longer unique. There was reason to suspect that, despite all the necessary coincidences, there would be many others.

Within three years several more pairs of identical twins presented themselves at the hospital. Not always were the donors suitable nor the illness of the recipient such as to give him a fine outlook for health, should the transplant be successful. In such cases operation could not be offered. By 1958, 7 kidney transplants had been done at the Brigham between identical twins. In addition, there was a twin transplant in Montreal, another in Paris, another in Oregon. By the fall of 1963, about 30 identical twin transplants had been done throughout the world, and by January 1970, the total had risen to 49.

Not all were as successful as the first case of Mr. R. H. In the Brigham group there had been three failures, one due to technical problems in the blood vessel anastomosis, in which the donor kidney had two tiny vessels of unequal length instead of one good-sized vessel. For this reason it has become routine to make an x-ray picture of the blood vessels of the aorta and the kidney arteries, known as an aortogram, to be sure which kidney is the more clearly available for transplantation. And, gradually, the three lingering questions could be answered, with increasing certainty.

Most hopeful was that the last question—will the ureter in its short and abnormal position escape infection?—could be answered in the positive. Under proper circumstances and with careful technique, it is possible to have a kidney transplantation in the pelvis function many years without any infection. Dr. Murray had shown this to be true in the laboratory; now it was proven in man.

The first question—whether the donor twin might develop glomerulonephritis or get sick later—could also be answered, likewise favorably. In the many twins who have donated a kidney, there have been no serious troubles except in one donor who developed mild glomerulonephritis seven years after donating one of his kidneys to his dying twin brother; both brothers are now well years later. The only death was from an entirely unrelated accident several years after the transplant.

But the second question has remained one of the central problems in the entire field of kidney transplantation—whether the kidney of the uninfected twin transplanted into the diseased recipient will be susceptible to further attacks. Unfortunately this question was answered unfavorably in the affirmative quite early in the experience with identical twin kidney transplantation.

Early in the twin experience, there were patients who developed glomerulonephritis in the transplanted kidney, as if some kinds of antibodies against that kidney were formed even though they were not allotransplantation antibodies (of the kind active in transplants between individuals other than identical twins). In several instances both diseased kidneys were removed as a preliminary to the kidney transplantation because of the possibility that the patient's own diseased kidneys might "sensitize" him against his new kidney tissue.

Most important, and coming to occupy a central position in the dilemma of kidney transplantation, was that this very first patient, Mr. R. H., died of coronary artery disease eight years after the transplantation, having developed glomerulonephritis in the transplanted kidney. Suffering from a fatal illness, he had been given eight good years; but in the end nephritis developed again. Four other twin transplants had shown glomerulonephritis in the transplanted kidney by biopsy, and later died of the disease.

Such a sad outcome would have little bearing on a kidney transplantation done between identical twins for injury or loss of the kidneys, infection of the kidneys, or tumor. But for this very special disease, glomerulonephritis, it had an ominous import indicating that the disease tends to recur even in the new kidney. Currently, enough kidney transplants in twins have lasted over ten years so that we can be reasonably optimistic about this matter. And yet these events have made the treatment of such patients increasingly a challenge. Some of the drugs used in the allotransplant procedure have become useful in identical twins, to prevent them from developing an entirely different type of immune response to the kidney, the autoimmune antibodies.

The total world experience with identical twin transplants has been 49 cases; there have been 15 transplants between nonidentical twins.

In the experience in identical twin transplants, fifteen years after the first twin was operated upon, the longest surviving patient from an identical-twin transplant is in her fourteenth year. Although difficulties in identical-twin transplants occur, the estimated survival of transplants from identical twins is 86 percent through the fifth year. The incidence of late kidney disease in identical twin transplants is diminishing (see page 164). In the late 1950's, identical twin transplants constituted the vast majority of successful kidney transplants. As of the present time they constitute about 2 percent of the 6000 or more kidney transplants recorded and analyzed in the International Human Kidney Transplant Registry.

How Young Can a Donor Be?

The successful transplantation of a kidney from a healthy twin to an individual suffering from chronic nephritis had a profound effect. There was a gradual changeover of many laboratories, in medicine, surgery, and immunology, toward a focus on the transplant problem. Just as Dr. Medawar's publication (in 1953) on actively acquired tolerance had shown that the immunologic barrier could be broken (though by a means scarcely practical in man), so also the identical twin transplants had shown that transplantation would become a clinically useful means of treating human disease (though by a means scarcely practical in most cases).

Of equal interest was that the twin experience had brought the dilemma of tissue donation into very sharp focus: was it morally right and ethically acceptable to injure one person to help another?

Among these questions of tissue donation (many of which are discussed in greater detail in Chapter 10), one in particular arose rather early in the twin experience and is worth an extra word of explanation. The question arose when twins arrived with all signs "go" for a transplantation: the sick twin critically, dangerously, and terminally ill, the well twin in excellent health with a pair of normal kidneys. There was only one stumbling block: they were below the age of consent, in their teens.

There is a very considerable web of legal precedent and statutory restriction surrounding the removal, disposition, examination, and operative manipulation of the tissues of the human body. Deep in this legal network is rooted the concept that a person under the age of 21 cannot give consent for an operation without parental approval in written form. Likewise there is the concept that a minor does not have the power to indicate that a portion of his body should be used to help another. Here was a legal tangle to unsnarl, and one that appeared for a while to be as much of a barrier as anything else in transplant biology itself.

On legal advice, and with the approval of the donor twin and his parents, a study was made of the emotional attachment between the twins. How much emotional damage would be done to the well twin were it to be made impossible (for reasons purely of legal impropriety) to help his sick brother by giving a kidney? Viewed in this light, the kidney donation became a positive act to promote the emotional well-being and long-term psychiatric health of the donor, as well as a step to help the recipient. This concept opened the door to the judges' chambers and helped to untie the legal knot.

As a result, the Supreme Court of the Commonwealth of Massachusetts handed down a judgment to indicate that such a transplant was within the letter and the spirit of the law. Professor Curran, then of the Department of Legal Medicine at Boston University, has written an account of this historic case:

. . . In most cases of minors, of course, parental consent is controlling in regard to medical treatment. However, in such cases the treatment is always potentially *beneficial* to the child. In transplantation of a kidney from a healthy twin to save the life of a sibling, there is a potential benefit to the sick twin, but what of the healthy donor? He will lose one of his two kidneys. At some time in the future such a loss could be highly detrimental should his remaining kidney be threatened.

At the hearing the justice heard testimony not only from the consenting parent, but also from the donor, who was fully informed of the nature of the operation and gave his full consent. Attorneys for the parties were, of course, fully aware of the issue of "benefit" to the healthy twin. On this point they produced the most significant factor in the case. They offered the testimony of a psychiatrist who interviewed both boys. He gave it as his opinion that if the operation was not performed and the sick twin were to die, it would result in a "grave emotional impact" on the healthy twin.

Justice Edward A. Counihan, Jr., who had heard the case, rendered his opinion on June 12, 1957, holding that the hospital and the surgeons could proceed with the operation on the consent of the parent, and that of both twins, without incurring civil or criminal liability for such action.

Justice Counihan found that the operation was necessary in order that the sick twin survive. He also found that the well twin had been fully informed and understood the nature of the operation "and its possible consequences" and had consented to it.

This decision, and the concept that went into its clarification, turned out to be of great assistance to other hospitals struggling with the same problem; similar declaratory judgments were handed down subsequently for donors who were under age. So long as the transplant had a high certainty of functioning normally—as in the great majority of the identical twin transplants—any question about the advisability of removing a kidney from a healthy person to assist another to survive life-endangering disease could be answered. The court decision solved the lawyer's dilemma, but did not answer the doctors' dilemma, still to be solved for each individual patient on his own merits.

When young identical twins (children under 12) were presented for the question of transplantation, it was necessary for the doctors of the hospital to say "No" despite possible legal approval, merely on the basis that a child so young could not really know the meaning of a tissue donation. He could not understand the possible harm to himself in the future and could scarcely be sophisticated enough to suffer lasting emotional upheaval should the decision be adverse. Furthermore, such donors are too young for a definitive evaluation of their own health. Older children (in their teens) could undertake such a project as this legally; but for small children, even though a life was lost by the saddening decision, the transplant was not advisable because of jeopardy to the young and healthy donor.

6

BATTERING
AT THE BARRIER

Whole Body Irradiation
as a Means of Immunosuppression

We have scotch'd the snake, not killed it.

—MACBETH

THE BALANCE OF SURVIVAL

On April 10, 1958, a patient with no kidneys was admitted to the hospital. This was not the first time that Dr. Merrill and the Kidney Study Unit had been forced to cope with this remarkable problem. Although a rare situation, one or two similar cases had been seen in the previous five years, and comparatively little could be offered to the patients. This patient, however, Mrs. G. L., arrived at a very special time. The findings in her case and the procedures used were, like those in Mr. R. H., to have a lasting effect on tissue transplantation.

The events of 1953 were in the background. Actively acquired tolerance had been demonstrated by Dr. Medawar; kidney transplantations both in the dog and in man had shown that the surgical operation could be performed and that the transplanted organ did its job.

The events of 1954, and the subsequent identical twin transplantations, were also understood and assimilated. It was clear that a human kidney, transplanted into another person, could maintain life for a matter of years, and a wasted, pasty-faced, headache-ridden uremic could become a healthy member of society. Over the four years intervening, about a half-dozen more twin transplants had been performed, including that involving the children discussed in the court case.

No one had progressed beyond the twins with much success. Laboratories were attempting to enhance graft acceptance by preliminary injection of masses of cellular debris or cellular extracts. The goal of the experiments was to "prepare the bed" for the graft by "binding" antibody or by some other as yet unknown biologic reaction. Unfortunately, most of these attempts resulted merely in sensitization, so that the subsequent graft was driven away even more hurriedly, as a "second set" response.

But the major attention at this time was being devoted to whole body irradiation.* The management of Mrs. G. L. ushered in the short and generally unsuccessful use of whole body irradiation. This was a phase in the development of transplantation when the balance of survival was much too often tipped against the patient.

The balance of survival depends on achieving suppression of antibody with just enough severity to permit survival of the allograft, yet without sufficient damage to threaten survival of the rest of the organism by rendering it vulnerable to invading bacteria. The achievement of this perfect balance with whole body irradiation proved to be extremely difficult. If the radiation was given at a sufficient dose to destroy all the antibody-producing cells so that a grafted kidney could survive, then it would appear that the transplantation would be successful. But if the dose had, at the same time, lowered the antibody defenses so far that the patient developed a severe infection, then even though the graft lived unmolested for some days or weeks, the patient would succumb to an infection caught after the irradiation. The old platitude that "the operation was successful but the patient died" was now given a new version—"the graft lived but the patient died." Al-

---

* *Whole body irradiation*, the exposure of the whole body, rather than merely a small area, to a beam of irradiation such as that from an x-ray machine or a cobalt source. The studies of Main and Prehn and of Barnes and Loutit were especially important in initiating this work.

though it was not known at the start of this period, whole body irradiation ultimately was to prove impractical when used alone, because this balance of survival was too precarious. Only rarely could it be achieved, either in the experimental animal or in man.

As part of the work of this period (and in an attempt to make whole body irradiation more satisfactory) a series of experiments were begun in which the entire body of an animal was irradiated. Bone marrow cells were then infused from the future donor of a kidney. The intent here was to repopulate the cellular factories of the bone marrow, damaged by irradiation, using cells that would later recognize the kidney graft as "self." This was the "beachhead" concept of grafting: bombardment first with irradiation, then a shore party of bone marrow cells to prepare the way for the main invasion by kidney.

This experiment, "irradiation-followed-by-marrow-then-kidney," gave a special sort of twist to the concept of balance of survival. Here a graft of bone marrow was given under circumstances in which it *might live* in the new recipient if the whole body irradiation had indeed destroyed the antagonistic cells of the reticuloendothelial system, including the lymph nodes, spleen, and bone marrow. But now, in addition, the graft of bone marrow *must live* so as to restore those very same cells to the blood and repopulate those same antibody-producing tissues which had been wiped out by irradiation to make the graft possible in the first place, in order to protect the patient against infection. This is a little as though one removed the bottom of a ship to make space for a large cargo of cork. The cork could now be loaded, since the ship had been damaged sufficiently to make room for it. But the cargo of cork *must* be put in and *must fit properly* in order to make the ship float at all. In this perilous experiment, the bone marrow cells must survive in the new host so as to permit the new host to survive the damage that made it possible for the bone marrow cells to live at all. A sort of circular relationship.

In the years 1957–1959, much of the scientific effort in this country was directed toward immunosuppression in the animal, as carried out by whole body irradiation. The laboratories at Cooperstown, New York (at the Mary Imogene Bassett Hospital) and at Richmond, Virginia (at the Medical College of Virginia), to name but two, were using these methods. Large doses of whole body irradiation (often far in excess of the lethal level) were given by means of an x-ray machine or a radiocobalt source. This was followed by an injection of bone marrow,* as just mentioned, and then by a kidney transplant taken from the same donor as the marrow. Our laboratories at Harvard were making a very modest start in this field as a collaborative enterprise between the Department of Surgery and the Department of Radiology under the direction of Dr. Dealy. We were using rabbits as well as dogs, and studying a variety of methods by which bone marrow infusion could render them able to accept skin grafts from the marrow donors.

In one of these experiments, carried out by Dr. Wilson and Dr. Sadowsky, rabbits were severely irradiated, and then given bone marrow from four or five other rabbits; small skin grafts then followed from these same rabbits. It was found that the irradiated animal, as a new host with new bone marrow cells aboard, "selected" which of the skin donors it would accept. Several of these rabbits accepted skin quite easily from the donor of one of the shots of bone marrow; in a few cases a rabbit would accept skin from two donors, suggesting that bone marrow had likewise been accepted from two.

But of the hundreds of experiments carried out to make kidney transplantation possible, only a handful were even partly successful. One of these, a dog named "Sam" at Cooperstown, New York, weathered the whole procedure and carried a successful kidney transplantation for 49 days.

Although these laboratory efforts were immense, and the results small, such advances made possible a better understanding of immunosuppression and paved the way for the later use of drugs. And of all the irradiation experiences, none was more important than that of Mrs. G. L.

THE CASE OF MRS. G. L.

Those rare patients who presented themselves at the hospital with no kidneys usually told the same story: an injury of some sort had

---

* Bone marrow can be ground up and injected through a needle into the veins whence it seeks out the bones for its dwelling place.

happened to a kidney which was then removed because of massive hemorrhage. A day or so later it was discovered, because there was no urinary output, that the patient was born with only one kidney. This accident, the injury and removal of a solitary kidney, has been recorded in the annals of surgery ever since nephrectomy was first performed. There is only one way to prevent such an event and that is to assure by x-ray examination or anatomical exploration during the operation that the patient has another normal kidney before removing the injured one. Yet, clearly, this will not always suffice. If the injured kidney has a bullet hole in it, its bleeding is going to cost the patient's life, and even if the bleeding has stopped, the kidney will be useless. The case of Mrs. G. L. was one in which the removal of the only kidney (and an abnormal one at that) was necessary to stem a life-endangering hemorrhage; her accident led to the initial application in man of immunosuppression for kidney transplantation by whole body irradiation.

Mrs. G. L. (PBBH 3M330) had undergone an operation a few days before her admission to the Brigham Hospital during which an abnormally placed kidney was found to be bleeding severely. After its removal it was discovered that the patient had no other kidney.

On her admission to the Brigham, dialysis on the artificial kidney was successful in lowering the blood urea concentration from very high values to those about normal. The patient improved immensely in her physical state and her emotional balance. Although she had been critically ill on admission, in a few days she was up and about, leading a normal life within the hospital, if life can ever be referred to as "normal" when no kidneys are present. Many days passed during her study and treatment, while plans for the solution of her problem proceeded.

Here was a patient who must have a kidney transplantation. There was no other way to solve her problem.* There was no identical

---

* The procedure, now frequently used, of daily dialysis on an artificial kidney for a period of many months or a year, to maintain life without kidneys, was impractical in 1958. At the present time, such repeated dialyses might be a supportable and defensible therapy for a period of many months or even years in such an individual. But still, and in the end, new kidney tissue must be supplied if the patient is to be freed of the burden of frequent dialysis treatments.

twin to donate a kidney. There was no sure way of making an allo-grafted kidney survive the rejection reaction. How then best to treat this patient?

All concerned agreed that although time was short and the year was early, some effort must be made to save this patient. The decision was a difficult one, and included consultation from many members of the surgical service, physicians, pathologists, and radiologists, as well as scientists from the nearby departments of the medical school and from neighboring hospitals, all anxious to help in any way possible.

A procedure was outlined for Mrs. G. L. which had never been carried out before in the human being, and has never been followed since in precisely this same form. She was given whole body irradia-tion by Dr. Marks to the extent of 600 roentgen units,* using a special two-million-electron-volt x-ray source in his department at the New England Deaconess Hospital. To receive this whole body irradiation, Mrs. G. L. lay on a stretcher about 19 feet from the irradiation portal so that her whole body was exposed to the x-ray beams (Fig. 9). The purpose here, as mentioned earlier, was to suppress those antibody-producing cells of the reticuloendothelial system (spleen, lymph nodes, bone marrow) that would reject the kidney about to be grafted; at the same time it was hoped that the precise dose was just right, so that her own antibody defenses against bacteria would not be de-pressed too much. The object was to achieve the balance of survival.

As soon as this irradiation was commenced, the patient was moved from one of the regular wards to the operating room itself, where she lived for almost a month. Because we knew that her defenses against infection would be lowered to a very dangerous level, it was essential to keep her away from any dangerous bacteria. The safest place in the hospital, from this point of view, is the completely aseptic environment of the operating suite. No person could enter her room without a complete change of clothes, gown, cap and mask, a scrub of the hands, and sterile gloves.

Shortly after the irradiation was completed, the patient was given

---

* The *roentgen unit* is a measure of x-ray intensity, named after Dr. Roentgen, the discoverer of the x-ray. It is expressed in terms of the ionization in air produced by the passage of an x-ray beam through a special ionization chamber.

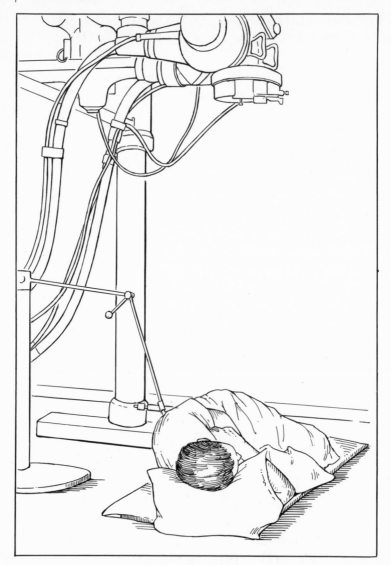

FIGURE 9. Whole body irradiation. The patient is shown here, curled up on a mattress several feet from an x-ray source so arranged that the whole body is included in the x-ray beam. With other types of equipment, the patient may have to be 15 or 20 feet away. The irradiation acts as a suppressant of the defenses which throw off the homograft.

In this figure whole body irradiation is shown from a rather small radiation device; this sort of equipment was often used 15 years ago. Whole body irradiation at present is usually given with supervoltage equipment at a much greater distance.

36 billion marrow cells* from 11 donors. This clinical procedure was similar to the rabbit work carried out by Dr. Wilson. Cells were being given from several donors with the hope that a "cross-acceptance" might be achieved, permitting acceptance of a kidney not only from one of these donors but possibly even from other sources.

The bone-marrow donations were taken by needle aspiration from the pelvic bone of various voluntary donors. Such a marrow donation does not harm the donor at all, since he has plenty of extra bone marrow, and it regenerates itself very rapidly. Mrs. G. L. had a very large and devoted family, and several of the donors of this marrow were her brothers. We were working along a number of lines at once: whole body irradiation was given as immunosuppression, closeness of genetic relationship was a guiding factor in the bone marrow donation.

As the days went by, it appeared inadvisable to take a kidney from a healthy normal donor. There were too many uncertainties and unknown variables in the plan. Therefore, a kidney that had to be removed from a young child having the hydrocephalus operation was placed in the patient's right thigh by Dr. Murray, after the manner of the operations initially carried out by Dr. Hume. Although the abdominal cavity is the preferred position for a kidney transplant, this patient had received such severe radiation dosage that it was deemed wiser to put the graft in the thigh where it could be done very simply and easily.

Just before the kidney graft, the patient received another 170 million bone marrow cells from the same donor who gave the kidney. Thus, by adding this procedure, the identity of donor for both marrow and kidney was achieved.

During the subsequent days many more marrow cells were given from her various donors. Evidently none of these marrow donations survived satisfactorily. Within a few days after the irradiation and the operation, the patient's own blood count of white cells was danger-

---

* Thirty-six billion is also written 3.6×10^{10}. Such large numbers of cells are counted by sampling a tiny fraction of the fluid and placing it under a microscope in a standard cell-counting chamber, and then counting this portion, or "aliquot," of the total injected mass.

ously low. But of more ominous significance was that her platelet*
counts had also fallen to very low levels indeed. Blood transfusions,
even of fresh whole blood, were not adequate to maintain these platelets in a normal range.

The sort of treatment being given here, after the irradiation
dosage, had been under close study in several laboratories since World
War II, because it is the sort of treatment that might be used for
survivors of an atomic bomb explosion. It was well known that bone
marrow transfusions might be an important treatment during a nuclear
war. Here was a patient who had received a lethal amount of radiation
to the whole body. Damage was severe, not only to the antibody-
forming cells but also to those components of blood that make it clot.
Blood transfusions and bone marrow transfusions were exploited to the
full.

Despite all these hazards, the kidney transplant itself began to
improve and show every sign of good function. It was making normal
urine, and in good quantities. By the fifteenth postoperative day, the
patient had made 1500 ml† of urine from the transplanted kidney on a
single day, and each day the urine was of better chemical quality.

A day or two later, abnormal bleeding began, and this was the
ultimate cause of failure. With Mrs. G. L. in the sterile environment in
the operating room, infection was not evident, and the damage to the
antibody-producing systems was evidenced only by the survival of the
graft. She was protected from the threat of infection, and the cultural
studies of her bedclothes and skin showed her to be free of dangerous
bacteria. All the efforts used to increase her blood clotting ability
failed to restore it to normal, and finally, thirty-two days after irradiation, the patient died of complications produced by the hemorrhage
and with some evidences of infection now just beginning to show
themselves. The kidney appeared to survive, but the patient could not
withstand the effects of irradiation, despite her courage throughout
this perilous course.

---

* *Blood platelets,* small bits of cells seen in the blood, formed in the bone marrow and
essential to normal blood clotting.

† *ml,* the abbreviation for *milliliters.* One thousand (1000) ml equals one liter, or
approximately one quart.

The important point for the study of transplantation turned on the microscopic examination of the kidney a month after the transplant. This examination, carried out by Dr. Dammin as part of the autopsy, was the most important aspect in the evaluation of the case of Mrs. G. L.

If a patient so severely injured by irradiation had *also* shown the microscopic appearances of kidney graft rejection, then the whole matter of kidney transplantation and immunosuppression would have appeared quite hopeless. Mrs. G. L. had been so severely irradiated that we could not save her. If *at the same time* she had been able to summon from within the depths of her body cells enough antibody to reject the kidney, then it would have appeared that no conceivable method of suppressing antibody production would ever offer a prospect of success for the transplantation of organs or tissues.

It was, therefore, with an unusual amount of apprehension that the staff awaited the findings of Dr. Dammin, as he studied the microscopic sections and the pathology in the kidney. During life, two biopsies had failed to show rejection. He now reported that even at the time of death there was no sign of rejection. Although abnormalities were present, due in part to the bleeding tendency, the signs of rejection were minimal. It was indeed possible to prevent rejection of a kidney in a human allotransplant. Now it was essential to make that immunosuppression gentler, more specific, and practical.

MORE FAILURES AND AN UNEXPECTED SUCCESS

During the period between May 1958 and April 1960, six patients were treated in this hospital by x-radiation as immunosuppression preliminary to kidney transplantation. The method was being explored likewise in other centers. Several different treatment schedules were used because there was a continuing effort to achieve precisely the right dose of whole body irradiation, gentle enough to permit survival yet strong enough to inhibit rejection.

Mrs. G. L. was one of these six patients. Of the remaining five, four also were failures. Finally, one of these patients was a startling success—a success that was to set the pattern for a few other isolated successful cases in which whole body irradiation was used alone for immunosuppression. In all of these patients the pressure of clinical necessity in a desperate situation (exactly as in Dr. Hufnagel's first patient) forced the decision to go ahead.

First, a word about one of the failures. This was the case of a 12-year-old boy (N. W., PBBH 3M994) sent to this hospital from Sweden. The boy had been born with one kidney, which was ruptured when he fell from a wooden horse on a merry-go-round, the rupture resulting in a hemorrhage which almost proved fatal and could be stopped only by removing the kidney.

After flying across the ocean and arriving at the hospital, the patient was given dialysis on the artificial kidney, and again his health was restored reasonably close to normal. Irradiation was given, at a dose of 700 roentgen units, followed by the infusion of 10.5 billion bone marrow cells. But this time there was an important change in the routine, seemingly an improvement: all of the bone marrow cells were taken from one donor, and this donor was the patient's mother. There was, by now, impressive evidence that nearness of genetic relationship was a helpful factor in any kind of allograft. To obtain so many bone marrow cells from the mother, it was necessary not only to withdraw the marrow from the pelvic bones, but the mother also underwent the removal of a rib. This rib was stripped of its many marrow cells, and these were injected into the bloodstream of her son.

Despite all the favorable factors, including the heavy irradiation and the maternal donation, it was evident within only a few days that the bone marrow did not take. The boy's blood count fell to perilously low levels and survival became unlikely. For this reason it was not justified to remove a normal kidney from an otherwise perfectly well person, his mother. The boy died without a kidney transplantation 25 days later.* This experience again seemed to emphasize the lesson that even with very dangerous levels of irradiation, and an ideal marrow donation, the method was rarely if ever going to be practical: the balance of survival was just too difficult to achieve.

Despite the failures, and the discouragement that pervaded the

---

* The skin graft from this boy's mother to his own arm showed no signs of rejection, confirming the conviction that radiation could achieve immunosuppression, as it had in Mrs. G. L.

use of whole body irradiation as the sole method of immunosuppression, there was a moment of triumph before the method was forsaken. Just as in the series of unmodified transplantations done by Dr. Hume and Dr. Murray, there was one isolated success which gave important impetus to forward research, and from which important lessons could be learned. This particular sequence of events was so remarkable that we have not ever duplicated it; it is still not adequately explained, and it has been repeated on only two or three other occasions in other hospitals.

A Case of Fraternal Twinning

Mr. J. R., a 23-year-old man (PBBH 3N55) was admitted to the hospital in the late fall of 1959, approximately nine months after the death of Mrs. G. L. Mr. J. R. came from Wisconsin, where he had been under treatment for several years because of chronic and progressive kidney failure. The kidney disease here was a very bad combination: a mixture of chronic glomerulonephritis with a superimposed bacterial infection of the type known as pyelonephritis.

Like so many other patients who were coming to the hospital at this time, Mr. J. R. brought his twin brother with him. One glance at this pair of young men sufficed to show that they were not identical twins. They were of different height, different hair color, and different body structure. On our inquiring more about the details of their birth, the obstetrician stated that they were born seven minutes apart and weighed six and a half pounds each. Evidently the mother had two placentas, one for each twin. This made it virtually a certainty that they were dizygotic or fraternal twins.

On the eighteenth day after their admission to the hospital, a skin graft was applied from the recipient to the donor. This was a skin graft "trade." If a skin graft from the kidney donor is placed on the intended recipient (from the well twin to the sick twin), one risks the hazard of sensitizing the sick twin to the donor's tissues. Here this was done despite the risk, to assess closeness of relationship. The skin graft from the sick twin to the well twin lasted for eighteen days, when a second graft was applied. This was a longer take than normal, but it was a prolongation previously observed in skin grafts between fraternal twins. The lack of identity of the twins was clearly established when the second set of skin from the sick to the well twin showed accelerated ("second set") rejection. The blood groups of these two young men were not identical, although they were very similar. The grafts on the sick twin's arm showed no signs of rejection for months—undoubtedly due to his debilitated and uremic condition.

Because of this closeness of relationship, and the unsuccessful experiences with large x-ray dosages of 600 to 700 roentgen units, the plan here was to give much less irradiation and no bone marrow. Dr. Dealy made the difficult measurements of radiation dosage, and calculated that about 450 roentgen units would be enough to inhibit antibody formation, but far less likely to produce a severe injury requiring marrow. The total irradiation was given in two doses, one of 250 and the other of 200 roentgen units, seven days apart.

After the second dose of irradiation, a kidney was removed for transplantation from the healthy donor twin. It had been shown that both kidneys were normal, and he had no evidence of disease elsewhere. His kidney was then placed in the abdomen, with vascular anastomosis to the large vessels of the pelvis, just as had been done in the identical twins. It was evident that these proceedings were carried out with a sense of confidence and assurance of success, traceable not only to previous experiences gained but also to the genetic closeness of the fraternal twins.

This time, and for the first time in the irradiation series, neither patient nor kidney failed or faltered. Although there was a brisk reaction to the whole body irradiation as shown by a fall in the count of white blood cells, the patient never developed an ominous irradiation sickness with bleeding and infection. The transplanted kidney likewise functioned well, and soon the patient was on the road to recovery. A proper balance of survival had been achieved with a *lower dose* of irradiation, and with *genetic closeness* of relationship.

The kidney produced a very large amount of urine right from the start. Indeed, on the first day it made 32 liters (about 8 gallons) of urine. Such a tremendous volume of urine could dehydrate a patient dangerously if this fluid volume were not restored by rapid intravenous infusion of sterile saline. A normal kidney is able to control the many gallons of fluid filtered through the glomeruli each day by reabsorbing most of it in the active tubular cells. Only a small fraction (1 to 2 percent) of the total filtrate of the day is actually excreted as urine. When the kidney puts out 32 liters per day, it indicates that the tubules are a bit sick and cannot perform properly as fluid reabsorbers.

In the next few days the kidney tubular cells regained their health and their "grip" on the filtered fluid. The concentration of salts rose in the urine and the volume diminished. Progress was good until the seventh postoperative day, when a very high swinging fever began, and the patient became acutely and critically ill from progressive infection in his two kidneys which were still in place.

The situation was difficult because the patient was still in the "trough" of his x-ray treatment; he could not withstand any such infection for long; at the same time, only a week had passed since kidney transplantation and he might not be regarded as an ideal operative risk. The phrase "operative risk," however, must always be tempered with a view toward the risk of doing *no* operation, which in this case was prohibitive. Therefore, in a difficult midnight emergency operation, Dr. Harrison removed both of the heavily infected kidneys from this critically ill man. This operation was carried out nineteen days after the whole body irradiation and eleven days after the transplantation. It was one of the most critical operations in the entire kidney transplant experience.

Surgeons have long noted that when a very difficult or dangerous operation in a critically ill patient achieves precisely the physiologic objective that is needed, then recovery from it is a remarkable combination of operative convalescence and release from illness. Such occurred here. The patient recovered very rapidly. He soon was feeling well, eating well, and had a normal temperature.

Six months after the kidney operation, skin was again taken from the recipient and rejected from the donor within a week. Likewise at six months the recipient *finally* rejected the test skin graft from the donor. Nine months after the operation, a test biopsy* from the kidney transplant showed some smoldering chronic rejection process. The

---

* *Biopsy*, literally "to see a sample"; refers to a sample of tissue taken for microscopic study.

patient was therefore put on cortisone in an effort to block this rejection response in the kidney, and given a small additional dose of whole body irradiation at weekly intervals for four more weeks. The threatened rejection was reversed—for the first time in man. His course since that time is one of continued excellent urine function and physical health in this, the first successful kidney allotransplantation between individuals other than identical twins.

Despite this success, the precise interpretation of the events that combined to make this transplantation successful has remained a source of controversy. The dose of whole body irradiation given was not large enough to produce a prolonged depression of cellular activity in the bone marrow and lymph nodes. It is surprising that such a mild dose should have achieved the necessary immunosuppression. Bone marrow infusions were not deemed necessary and were not given. Based on other human data, and on information from animal experiments, one would not expect such a small amount of irradiation to achieve prolonged kidney survival alone. Indeed, in animals studied by Dr. Hume in Richmond and by Dr. Ferrebee and Dr. Thomas in Cooperstown, proportional amounts of radiation far in excess of this, and yielding an extremely high fatality in dogs, still were unassociated with prolonged success in kidney transplantation in the vast majority of instances. Therefore, one must seek some other possible explanation for the survival of these grafts between twins who were not identical.

One explanation might lie in the concept that in all transplantation experiences there are odd "freaks" in which prolonged success is surprisingly attained. Possibly this was just a random success. Eight years later one or two of the early spectacular successes in heart transplantation also appeared to be based on a chance compatibility, although in those instances (see Chapter 13) there was no likeness of relationship to provide the explanation, but rather a random histocompatibility based on similarity of tissue types.

A somewhat more appealing explanation might be that the twins shared a common blood supply in their mother's womb, like the bovine twins studied by Owen, and Mrs. McK. (p. 55). Strong evidence against this explanation is that the R. twins were not tolerant of each other's skin. Indeed, the kidney donor had twice rejected skin from the recipient. Later on, at a time when the kidney recipient was tolerating his kidney with no additional immunosuppression by drugs or irradiation, his own lymphocytes were injected into the skin of his donor brother and produced a violent local skin reaction. It was thus evident that we were witnessing graft acceptance of the general type called "adaptation" (see page 64). Without any genetic change in the tissue of either person, and possibly through a protective coating by blocking antibodies, the graft had become adapted in such a way that the host no longer reacted against it even though its own genetic constitution had not been changed.

All these factors, as well as the small dose of 450 roentgen units of irradiation, suggest that success in Mr. J. R.'s case was simply an example in which the balance of survival was achieved with mild immunosuppression (by low dose whole body irradiation and without bone marrow donation), a success in large part due to the two persons being of very close genetic relationship—fraternal twins.

Now, ten years after his transplant, Mr. J. R. remains living and well. He has completed his studies for a Ph.D. in philosophy at the University of Indiana, and has married. His health has been good save for a brief time in 1968 when he excreted some protein in his urine and the question was raised that he might then be developing glomerulonephritis. He was treated with cortisone for three months, and now, two years later, he has a negative urinalysis and is doing well.

The French Experience

Transplant studies in England, Scotland, Denmark, and Australia have already been touched on, especially the work of the French surgeon Dr. Carrel. Activity of other French scientists and surgeons has always been very intensive in the study of transplantation, and particularly in the use of irradiation for immunosuppression. This is, therefore, a fitting point at which to discuss the French history, at least briefly.

We are indebted to Prof. Hamburger of the Hospital Necker in Paris for some additional details about the French experience when few of these events were recorded as medical history and only sporadic publications revealed the early steps essential to progress in the relief of people suffering from late kidney failure.*

At about the time that Dr. Ullmann (see Chapter 4) was doing his transplants in Vienna, Dr. Jaboulay in France was doing kidney grafting of a highly experimental sort. The first two examples were the transplantation of kidneys from a goat and a pig. According to Dr. Hamburger it was this early experience in France that kept up the French level of interest in transplantation as a possible future application of science to sickness.

By the late 1940's a series of experimental kidney transplants was performed by Dr. Hamburger and his group, and then, on Christmas night, 1952, there was a major change in the climate of transplantation in France because of a clinical transplant carried out as an outgrowth of sound experimental work with at least a possibility of success.

This was the case of Mr. Marius R., a young man 16 years of age who had fallen three floors from a scaffolding. He had ruptured a kidney and it had been removed. From the time of the operation forward, no urine appeared, and it was only then that it was discovered that the boy had no second kidney and had been born with complete atrophy of renal tissue on the side opposite to the injury.

Six days later, the decision was made to attempt transplantation of a kidney from his mother. The transplanted kidney soon began to produce a large amount of urine, and for more than three weeks it continued to function well. The boy's general condition seemed to be fine, and he was up and about, getting ready to go home. At the beginning of the fourth week after the operation what we now recognize as a typical bout of acute rejection was observed, but the kidney had stayed in place, functioning much longer than in any case previously known to the French surgeons. Dr. Hamburger, in publishing these results in the French literature, suggested that the close relationship between the donor and the recipient might have been the cause of the prolonged survival of the kidney. Analysis revealed that all the blood groups and subgroups of the patient and of his mother were

---

* Dr. Hamburger also brings up for discussion the interesting question of chauvinism in medical history—the tendency of each country to believe that its scientists have carried out *the* important work. These notes from Professor Hamburger make it possible to enter some of the early French experience in proper prospective.

identical; it was disappointing to the French surgeon, just as it had been to the Americans working at about the same time, that even with genetic closeness and blood group identity, permanent acceptance of the kidney was not achieved.

In 1959, Dr. Hamburger was presented with a patient reminiscent of Mr. J. R. (page 119). This was a patient suffering from chronic glomerulonephritis, who had a nonidentical or fraternal twin. Dr. Hamburger treated this man with exactly the same routine that had been followed in the case of Mr. J. R. Irradiation was given by Dr. Tubiana at the Institute Gustave-Roussy, from a cobalt source, totaling 450 roentgen units. The kidney graft was then placed from the well twin to the sick twin. After the operation the patient got along well for a while. Then he developed a typical immunogenetic rejection crisis: he became much sicker, his fever rose, the volume of urine was reduced, and the level of waste products in the blood was elevated. More irradiation was given, and this rejection crisis rapidly reversed. This experience was the first successful venture in allotransplantation on the continent of Europe, and it marked the beginning of the transplant experience abroad. Dr. Hamburger writes:

> The patient, Georges S., is perfectly well and active today, exactly ten years after having received the renal allograft. We also thought at that time, despite the skepticism of others, that results obtained in our group were perhaps better than in other groups for the sole reason that we were using this leukocyte selection test (see page 215).

Pursuant to the work of Dr. Hamburger and his group, Dr. Küss, also of Paris, carried out a graft from a sister to a brother, with remarkable success. The patient was 41 years old. He was given whole body irradiation very much as Mr. J. R. had been at the Brigham Hospital two years previously, and as Dr. Hamburger's more recent patient had been. The transplant was performed on January 17, 1960, and the patient got along well.

Drs. Hamburger and Küss carried out most of the work on transplantation in Paris during the next few years, and their work constituted the background for the widening French experience. In the first few years of his work Dr. Hamburger reported 25 allotransplants performed with the help of whole body irradiation for immunosuppression. Drugs were used only in a few of these initial transplants. In this group of patients, he relied on closeness of genetic relationship to a greater extent than our staff did at the Brigham Hospital or the physicians in Edinburgh and London. The patient's mother was the donor of the kidney on 12 occasions, and siblings were donors in 9. Of a total of 25 patients who had allotransplants in the first group, 7 were still alive one to three years later, 2 had died after 22 months, and 2 were living over two years (one, the fraternal twin, over four years).

Dr. Küss, at the same time, reported 10 patients operated on, using total body irradiation as immunosuppression in every instance. Of these patients, only 3 had shown a prolonged survival, and 1 had lived for 18 months.

At the same time, Dr. Jean Dausset was beginning work on antibodies formed against human white cells injected into unrelated persons. This study later led to "leukocyte testing" and tissue grouping, which were brought to this country by Dr. Terasaki and formed the basis of tissue grouping methods used throughout the world. Dr. Hamburger and his French colleagues are quite properly proud of the fact that by 1955 they were combining immunologic concepts of tissue grouping with transplantation and in that regard were far ahead of their colleagues in Great Britain and America. He writes:

I remember how skeptical my American friends were when I told them we were working extensively on the subject of tissue grouping and that a careful immunologic selection of the donor based on leukocyte testing might be one of the keys for the eventual solution of the transplant problem.

The French work continued to prosper on the basis of leukocyte grouping, and in 1962 a transplant was carried out with the first cousin as a donor. This patient has done extremely well and is now living and well, a young physician, and constitutes the longest surviving nontwin kidney allograft in the world.

Building on these historical first steps, the French workers have continued to establish a fine series of transplants in critically ill patients, rehabilitated and returned to normal living by kidney transplantation. They have continued their interest in the immunologic aspects of transplantation, and were among the first to report that chronic rejection resembles glomerulonephritis itself.

Dr. Hamburger disclaims any personal credit or priority for kidney transplantation in France even though he is clearly one of the great figures in the field and one of the prime movers in this work on the European continent. He also feels that there should be no such thing as national pride in medical history, and he closes one of his letters with the words:

. . . this kind of thing is really unimportant. None of us in Europe or in America is working for personal or national credit. The only important thing is that patients benefit from medical progress obtained by common effort throughout the whole world.

The many disappointing failures with whole body irradiation and the difficulties in achieving a balance of survival after the sledge-hammer blow of damaging x-rays made it clear by 1958 that a method gentler than whole body irradiation must be found. This should make it possible to transplant organs without rejection, breaching the immunogenetic barrier in a milder and more readily controlled way.

7

BREACHING THE BARRIER

Immunosuppression with Drugs

Every excess causes a defect; every defect an excess. . . .
Every faculty which is a receiver of pleasure has an equal
penalty put on its abuse. . . . With every influx of light
comes new danger. . . . There is a crack in everything God
has made. It would seem there is always this vindictive
circumstance stealing in at us unawares . . . this back-
stroke, this kick of a gun, certifying that the law is fatal; that
in nature nothing can be given, all things are sold.

—EMERSON, *Essay on Compensation*

THE NUCLEUS, NUCLEIC ACIDS, AND THE
NEED FOR A SHARPER TOOL

The price of immunosuppression is damage to the normal chemistry of protein synthesis and antibody production. The development of allo-transplantation under immunosuppression came about at the end of a decade in which the chemistry of the nucleic acids had been a central and most important development in biology.

The occasional stray success with transplantation after whole body irradiation and the rare successes in animal work suggested that success might be achieved by suppressing immunity to allotransplants. But the method used was not quite right; there must be a better way to interfere with the production of antibodies. The antibody proteins are made in the cell as new proteins, through the action of the nucleic acids.

These nucleic acids, which are found in the nucleus of each cell, are substances of very high molecular weight, long thin strands made up of many units strung end-to-end like pearls in a necklace. These subunits of the nucleic acids are known as "nucleotides," and each consists of three components within itself: a five-carbon sugar, a basic substance—a purine or a pyrimidine—and a phosphorus linkage. These three units together form the nucleotides; when the nucleotides are strung together in long chains, nucleic acid is formed. If the sugar involved is ribose, then the nucleic acid is called "ribonucleic acid" or RNA. This is most commonly found in the substance of the cell, outside of the nucleus. If the sugar is deoxyribose (only slightly different from ribose), then the nucleic acid is called "deoxyribonucleic acid" or DNA. DNA exists entirely within the nucleus of the cell, and it was shown many years ago that each time the cell divides the amount of DNA is *exactly* doubled. This suggested that somehow this long thin molecule carried a message from each cell to its daughter offspring. In the past decade the details of this message have been elucidated.

It has been shown that DNA is of the greatest significance both in genetics and in protein synthesis because the precise arrangements of its nucleotide units seem to constitute a "code" which determines the nature of proteins made in that cell; a string of nucleotides is translated into a string of amino acids.* This translation takes place through the agency of RNA, which carries the message out of the nuclear office and into the cellular factory outside of the nucleus, called "messenger RNA."

Both RNA and DNA have been known to biochemists for many years. The precise geometrical structure of the DNA molecule appears to be a double-stranded helix, first postulated on the basis of x-ray crystallographic evidence by Dr. Crick and Dr. Watson. During division of the cell these two strands unwind and each makes up a matching daughter strand so that, as the total amount of DNA is doubled, so

---

* *Amino acids,* nitrogen-carbon compounds of low molecular weight which, put together by the thousands, make up the proteins.

also its precise chemical structure is duplicated in the daughter cell. The daughter cell can then make protein exactly like its parent. The reader will recall that one of the features of Burnet's theory of clonal selection in immunity was that certain colonies or clones of antibody-forming cells were endowed with the property of making specific antibody proteins against a certain specific kind of foreign protein. Each cell, as it divides, gives rise to two cells each of which has this same DNA-RNA "code" which yields one specific antibody protein. It was for this reason that Professor Burnet termed immunology a genetic process.

It would be expected that any procedure which poisoned or distorted the DNA-RNA sequence for the synthesis of protein might have a profound effect on the ability of the organism to throw off a kidney transplantation. X-ray treatment was a very blunt and brutal blow, damaging this synthetic sequence of the nucleic acids throughout the whole body, in order to achieve the single specific effect of reducing antibody production.

X-ray treatment is also effective in treating cancer, and for the same reason—namely, that it damages the cells so that they cannot reproduce their own proteins and their own kind. It might be expected that some of the drugs useful in treating cancer would also interfere with the production of antibodies.

One year after the unsuccessful experience with transplantation of a kidney following whole body irradiation of Mrs. G. L., there was published a brief report that would change the whole face of the transplant problem.

SCHWARTZ AND DAMESHEK SHOW THE WAY

The British journal *Nature* is similar to *Science* as published in the United States. Both publish brief letters to the editor and other short articles. When a scientist makes an interesting and important finding, he can present it in these journals within a few weeks or months, and thus avoid delay in spreading the word to others who might be interested. In *Nature* on June 13, 1959, an article appeared describing a study conducted by Dr. Schwartz and Dr. Dameshek of the Blood Research Laboratories of the New England Center Hospital–Tufts

University Medical School in Boston. Dr. Schwartz and Dr. Dameshek had concerned themselves with stopping antibody formation, using drugs. This was termed "drug-induced immunologic tolerance," or immunosuppression with drugs.

The description of this work is so brief and yet so clear that it is best to quote the authors directly. They refer to some of the background in transplantation, particularly the work of Drs. Billingham, Brent, and Medawar on actively acquired immunologic tolerance (p. 60) and observe:

The term "actively acquired tolerance" first used by Billingham, Brent and Medawar, was defined as "an induced, specific, central failure of immunologic response brought about by an exposure of animals to antigenic stimuli before maturation of the faculty of immunologic response." Tolerance of this type to homografted tissues and organs as well as to simpler antigens has been induced in laboratory animals by many workers. In all such experiments, this has been carried out in the newly born or immature animal. The mechanism of this phenomenon is obscure; but the results of the present study indicate that the foetal state is not essential for its induction.

These scientists proceeded to describe their very simple experiment, involving New Zealand white rabbits. The animals were injected with an antigen consisting of human serum albumin* which could be followed by tagging it with a radioactive iodine atom. The normal animal quickly removed this foreign protein from its serum, showing a marked reduction in the radioactive counts. One group of rabbits was then given a daily injection of a drug named 6-mercaptopurine, previously used in the treatment of cancer (Figs. 10 and 11). For many weeks afterward the animals no longer reacted normally. They did not remove the antigen from the circulation as expected. This blockade of normal immunity persisted for a long time. With subsequent injections of the same antigen, not only was there no "secondary response" but, even more important, there was not even a normal "primary response" of immunity.

Writing of the response of antibody production, the authors com-

---

* *Albumin,* the "white protein"; an important protein of human blood serum formerly thought to be similar to that found in egg white.

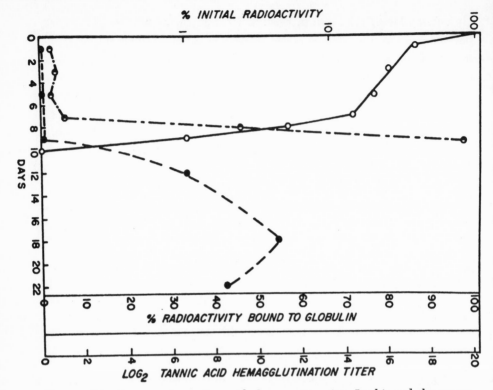

FIGURE 10. Immunosuppression with 6-mercaptopurine. In this and the accompanying figure (Figure 11) are shown immunologic studies carried out in two rabbits injected with radioactively tagged human serum albumin, by Schwartz and Damashek.

Here the downward sloping solid line (connecting the open circles) shows the disappearance of the tagged human serum albumin, given as a test antigen. It will be noted that in the normal rabbit (shown here) the material is removed very rapidly after the seventh or eighth day and disappears completely by the tenth day. At the time of its disappearance, antibodies begin to appear in the blood, as shown by the dotted lines.

mented: "It is evident that this . . . response can be blocked by an antimetabolite.* . . . In the drug-treated animals it is apparent that although antibody production *in general* is not blocked, a gross dysfunction of the information-storing device has occurred."

This "information-storing device" is the system of protein syn-

---

* *Antimetabolite,* a drug interfering with normal metabolism by entering directly into a normal metabolic reaction; 6-mercaptopurine is an antimetabolite.

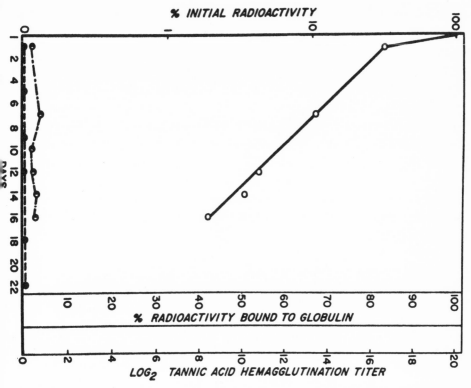

FIGURE 11.   To be contrasted with the data shown in Figure 10. Here the albumin disappears gradually and is still present at 16 days in the animal treated with 6-mercaptopurine. The antibody levels, shown as the dotted line at the bottom of the figure, do not rise. This is in marked contrast to the disappearance of antigen and appearance of antibody shown in Figure 10. This was the initial demonstration of abolition of an immune response using 6-mercaptopurine. It was on the basis of these findings that drug immunosuppression was adapted for use in the dog and then in man.

thesis in the cell resulting from the DNA-RNA coding system, which permits the daughter cells to make the same kind of protein the parent cell did prior to division; the "sensitive clones" (to use Professor Burnet's term) thus might be referred to as storing the information required to make a specific protein antibody.

Whatever the interpretation, the important fact remained that a drug had blocked the immune response. The authors concluded: "In any event, these experiments indicate that the term 'acquired immunologic tolerance' previously used only for the response of the immature animal needs to be broadened to include drug-induced tolerance." The authors might have added the words "in the adult organism," for they had shown that in the adult rabbit there could be induced a state of tolerance to this extremely unnatural antigen— *human* serum albumin. Herein lay the significance for the transplant problem. Transplant patients are adults; even if they are children, they are immunologically to be considered as adults, because they are many years removed from that state within the mother's uterus or during the first few days of life when tolerance is easily achieved, as shown by Dr. Billingham. If such a drug as 6-mercaptopurine could make the *adult* animal tolerant to a foreign protein, then indeed it might be useful in transplantation.

Important as this finding was, like so many other things in science its origins could be traced to previous work by these same scientists and other work of other investigators undertaken many years before.

One of the earliest efforts to modify immunology with drugs was reported in 1916 by Dr. Hektoen of Chicago who studied the effect of simple organic compounds, such as benzene and toluene, on the production of antibodies. Dr. Hektoen, likewise, was one of the workers who, shortly after World War I, studied the effect of mustard gas and similar compounds called "nitrogen mustards" on cellular systems. He showed that mustard gas delayed the appearance of antibodies to certain types of red blood cells injected into rabbits.

Furthermore, Dr. Baker and his collaborators (likewise of Chicago) reported in 1952 some studies on the use of nitrogen mustard to help promote the success of kidney transplants. They were almost a decade ahead of others with this concept. But the results were discouraging, and the experimental model used would not permit precise quantification of the effects obtained.

Another student of this subject was Dr. Uphoff, working at the National Institutes of Health, who carried out an experiment which was in a sense a direct precursor of the work of Dr. Schwartz and Dr. Dameshek. She used another cancer drug called amethopterin, giving it to mice that had been irradiated and received bone marrow infusions. She showed that this medicine prevented the "graft versus host" reaction which makes these animals quite sick. Her first publication on this subject (in 1958) was made in the same journal in which Dr. Schwartz and Dr. Dameshek had published a preliminary short note on their rabbit studies.

A year after their initial publication in *Nature,* Dr. Schwartz and Dr. Dameshek described a further step of applying 6-mercaptopurine to the take of allografted tissues, rather than to injected artificial antigens such as human serum albumin. Again they used rabbits; the 6-mercaptopurine was given, and skin grafts were placed on the animals from other rabbits. They showed that the drug would triple the survival time.

All these things constituted the first clear demonstration that some sort of immunologic change in the direction of tolerance could be produced with drugs that interfere with the DNA-RNA protein-making sequences within the cell. This finding was soon noted by transplant scientists eager to get on with the problem of immunosuppression for organ transplantation. Within a year after the publication of the work of Dr. Schwartz and Dr. Dameshek, patients with transplanted kidneys were being treated with this family of drugs.

SAND IN THE MACHINERY

Four of the drugs commonly used for immunosuppresion in transplantation are 6-mercaptopurine (and its close relative azathioprine), azaserine, actinomycin, and cortisone. Other drugs are being used to some extent; better drugs will be discovered; and other chemical methods are certain to be effective. But each of these four drugs characterizes a certain class of drug action in immunosuppression. The four drugs are rather different, but they all achieve the same final result.

6-MERCAPTOPURINE (AND AZATHIOPRINE)

As one might guess from its name, 6-mercaptopurine is indeed a purine, and therefore it resembles the basic compounds which are normal parts of nucleotides and therefore of DNA and RNA. When 6-mercaptopurine is linked with another chemical structure, an imidazole, a drug is formed which is closely related to 6-mercaptopurine but is somewhat less toxic* and more useful in transplantation. This is

---

* *Toxic,* poisonous.

azathioprine, or Imuran. Currently it is the most widely used drug in transplantation research and practice throughout the world.

Evidence is somewhat conflicting as to the precise chemical mode of action of 6-mercaptopurine and azathioprine. They both contain a normal purine to which a sulfur atom has been attached. Were this to be incorporated into DNA, it would alter slightly the electrical, chemical, and structural features of the molecule. This might well interfere with the normal synthesis of protein, in which case 6-mercaptopurine would be a "sham" or "decoy" chemical compound easing its way into a chain in which it did not belong. This is a familiar principle in the pharmacology of drug action, and there are many commonly used drugs which act in this manner: they resemble very closely some normal chemical or hormone and thus block its action.

One might make an analogy with the bullets in a machine gun belt. As the ammunition belt rattles through the gun, many bullets, all exactly the same, are fired from the cartridges. If a cartridge were to be placed in this belt that was twice as large as the others and totally different, the belt would not fit into the gun mechanism at all. It would not damage the machinery because the gun could not accept it or start to fire it. It would just stop the gun.

If, however, a cartridge were placed in the belt that was almost exactly like the others, but just a little larger, then the belt might slip through into the firing position and engage properly with the mechanism. When the bullet was discharged, it would then jam the barrel and wreck the gun completely.

Some of these drugs, such as 6-mercaptopurine and azathioprine, are known collectively as "antimetabolites" because they appear to have this property of entering into metabolic reactions. They closely resemble the normal purine bases, and they are incorporated into the DNA molecule to the extent of about 1 percent of the total. This seems to disturb the DNA-RNA sequence just enough to interfere with the synthesis of antibody proteins. In much larger doses it interferes with cellular duplication so much that it tends to slow down the growth of a cancer.

AZASERINE

Methods of pinpointing the mode of action of such drugs, have become very advanced with respect to the second class of these drugs, characterized by azaserine. Dr. Buchanan, of the Department of Chemistry at the Massachusetts Institute of Technology, has demonstrated the mode of action of this drug in remarkable detail. Many of the experiments narrated in this book have been of a biologic nature, such as grafts from one animal to another, transplants into the embryo, and the suturing of kidneys. Here is an example of a purely chemical experiment which elucidates the precise chemical mechanism of action essential to the success of transplantation.

To achieve this, Dr. Buchanan first synthesized azaserine containing a radioactive carbon atom. He then purified one of the enzymes* involved in the synthesis of the nucleotides—namely, the one that transfers nitrogen from glutamine† into the nucleotide synthesis. To change our analogy, this enzyme might be thought of as a worker standing along an assembly line, taking the nitrogen atom from glutamine behind him, and putting it into the nucleotide substance as it goes by.

Dr. Buchanan showed that azaserine "locks on" to this enzyme, forming an extremely stable bond. The pieces of this whole compound could be separated by chemical digestion, and he could then study the precise chemical structure of each one of these smaller pieces. By this complicated and exacting procedure, Dr. Buchanan and his collaborators showed that azaserine attaches itself to the sulfhydryl‡ group of the enzyme and, once having arrived there, stays put. The drug acts to damage this mechanism, as though the worker in the assembly line got his wrench caught in the conveyor belt, and it was pulled off into the machinery, damaging the whole assembly line beyond repair.

ACTINOMYCIN

Dr. Reich and colleagues at the Rockefeller Institute have studied the exact mechanism by which actinomycin acts. This drug characterizes the action of a third and entirely different group of drugs. The suffix

---

* *Enzyme,* a protein substance that engineers or catalyzes the reaction between two other chemicals.

† *Glutamine,* a nitrogen compound.

‡ *Sulfhydryl,* a sulfur-hydrogen unit of the molecule.

"mycin" means that the drug comes from a yeast fungus or mold. It is closely related to the familiar antibiotics which have the same root in their names, such as streptomycin, erythromycin, and chloromycetin. All of these drugs are extremely toxic, and are used in minute doses so that the bacteria are damaged more than the patient. Certain of them, of which actinomycin is an example, are also damaging to cancer cells, and are used in the treatment of cancer.

It had been known since 1962[*] that actinomycin prevents the reaction by which molecules of DNA form a matching RNA molecule, to take the message of the protein code from the nucleus to the cell. The chemists visualize the RNA molecule as being synthesized in close contact throughout the length of a portion of the DNA molecule. Dr. Reich and his collaborators have shown by extremely ingenious methods that the actinomycin molecule binds itself onto the side of the DNA molecule, so that the RNA can no longer fit on it for assembly. Dr. Reich has shown exactly where this "clinker" fits into the elaborate helix structure of DNA, discovering the exact binding site by very precise chemical and physical studies. The exact binding angles, by which the various atoms are attached to the carbon skeleton, give a clue to the chemist as to where the DNA molecule and actinomycin might fit together. Thus, actinomycin acts much farther along the pathway to antibody synthesis than either azaserine or 6-mercaptopurine, both of which act on smaller molecular units.

That actinomycin in small doses interferes with the production of transplant antibodies without producing an immunologic cripple (i.e., a patient vulnerable to every kind of infection) indicates again how remarkably exposed in the cell is the production of transplant antibody protein. Using drugs, the "balance of survival" is remarkably often achieved.

CORTISONE

Of the four drugs, the one familiar to most people is cortisone, a potent hormone of the adrenal glands. Pure compound E, cortisone, or cortisol (the three terms are synonymous) was first discovered in adrenal secretions by Dr. Kendall of the Mayo Clinic and by Dr. Reichstein of

---

[*] Goldberg and Rabinowitz, 1962.

Basle, Switzerland, simultaneously in 1936. It is now synthesized as a pure chemical and is widely used in medicine.

Around 1950, it was shown that hormones of this family block or disrupt a whole variety of immunologic responses. For example, a patient with hay fever, hives, asthma, or poison ivy will often have a dramatic recovery when given cortisone. The drug is evidently blocking the interaction between the antigen and the antibody that is responsible for the patient's symptoms. It also impairs the passage of cells through blood vessel walls. As used in the transplant problem, cortisone is therefore a drug that interferes with the actual ability of the antibody to react against the antigen. The precise chemical mechanism of its action, in the sense that Dr. Buchanan and Dr. Reich have elucidated the action of azaserine and actinomycin, is unknown.

When very large doses of cortisone are given, the total number of cells in the antibody-producing tissues is much reduced; lymphocyte counts are reduced, and the lymph nodes actually get smaller. Cortisone has many other effects observed in transplant patients under treatment. One is its effect, evident from the foregoing, of making people more susceptible to infection. In addition, there is a peculiar effect of producing a heavy-jowled appearance of the face with thin skin, a ruddy complexion, and a round "moonface" seen in people suffering from a disease in which too much cortisone is produced. This disease was first described by Dr. Cushing and is known as Cushing's disease. For this reason the rather odd word "cushingoid" is used to describe the appearance of a patient who is taking large amounts of cortisone; while not harmful in itself, it is sometimes a bother to the patient and rather startling to his friends.

OF DOGS AND MEN; NEWS TRAVELS FAST

Only a few months after Dr. Schwartz and Dr. Dameshek made their work public, new research projects attempted to apply these drugs to the transplantation of kidneys. These were first undertaken by Dr. Calne, a young surgeon working at the Buckston Browne Research Farm of the Royal College of Surgeons of England, and by Dr. Zukoski working with Dr. Hume in Richmond, Virginia. The direct line of influence and the speed with which Dr. Calne went to work on the problem are made clear in his statement: "Following the report of Schwartz and Dameshek that 6-mercaptopurine can make rabbits tolerant to human serum albumin antigen, I have used this drug in an attempt to modify the rejection of renal homografts in dogs."

Dr. Calne's initial experiment consisted in placing an allografted kidney in the lower abdomen of a dog, joining it to the iliac* blood vessels. These animals were given 6-mercaptopurine. Although they did not survive for more than two weeks, the kidneys did not show the signs of rejection (Fig. 12).

Realizing the significance of this finding, Dr. Calne then set out on a second series of experiments a few weeks later. This time he performed a bilateral nephrectomy, using the type of experiment in which the survival of the animal itself must depend on the survival of the kidney. Dr. Calne also modified the dose of the drug, and he encountered two rather long-term survivors, one at 21 days, and one at 47 days. This last dog, living for 47 days wholly on an allografted kidney maintained by 6-mercaptopurine, was unique. There never before had been such an animal, holding a kidney without rejection, and on the basis of very low dosage of a drug. Dr. Calne published his report in *Lancet* in February, 1960. It ends with the words:

My observations with 6-mercaptopurine suggest that this drug can modify the rejection of renal homografts in dogs. It could have advantages over total body irradiation in being less hazardous, and possibly less crippling immunologically, though it seems to increase liability to infection and cause hepatic biliary stasis. . . . Its use might thus offer an approach for renal homografting in man, especially in chronic uremic patients in whom homograft rejection is already depressed.

At the time that Dr. Calne was working out these experiments and writing his brief description, he was also making arrangements to spend a year of study in America. He arrived for work at the Harvard Surgical Laboratories as a holder of a Harkness Fellowship of the Commonwealth Fund, on July 1, 1960. Dr. Calne's arrival here marked

---

* *Iliac artery*, a large blood vessel coming from the aorta and coursing around the brim of the bony pelvis to supply blood to the legs. It is the artery on which most kidney transplantations have been placed.

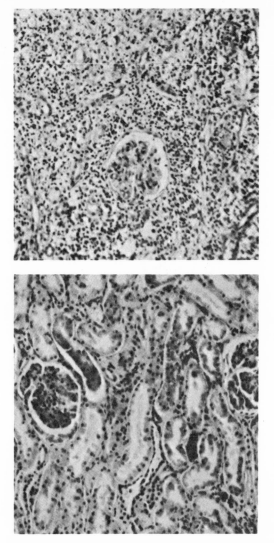

FIGURE 12. The effects of immunosuppression on a kidney allograft. Photomicrographs published in 1960 by Dr. Roy Y. Calne in *Lancet*. This was the first article to show the effect of immunosuppression on kidney transplantation in the dog. It was published just eight months after the description by Schwartz and Dameshek of the effect of 6-mercaptopurine on antibody production.

In the picture above is shown the confused mass of rejecting cells which have invaded the kidney. These appear as little black dots infiltrating and almost obliterating all the normal kidney tissue except for one round island of cells, a glomerulus.

Below is shown a picture made 47 days after the same type of kidney transplantation, but in a dog treated with 6-mercaptopurine. Here the normal tubular structure of the kidney is preserved; two of the glomeruli are plainly seen, and look quite normal.

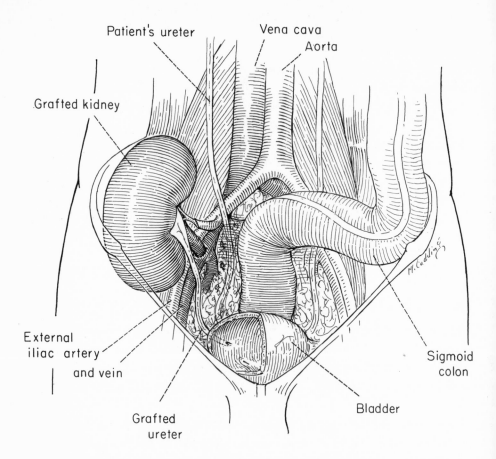

Patient's ureter

Vena cava

Aorta

Grafted kidney

External
iliac artery
and vein

Sigmoid
colon

Grafted
ureter

Bladder

FIGURE 13. Sites and sutures: kidney allograft. This diagram shows the location of a transplanted kidney in the pelvis, receiving its blood supply from the iliac vessels and with the ureter draining directly into the bladder.

the coincidence of three very important factors, the sort of conjunction that often produces important advance in scientific research. First was the mounting conviction that drug immunosuppression was preferred over whole body irradiation. Second was that in our laboratories Dr. Murray had already established, as a routine and practical procedure for study, the bilaterally nephrectomized dog with an allotransplanted kidney in place. Third was the ready availability of a suitable drug of known chemical structure in adequate quantity, backed by an industrial laboratory of the pharmaceutical industry keenly interested in further collaborative research—that of Burroughs, Wellcome & Company.

As a result of the conjunction of three important collaborators—Dr. Murray, Dr. Calne, and Dr. Hitchings of the Wellcome Laboratories—the next two years were to mark the most sudden advances in this field that had yet occurred. The first patient to have a human kidney transplantation from an unrelated donor, with a prolonged successful outcome under this type of drug-induced immunosuppression, was operated upon only twenty-six months after Dr. Calne's publication in *Lancet*. Several patients were treated with 6-mercaptopurine and azathioprine even before that. None of this advance could have occurred without extensive research carried out in dogs to explore the use of the drugs in kidney transplantation.

Dogs in Massachusetts, and "New Hampshire"

The standard animal model* was the basis for advance in the field of kidney transplantation and later transplantation of other organs, both in our laboratories and elsewhere in this country and abroad. This was the dog, bilaterally nephrectomized with an allotransplanted kidney in place. The preparation was first conceived by Dr. Ullmann, used by Dr. Carrel, and then put on a modern laboratory basis by Dr. Simonsen and Dr. Dempster. Such an animal requires very careful preparation, postoperative care, professional management, and nursing supervision. Research would be much easier to do in rats, mice, hamsters, or rabbits, in which experiments might be done by the thousands rather than the tens or hundreds. But such small animals do not have blood vessels large enough to permit a simple anastomosis for kidney transplantation. Dogs, or larger animals, must be used. The freedom to obtain, study, and operate on such animals has been an important component of advance in transplantation research.

While Dr. Murray and Dr. Calne were starting their work on drugs, the research workers of the Burroughs, Wellcome Research

---

* *Animal model,* an experimental arrangement in animals established to reproduce or study a situation often found in sick people.

Laboratories in Tuckahoe, New York, under Dr. Hitchings began to synthesize new compounds that might improve on 6-mercaptopurine. Within a few months, his laboratories developed azathioprine. It was found to be less toxic than 6-mercaptopurine, and it could be given as a pill, rather than by an injection.

Now, for the first time, after ten years of work, it became increasingly commonplace to have animals in the laboratory that were living normally, one, two, six, eight, or twelve months after kidney transplantation, with both their own kidneys removed and only the transplant functioning. This ideal result could not be achieved every time. There was still a high rate of loss and a high mortality from infection of the lungs, so common in dogs. But the increasing frequency of success provided new impetus to the work. As dogs lived for many months or years on the drug, the question was naturally raised whether the drugs could ever be stopped. It was also appropriate to inquire whether or not such animals had indeed achieved an unusual tolerance for foreign tissue, or whether the transplanted kidney itself had undergone some sort of adaptive change. The story of one animal illustrates many of these matters.

Each of these laboratory dogs is named to assist in its identification. The dog named "New Hampshire" (see Fig. 13A) pursued a singularly successful course. His story is an example of an important case history, even though the patient is four-footed.

"New Hampshire" was a 15 kg mongrel male, yellow and white in color, and of friendly habits. He was operated upon by Dr. Alexandre of Louvain, Belgium, who was working in our laboratories with Dr. Murray, on January 17, 1962. A bilateral nephrectomy was carried out, and a kidney allotransplant placed on the iliac blood vessels in the pelvis. The animal was put on azathioprine treatment. He did extremely well right from the beginning.

About sixty days after the transplant, a small patch of skin was taken from the animal that gave the kidney, and placed on "New Hampshire" as a skin graft. Much to the surprise of all concerned—because the kidney graft was working extremely well at the time—"New Hampshire" decided to do away with this skin graft, and it was promptly rejected. And at the time of this skin rejection, "New Hampshire" showed an increase in the blood urea concentration, indicating

FIGURE 13A.   Immunosuppressed recipients. Above is shown Mr. William Berry of the Laboratory for Surgical Research of the Harvard Medical School, with "New Hampshire," whose story is told in the text. The animal is off immunosuppressive drug, carrying the kidney graft well.

Also is shown Miss Marianne Mattlaer with "Mona," who had a kidney graft followed by the birth of healthy puppies two years later while Mona was still taking azathioprine immunosuppression.

Research in large animals such as dogs, cats, goats, sheep, pigs and monkeys has been essential to the development of transplantation.

that the kidney was going through a rejection crisis while the animal's body was busy making antibodies against the skin. Presentation of the skin antigens from the same donor excited within the animal a tendency to reject the kidney also. This was treated by giving the animal small doses of actinomycin.

On the one hundred-eightieth day, the experiment was again performed. Skin was taken from the kidney donor. It was rejected by "New Hampshire" *in spite of the fact that the kidney from this same donor was still working very well.* However, this time there was no rejection crisis in the kidney transplant.

On the two hundred-eightieth day, the experiment was again repeated, and again the skin was rejected; but this time, as on the second occasion, there was no tendency to reject the kidney. Here was a truly remarkable situation. The "adult acquired tolerance" was so very specific that it seemed to apply to the kidney alone!*

Then about the three hundredth day, the research team considered the possibility of stopping the azathioprine being given to "New Hampshire." Up to that time, no animal had carried a kidney graft successfully after the drug had been stopped, save for a single animal reported by Dr. Pierce and his group from the University of Minnesota. In that particular animal, nephrectomy had not been done at the time of transplantation, so it was not a fully comparable experiment.

In any event, the drug was intermittently stopped, and the dose lowered gradually for one hundred days from the three hundred-twentieth to the four hundred-twentieth day after the transplantation. Then, on that day—almost fourteen months after the initial transplantation—the drug was stopped altogether.

"New Hampshire" kept his kidney. He is still bounding around the laboratory, feeling very well. He is well known to all experimenters in this field, has been photographed many times, and has played on television. It is now over eight years since the transplantation. The drug has been stopped for over six years. "New Hampshire" continues to do well and continues to give hope that as our sophistication improves in the clinical use of immunosuppression, it may be possible to stop dosage of the drug in patients, as well as in dogs, after a prolonged transplantation success.

---

* Later on it was shown that in some animals even the second kidney from the original donor is rejected.

Several other laboratories were simultaneously active in this field, following the work of Dr. Calne and based on the studies of Dr. Schwartz and Dr. Dameshek. Dr. Zukoski, working with Dr. Hume in Richmond, showed that there was an average survival time for kidney grafts in dogs treated with 6-mercaptopurine of 23.7 days. This was to be contrasted with a control average of only 7.5 days. This finding was a strong confirmation of the work of Dr. Calne.

In Minnesota, Dr. Pierce reported that 15 of 51 animals, treated with 6-mercaptopurine for a kidney allograft, survived beyond 15 days. One of these animals was the very long-term survivor mentioned above, in whom the drug was stopped.

In the next year or two many other laboratories followed a similar approach, using these drugs, or others like them, to promote allograft survival of kidneys in animals. In addition, work was commenced on the liver, the spleen, the heart, the lung, and other glands and organs, using drug immunosuppression as the basis.

The drug had shown itself useful in the laboratory; it was time for another cautious visit to the sick.

8

FROM THE LABORATORY
TO THE HOSPITAL

Seeking to Establish a New Routine

*To be really useful, an astronaut must be a trail blazer,
doing something which, under proper conditions and with
the right equipment, others can also accomplish. He is not
an adventurer—however high and exciting the venture he
undertakes—but one who seeks to establish a new routine.*
—Editorial, *New York Herald Tribune, July 22, 1961*

A Visit to the Sick

By mid-1961 it appeared that the balance of survival was more readily
achieved on drug treatment than with the heavy blow of whole body
irradiation. The transition from the use of whole body irradiation to
the use of drugs for immunosuppression occupied only a few months.
The patients considered for transplantation were those whose outlook
for survival was only a few weeks at the time of the transplant; most of
them were suffering from chronic renal failure due to glomerulonephritis or pyelonephritis. During this time some patients who had been
started on irradiation were actually given drugs later on. This sequence was followed in several of the French cases in whom drugs
were used some weeks or months after initial whole body irradiation.

148

It was immediately clear that the drugs were a major advance, although spectacular success was not achieved in the early cases.

Unlike irradiation, which was given all at once or in a few divided doses, the immunosuppressive drug could be given daily, in very small doses. If the body's defenses were depleted too far (as shown by a low blood count of white cells or platelets), the dose of the drug could be lowered, or completely stopped for a few days. The doctor could simultaneously follow the progress both of the kidney and of the body's defenses against it. This was gentle treatment in sharp contrast to high-dose whole body irradiation after which no further improvement could be expected until the natural course of the irradiation damage had been run over a period of weeks.

The first patient given 6-mercaptopurine for immunosuppression in kidney transplantation was Mr. L. S. (PBBH 4P503), operated upon April 14, 1960. Azathioprine was soon substituted for 6-mercapto-purine, and the first patient to be treated with azathioprine for immunosuppression in kidney transplantation was Mr. D. T. (PBBH 0-15-05) operated on in March 22, 1961. These two patients represented the first human application in the world of drug immunosuppression hinted at immunologically in the work of Dr. Schwartz and Dr. Dameshek and demonstrated to be useful in animals by Dr. Calne. Virtually every kidney transplantation throughout the world since 1961—all of the heart and liver transplantations, and all the allotransplants of any other organ—have been carried out with basic immunosuppression using azathioprine. Whatever the legal or ethical aspects that surround clinical experiments and therapeutic innovation, there must always be a first time and a first patient. It was a fortunate circumstance that in 1961, the right people happened to be assembled in an appropriate hospital and presented with an effective drug, to give the first cases of kidney allotransplantation under drug immunosuppression a reasonable chance of success. Neither of these patients survived for long, but soon there would be a successful experience. It was toward such an outcome that all this work had been devoted.

The doctors in all of these hospitals were seeking to establish a new routine that would be safe, practical, and effective. All of these experiences were based on the assumption that it would be possible to obtain long-term survival in a patient, maintaining him in good health, with both his own diseased kidneys removed, an allotransplanted kidney in place, and achieving immunosuppression by means of a drug. This assumption of clinical success was based wholly on the animal work in the laboratory; and its reality—which stimulated so many other workers—was first achieved in the case of Mr. M. D. He was operated upon April 5, 1962, and for the first time gave substance to the growing conviction that drug immunosuppression would make allotransplantation possible.

THE CASE OF MR. M. D.

Mr. M. D. (PBBH 1-19-87) was 24 years old at the time of his admission to the hospital on January 21, 1962. Like so many other patients before him, he was referred to the Kidney Study Unit because he was suffering from chronic glomerulonephritis. In the twelve years since the artificial kidney was first used, many procedures had changed. Besides the use of dialysis on the artificial kidney, it was possible to wash the surface of the peritoneal cavity and remove waste products in this way, called "peritoneal dialysis." Here the peritoneum itself, a thin membrane that covers the abdominal viscera, is acting as the dialysis membrane. This procedure was much easier and less expensive than the artificial kidney because the patient did not have to stay in the hospital. Although the equipment required was very simple, the danger of infection was always present. New procedures had also been developed that made it possible to carry out brief and simple artificial kidney dialyses daily, keeping the patient up and about, feeling very well, and often at home.

Upon admission to the hospital, Mr. M. D. was treated initially by peritoneal dialysis to bring his body chemistry closer to normal and to improve his health and strength. The patient was in and out of the hospital six times during his first month. A plastic button was placed in the abdominal wall so that the small tube for peritoneal dialysis could be inserted without pain or inconvenience. The peritoneal dialysis procedures appeared to become less and less effective in washing waste products out through the peritoneal cavity. The patient then became a candidate for kidney transplantation. He had no twin, and family members were not readily available as donors. He began the wait for a donor.

On April 5, 1962, there arose one of those coincidences, the recognition of which is so important in any kind of clinical advance. This was the case of a 30-year-old man who was undergoing an operation on his heart. His heart was opened and repaired under hypothermia, in which the patient's whole body is cooled. This heart was severely diseased, and by cooling the patient while asleep, some of the risks could be reduced. At the close of the operation, this heart would not resume its normal beat. The patient died on the operating table after a prolonged effort to help the heart to beat again. At the time he died, his whole body was cooled well below normal body temperature, and both of his kidneys were functioning well. Because of the hypothermia, both of the kidneys were already cold when their blood supply was shut off by the patient's death. Therefore, they were well protected and well preserved through the inevitable period without blood flow.

During the previous week Dr. Murray, Dr. Couch, and Dr. Wilson had taken turns sleeping at the hospital to provide a twenty-four-hour watch in case the sudden demise of some severely injured person should provide a kidney for Mr. M. D. There were three "false alarms" before this ideal and remarkable opportunity presented itself.

It took a few minutes to complete the necessary arrangements with a very helpful and understanding family. One kidney was removed forty minutes after death, and was then cooled further to 4°C. Again the transplant operation was carried out by Dr. Murray. Immediately kidney function resumed.

The total length of time from the death of the donor to establishment of new circulation in the kidney transplant was two hours. At normal temperatures such a length of time would be damaging to the kidney; but in this situation, with the donor's organs cooled at the time of death, two hours was not too long. These circumstances were clearly recognized at the time as being very favorable for Mr. M. D.

The patient was immediately placed on azathioprine, and was maintained on this drug.

For a few days after the transplant, there was no more urine function even though some began during the operation. Then, on the eleventh postoperative day, urine began to flow in good volume, and by the eighteenth day the patient passed 6000 ml of urine in one day. Progress was satisfactory for the next three weeks.

On the thirty-ninth day, the patient's body made an effort to reject the new kidney, producing an immunologic rejection crisis with high fever and severe illness. This was treated with actinomycin in addition to azathioprine. When this crisis subsided, it was clearly necessary to remove both of the patient's own kidneys in order to lower his blood pressure. On the fiftieth and then on the sixty-second postoperative day, two operations for nephrectomy were performed by Dr. Harrison, each time removing one of the patient's own degenerated kidneys.

Four months after the transplantation, there was another immunologic rejection crisis. The drug did not seem to be holding the kidney satisfactorily, so cortisone also was given. The patient then developed pneumonia, a frightening complication in any patient on immunosuppressive drugs. Some confidence in treating this infection was born of the fact that in many hundreds of dogs it had been shown that ordinary kennel infections, such as distemper and pneumonia, could often be thrown off even though the animals were on drug dosage.

So it was with Mr. M. D. The pneumonia subsided under treatment with antibiotics, and the patient was finally discharged from the hospital. He returned to his work, feeling well and working effectively, with normal blood pressure, even though the level of urea waste products in his blood was slightly elevated above normal, and he could not be said to have completely normal kidney function. As a patient suffering from chronic kidney disease, he had been restored to a useful life. Just as in the case of Mr. R. H. and Mr. J. R. (the two other "firsts"), Mr. M. D. was of very special importance because his was the first successful kidney transplantation in man, under drug immunosuppression, from an unrelated donor.

Then as if to put the entire procedure to its severest test, Mr. M. D. developed acute appendicitis eighteen months after his transplant. The appendix lay right next to the transplanted kidney. It was badly infected and partially perforated. It was removed.* The pa-

---

* Under the microscope this appendix showed suppression of its normal lymph tissue response to inflammation—demonstrating the local effect of immunosuppression.

tient's course was stormy for a while, but he finally went home as well as ever—still on the drug.

But this was not all. This kidney, the first to show long-term function after transplantation on drugs, displayed a continuing though nonprogressive reduction in function. Although Mr. M. D. was home and at work, his condition was not quite perfect. Therefore on January 22, 1964, twenty-one months after his transplant, a second kidney was placed in the patient. This time the new kidney (like several others) had been removed by Dr. Matson from a child having the hydrocephalus operation. The kidney was placed on the other side of the pelvis.*

As knowledge of the case of Mr. M. D. began to spread in late 1962, an increasing number of patients were operated on in several centers.

Of the 13 patients operated on at this hospital in the interval between April 1960 and April 1963, 10 received kidneys from recently deceased persons, or from young patients who had to lose their kidneys anyway in the treatment of hydrocephalus. Only 3 of these patients had living donors, and these 3 appeared to get along the best.

In a more recently commenced series of operations reported by Dr. Waddell and Dr. Starzl in Denver, Colorado, 29 of 46 patients, or a little more than one half of the group, showed good kidney function for at least 3 months. In addition, workers at Richmond, Virginia (under Dr. Hume), and in Boston at the Massachusetts General Hospital (under Dr. Russell) were obtaining results greatly improved over those reported several years previously. One of the early workers in the field was Dr. Goodwin, working with a team at the University of California at Los Angeles. He had reported 13 renal transplantations done since 1956. It is interesting that one of the long survivors in Dr. Goodwin's experience had a kidney donated from another patient from whom it had to be removed because of cancer lower down in the

---

* Mr. M. D. finally died on July 2, 1964, twenty-seven months after his first operation, of general infection and severe liver damage. Although his second kidney was functioning fairly well, infection and liver damage took their toll. Later improvements in immunosuppression and histocompatibility matching eventually reduced these hazards, but by 1970, eight years after the historic operation on Mr. M. D., infection remains the principal hazard to survival in a patient on immunosuppressive drugs.

ureter. This was the same sequence, it will be recalled, that occurred in Dr. Scola's patient at the Springfield Hospital in 1951.

Dr. Kolff, the original developer of the artificial kidney, was then in charge of a group carrying out renal transplantations at the Cleveland Clinic Foundation in Cleveland, Ohio. Up to September 1963, he reported 9 transplants of which 6 were still doing well at the time of the report.

In England, Dr. Calne was carrying on his work, now at the Westminster Hospital. He was one of the surgeons who had used kidneys from cadavers *only*. Of 8 patients operated upon, 2 were still living, but only 1 with good function.

Professor Woodruff and his group in Edinburgh reported 11 patients who had been operated upon, with 5 still doing well. Two of these 5, however, were identical twins; the allografts were from parental donors.

Dr. Shackman at the Hammersmith Hospital in London reported on 12 transplants in 11 patients, one patient (like Mr. M. D.) having had two transplantations. His group was able to report a very long survivor, a man in his twenties who survived two and a half years after kidney transplantation from his younger brother. X-radiation to the extent of 100 roentgen units was used. This patient, operated on early in 1961, represented the first long-term survivor in a nontwin transplant. The group at Hammersmith Hospital had used whole body irradiation patterned somewhat after the treatment of Mr. J. R. (page 119) and the experiences in Paris.

Immunosuppressive drugs had provided the most practical and safest way of achieving transplant acceptance. Each year the results improved. The drugs were gentler than whole body irradiation, but they were still toxic and far from perfect. New and better methods had to be developed.

Before turning to the present posture and clinical results of kidney transplantation over the world, we should pay brief attention to two very large subjects: home dialysis and the psychologic aspects of kidney transplantation.

At Home with Dialysis

The introduction of the artificial kidney by Dr. Kolff in 1946 (see Chapter 4) led directly to kidney transplantation. The presence of this substitute for the kidneys made it possible for people dying of renal failure to be kept alive until a transplant could be done. By 1965, dialysis services were being expanded in many centers of the country and thus made long-term maintenance possible with an approach to normal living on dialysis. This required two or three special developments.

First, disposable plastic materials and readily mixed sterile solutions were needed so that dialysis could be done on an expanded scale, in some cases daily.

Second, in the interest of economy, home dialysis programs were essential to provide a means by which patients, with the help of family (with minimal assistance from doctors or nurses), could operate dialysis apparatus in their own homes. This required the perfection of sterile equipment and supplies and providing the necessary salt solutions in a transportable and disposable form. After a period of training, the patient could then have frequent dialysis without coming to the hospital at all.

Third, a surgical method had to be developed for ready access to arteries and veins for hookup to dialysis without the attendance of a surgeon.

Many laboratories and hospitals played a role in the perfection of all these elements, but none surpassed that of Dr. Scribner and his group in Seattle. A special plastic wrist-shunt was invented to connect the artery and vein of the wrist by a small bit of tubing installed by a minor surgical operation to remain in place for months or years. Any trained person could then put a patient on the artificial kidney. It became a nursing routine and home dialysis became a reality.

At first it appeared that this way of life was in competition with transplantation. Instead, it provides an alternative for patients who cannot receive a transplant. Many patients on home dialysis, who later had successful kidney transplantations, have agreed that it is better to have a working kidney (and be free of apparatus and critical treatments several times a week) than to be on home dialysis. But transplantation carries a greater immediate risk. In the sense of long-term alternatives, the methods are not really in competition. Instead, they complement each other. No hospital can run a successful transplant service without dialysis for preoperative care and as a standby should the transplant fail. And no hospital can conduct a dialysis service without being able to offer selected patients the alternative of transplantation.

One of the principal reasons that kidney transplantation will dominate transplantation for decades to come is that the artificial kidney exists as a viable alternative to transplantation, as a way of keeping patients alive and at work while awaiting a kidney for transplant, and as a way of taking care of patients in whom the transplant has failed.

In addition, some patients have coexistent diseases such as cancer, advanced degeneration of blood vessels, brain diseases, or diabetes, which make kidney transplantation (especially from living donors) unwise. For these patients chronic dialysis becomes a permanent way of life.

It is historically significant that the hospitals doing kidney transplants began with dialysis and advanced as fast as they could in establishing additional dialysis units and home dialysis programs. They understood the need to have artificial kidneys before kidney transplants could be employed. By contrast, those physicians who had developed dialysis as the only treatment (thinking it would make transplantation unnecessary) found after a few years that they must mount a transplant program to give their dialysis patients an alternative—to release them from frequent medical treatment and let them return to the mainstream of society.

How Does It Feel?—Emotions of the Transplanted

The transplantation of an organ from one person to another to escape imminent death invokes a remarkable series of emotional stresses and perturbations of the human condition. With the widespread development of kidney transplantation and the growth of large renal centers where there were many patients on dialysis before and after operation (with or without living donors) there has developed a new set of problems.

Prominent among these problems is the attitude of spouse and family when a person threatened with death, and assumed to be dying, is suddenly returned to life. It is a remarkable phenomenon: the family had written off the patient. They had adjusted their emotional life to his anticipated demise. Although sympathetic to his suffering and desirous of alleviating it, and helpful and supportive in treating it, they nonetheless had, deep within their subconscious, already assigned him to a place other than the land of the living. They are thus shocked when the passive patient returns, demanding, to their midst, very much alive. This is the phenomenon of "premature mourning."

Our attention was called to this in some instances where a spouse had taken most devoted care of the patient through a long and tragic illness, then, upon recovery, they were divorced. When the patient came to life with his new kidney and began to evince new desires, new plans, new wishes, new aspirations, the spouse lost her dominant role as nurse and caretaker and became insecure, not quite so sure that his new plans were good ones and possibly fearful of her own rejection. Several of these divorces occurred between couples who, when the one was extremely ill, appeared to be totally devoted to each other. This crisis is one that might be prevented with better counseling and understanding for patient and family and better psychiatric insight by physician and surgeon.

Another emotional problem is that of "excessive gratitude." Most surgeons have seen this in occasional patients with other diseases or operations. It is the privilege of every surgeon a few times in his life to save a patient who is aware of the total situation. He sees his bodily deterioration repaired, rectified, and then followed by convalescence and normal living. Some patients are deeply disturbed by this. They feel it is a debt they never can repay. They may even become antagonistic toward the physician or surgeon, feeling that their excessive gratitude indicates a sort of dependent relationship which is distasteful. No amount of gifts or letters or expressions on Christmas cards can quite indicate what such total salvation means to the patient. He is eternally burdened.

In kidney transplantation the problem of excessive gratitude is not directed toward the physician or surgeon but is instead directed toward another person—the donor. The donor may be a parent with whom there have been feelings of rivalry or outright conflict in the past. It may be a sibling toward whom the patient feels close bonds of affection, but with whom nonetheless there have been many periods of friction, especially in childhood and adolescence. Now, all of a sudden, the patient finds that he is in a dependent relationship to this donor for the rest of his life, owing every minute of his life to the generosity of that person.

The selection of a donor within the family depends on many social and emotional factors, as well as the histocompatibility data which later determine his acceptability. Dr. Eisendrath, psychiatrist to the Brigham Transplant Unit, writes:

The preselection of the donor within the family, as complicated as human behavior itself, is largely determined beyond the view of the transplant service. The problem of motivation is complex, for no family is completely free of obligations based on guilt, shame, debt, or fear. Thus important, although unseen, selection is activated within the family. One family member may not be considered because of a previous disagreement and mutual dislike, another may have too many economic responsibilities, while another might be anxious and willing to give. Occasionally, a parent is kept ignorant of the possibility of a transplant by the patient, or spouse, to avoid undue tensions on the parent or for fear of being turned down. In one instance, a cadaveric kidney was selected instead of a maternal kidney because the man wanted to avoid upsetting his wife—and himself. In this instance, the mother of the patient had a domineering personality, and both the patient and his wife feared being "owned by her" if she were asked to be the donor. Furthermore, a careful balance between the two women had been maintained by this manipulative patient who skillfully played one woman against the other. The mother, as a donor, would have endangered this balance.

In another instance, a black sheep brother quickly offered to donate a kidney to his well-established, respectable brother in the hopes of re-establishing himself in the family circle and to prove his worth. While in a contrary situation, and to our knowledge a unique one, a suitable prospective donor, the mother of the patient, decided against giving her kidney because she felt "pushed into a corner from which there was no escape," and a sister was chosen in her stead.

Subsequent evaluation of the donor's total experience reveals many hidden aspects of kidney donation. Dr. Eisendrath asked a number of donors to express their thoughts and beliefs about the whole experience.

Donors were asked to comment on their beliefs, the worth of donating, and whether or not they would go through it again, knowing what they knew now. They were also asked if they themselves had derived something from the experience. Here again, replies were quite consistent, irrespective of the results of the transplant. There was almost complete unanimity of belief that the donor would do it again and that each had derived some sense of worthwhile accomplishment or helping to save a life. Sometimes, the answers were moving.

A 39-year-old woman who donated her kidney successfully to her sister said that it had been a "thrilling experience" and quoted Emerson: "To know even one life has breathed easier because you lived—this is to have succeeded."

A 57-year-old mother told how her donation was the first contact she had had with her estranged son in more than six years. He had married against her wishes, and when she found he was dying, she offered her kidney. They spoke only once during the eight months between the time of transplant and his subsequent death, but during that one contact, he thanked her for what she had done.

A 48-year-old father who successfully donated to his son, who died, however, of meningitis more than two years later, said he had "gained the courage to give his life."

A mother who successfully donated to her daughter spoke of "so much satisfaction" and how she had become "less selfish."

A 60-year-old father said, "Many people have commented on my bravery. It is, of course, no such thing. When something has to be done, it has to be done. I was glad to do it, and I could not have lived with myself if I had not."

There were many other positive responses in which people believed they had "become more understanding of others," developed deeper religious faith, and had "greater satisfaction in doing something important." One man said it was the most important thing he had ever done in his life. They mentioned how "proud" they were of what they had done, and how "pleased and happy" their gifts had made them. One donor was elected

Exemplary Mother of the Year by the community after she had donated a kidney.

There were four comments which had negative connotations under this heading, all involving unsuccessful transplants.

One mother whose daughter died of sepsis in the first month after transplant wrote that she was too upset to reply to the questionnaire. She had been unable to resume her career and was affected by Graves' disease. A brother wondered, in passing, how much of his own life he had lost through the two years of life gained by the recipient of his kidney. He did not, however, regret his donation. A 67-year-old mother who gave her kidney to her son—which his body later rejected, who is now awaiting a second transplant—stated that she was "concerned that I saved him only for worse suffering. . . . I was let down with the failure of the kidney and couldn't urge anyone else to do it." But she said she would "do it again myself." A mother who donated her kidney to her daughter—who died shortly after operation—believed that she had not had the situation well explained, that not enough experienced doctors were involved, that the transplant was not worth it with the limited success of a period of 60 days, and that she would not do it again with the then limited chances of success. However, she concluded that she would if the chances were greater, and she hoped that her sacrifice would benefit someone else.

An interesting and ambivalent response came from the twin brother of a successful recipient, who said, "I believe kidney donors should be recognized with a Presidential award of a lifesaving medal," and requested us to write his employers telling them of his fortitude, so that he would get a raise.

Taking an organ from one person and having it work within another, might present an "identity crisis," the patient thinking he is part of someone else, and identifying with that other person or worrying about the fate and life of the other person. In kidney transplantation it has not been a very frequent or disturbing matter. If cardiac transplantation becomes commonplace, the aspect of identity, or misidentification with the donor, might present a new problem. The donor is necessarily a recently deceased cadaver. His death has made the patient's life possible; his heart is beating and seems to be a sort of manifestation of someone else's "self" in the patient.

More important than any of these emotional crises, and much more difficult to deal with, is the overriding insecurity of the transplanted patient who realizes that his kidney may be rejected and he may be thrown either into severe illness or back into dialysis, or may develop a fatal infection. The patient in this circumstance is no different from any other who feels insecure and worried about the progress of his disease and his treatment. The only difference lies in the fact that the kidney transplant patient is apt to know a good deal about his disease. He is not easily fooled or comforted by meaningless reassurances. He knows about the volume and quality of his urine. He knows how he feels. He knows how much cortisone is being given, and if he is rejecting. He may be a patient in a transplant unit where there is common conversation and exchange of information about the state of one another's transplanted kidneys. No matter how brave or stoic a person might be, he cannot help but worry about the state of a transplanted kidney which he can feel in his lower abdomen and sense as a functioning organ.

These feelings must be dealt with as they are in any other sensitive, intelligent patient. The doctor must discuss everything in detail, hold nothing back, never remove hope, always explain and show by analogy and comparison how these things happen and how the future can be secure. At present, with the easy removal of rejecting kidneys, and frequent home dialysis to fall back on, and with hundreds of patients doing well after a second or even a third kidney, these worries are much easier for the physician and surgeon to expiate. In liver or heart transplants there is no such crutch to fall back upon; the onset of rejection forebodes a fatal outcome.

THE WORLD SERIES

As clinical kidney transplantation approaches its twentieth year since the first series of unmodified recipients operated on by Dr. Hume, and its tenth year since the first use of immunosuppressive drugs in the laboratory, it is possible to review the series of kidney transplants done throughout the world. In 1963, an International Human Kidney Transplant Registry was established in Boston, conducted by an advisory committee representing eleven hospitals in North America, and including in its corresponding membership many hospitals in western Europe, Australia, and New Zealand. The Harvard Computing Center with its elaborate modern computational methods has made it possible to gather continuously, and report annually, the data on world kidney transplantation. A special flow sheet was perfected that can be used in any hospital to record the clinical course of the patient. It is then sent to the Boston Center where the data are fed into the computer memory circuits for analysis and retrieval.*

By January 1971, 4683 transplants were recorded, of which 4490 presented sufficient data for complete analysis. Thirty-six percent of these kidney transplantations were performed in the years 1968 and 1969, an upward trend of operative performance that is still rising, though not as rapidly as it did in those years. We do not have records of the number of kidney transplantations performed in eastern Europe, Russia, or China, and there are some hospitals in the Western area that have elected not to report to the Registry. It is estimated that about 6000 transplants of kidney have been done throughout the world. About 2 percent of the entire world series (approximately 90 cases) were transplants carried out between twins, of which about one half were monozygotic or identical twins. The longest surviving kidney transplantation in the world is that of the identical twin now in her fifteenth year, and the longest surviving transplant from fraternal or dizogotic twins is in its tenth year. At the present time grafts between identical twins have a 90 percent chance of excellent function through the first year with very little decrease after that.

Of this entire series of operations, 52 percent were transplants taken from unrelated donors, largely unrelated cadaver donors. A very small group (about 1.5 percent) were kidneys removed from unrelated living donors.

Forty-six percent of this world series were transplants done from family donors as follows: mother—16 percent, brother—11 percent, sister—10 percent, and father—9 percent.

Based on this relationship of donors, it is possible to predict the estimated transplant survival at one year. This figure is for survival of the transplanted kidney, not the patient! Patient survival is much higher than this, as nonfunctioning kidneys are now removed before they have time to do serious damage to the host. The data show that

---

* This Registry function has now been taken over by the American College of Surgeons, which, supported by the National Institutes of Health, maintains an international registry for all sorts of transplants, not kidney alone.

with a sibling donor there is a 91 percent chance of good kidney function at one year, with a parent 83 percent, with another blood relative 67 percent, and with a cadaver donor 42 percent. The two-year survival data, estimated from a somewhat smaller number of cases, indicate a 77 percent likelihood of good function with closely related family donors, and 40 percent with cadaver donors. Improvement in statistical likelihood of survival, using family donors, is still being noted from year to year, whereas with the cadaver donors after years of gradual improvement the situation seems to be fixed and unchanging, pointing up the need for improved methods of immunosuppression. The role of tissue typing has not yet been widely felt in very late results; the effect of tissue typing (see Chapter 11) has not been clear-cut in the success of cadaver-donor kidneys, save for the avoidance of transplants where there was an unfavorable direct crossmatch.

Kidney transplantation, formerly performed in only a few centers studying the matter intensively, is now diffused in a worldwide community of hospitals. It is possible to compare the results in large centers with those from smaller centers with much less experience (those who had done fewer than 30 transplants prior to January 1967). Diffusion of knowledge about transplant science and the care and selection of such patients has been successful. There is no gross difference in the results between these two types of transplant units. Before starting transplantation, doctors visit, study, and work in the established centers. They carry these procedures home and start from a base far advanced over the starting point of their predecessors. There are many national and international meetings where this new field of work is reviewed and widely discussed. Some of the new smaller centers have made important contributions to the field of clinical transplantation and have conducted important studies in basic transplant immunology. A myriad of publications and books and the formation of a new journal devoted entirely to transplant science have further advanced the status of both the beginner and the old hand in this work.

The computer can be asked many questions, quickly yielding numbers impossible without such electronic aids. It is possible to contrast all the transplants done throughout the world prior to 1967 with those carried out after that date. In all categories of transplantation there is an improvement of approximately 20 percent in transplant survivorship for the first year when comparing the early series with the later series. Outside of the twin kidneys, these data demonstrate clearly that the finest clinical result now obtainable with kidney transplantations is based on the use of tissue typing and the employment of a well-matched sibling donor. Using this set of criteria the chances for survival of both kidney and patient approximate 87 percent at four years. This figure, more than any other, epitomizes the achievement in transplantation through the years covered by our narrative.

Turning from this large assemblage of allografts, there have been approximately 45 transplants in identical twins since that first one in 1954. In this group, recurrent glomerulonephritis has been the major and most prevalent problem. The disease has occurred only in those cases in which the operation was performed for chronic glomerulonephritis in the first place. If the kidney transplantation was done for an identical twin suffering from some other disease (such as kidney infection or pyelonephritis), glomerulonephritis has never occurred in the transplanted kidney. This is proof positive that the recurrent glomerulonephritis results from the same old set of causes that had given the patient this disease in the first place. These causes may include the existence of antigen-antibody complexes in the recipient's circulation which lodge in the new kidney and destroy it much as they did the old one.

The recurrence rate of glomerulonephritis in the transplanted kidney of identical twins, although apparently falling, is still quite high. In our series of 16 such transplants carried out by Dr. Murray for chronic glomerulonephritis, 8 of the 16 developed recurrent nephritis, and 7 of these 8 died of this recurrence. By contrast, in the 6 identical twin transplants done for other diseases, there were no instances of recurrent glomerulonephritis and no deaths.

Some of these cases of recurrence of glomerulonephritis in identical twins occurred as long as five years after the transplant. Evidence from current immunologic studies suggests that an antiglomerular basement membrane antibody* is present in some of these patients

---

* *Antiglomerular basement membrane antibody,* a protein antibody or immunoglobulin (see Chapter 9) that lodges in the underlying or basement membrane of the glomerulus of the kidney. It is responsible for producing a kidney inflammation that closely resembles glomerulonephritis.

and continues to react against the tissue of the new kidney. It is estimated that 15 percent of patients with glomerulonephritis demonstrate such an antiglomerular basement membrane antibody. When an isograft is carried out, as between identical twins, immunosuppression is not employed initially, and any of this antibody present is free to react against the new kidney. When an allograft is performed between any two other individuals, the reaction of this antibody against the new kidney may be abated to some extent by the same immunosuppressive drugs that are helping to protect the kidney from rejection. This evidence has led to the use of some immunosuppressive drugs even in identical twin transplants once the transplanted kidney begins to show signs of recurrent disease.

At the present time, when identical twins present themselves for transplantation, blood from the sick or recipient twin is analyzed for the presence of the antiglomerular basement membrane antibody. If it is present, the patient is treated with immunosuppressive drugs—azathioprine, cytoxan, or cortisone—following the removal of his two diseased kidneys, until the antiglomerular basement membrane antibody disappears from the blood. Then the transplant can be carried out with a better likelihood of success. In one group of identical twin transplants only 15 percent showed the presence of this special antibody. The others were transplanted much as before, the surgeons watching the transplanted kidney for signs of recurrent nephritis.

To understand these new applications of immunology, the nature of tissue grouping, and the future possibilities for transplant methods that might release patients from the dangers of toxic immunosuppressive chemicals, we must return again to basic transplant science and review modern molecular immunology, as it too has advanced, evolved, and changed over the past decade since the theories of Burnet (described in Chapter 2).

9

THE NEW IMMUNOLOGY

How Do Molecules Become Weapons?

*Before these weapons of the gods, you must have seen how
the proudest palaces and the loftiest trees fall and perish.*

—HERODOTUS

ANTIBODY IMMUNOGLOBULINS—
THE CHEMISTRY OF REJECTION

A central concept of modern immunology is the assignment of antibody activity to several species of large molecules that can be identified and isolated as proteins and their behavior analyzed in detail.
Within the past few years several of these proteins have been characterized in sufficient detail so that molecular models can be constructed,
and in some cases the proteins have been partially synthesized—or
rather reassembled—from large component parts.

All protein molecules are composed of long chains of amino acids
linked end-to-end, cross-linked in a variety of shapes. The antibody
proteins that confer immunity on the organism are proteins of the
globulin type. They are therefore called immunoglobulins and are
regularly composed of four chainlike proteins linked together in two
big heavy chains and two small light ones. Most immunoglobulins

share this configuration of four protein chains joined by cross-linking, and there is close similarity or even identity amongst them as to the detailed composition of one end of this large four-piece molecule. But at the other end of the four-chain aggregate there is an almost infinite variety of detailed molecular structures. Figure 14 diagrams such a molecule, showing its two heavy chains, its two light chains, the lot joined together with sulfydryl or disulfide bonds (with sulfur atoms) and indicating where the constancy and the variability are found. Normal human blood contains hundreds or thousands of slightly different immunoglobulin molecules. Each is distinct in the precise sequence of amino acids joined together at the variable end of the chain and the precise shape that they offer an antigen with which they might combine.

Each specific immunoglobulin structure is somehow related to the chemical configuration of the antigen with which it must react. Although all immunoglobulins possess the same basic four-chain structure, their infinite variety in detailed sequence at the variant end seems to be related to their specificity—their ability to react with an almost limitless variety of specific antigen molecules.

This leads to a question that is at the heart of our understanding of the formation of antibodies: how can an entirely new substance—an antigen molecule—previously unknown to the organism, be fitted or matched up with a specific immunoglobulin *after* it arrives on the scene? How can immunoglobulins be formed through the DNA-RNA genetic coding mechanism (responsible for the synthesis of all proteins) so that they will be able to match the variety of antigenic substances that threaten the host? Such antigenic substances might be the cell membranes of bacteria, chemicals used as drugs, or injected proteins. As far as the transplant patient is concerned, these antigens are found on the surface of transplanted cells such as those in the kidney.

To answer these questions one must either theorize that protein structure is not fixed by its genetic (DNA-RNA) background and can mold or adapt itself to the new antigens as they enter the body from the outside world, or postulate that there are already present in the genetic constitution of each person enough different genes (i.e., nucleotide combinations in DNA) to provide *in advance* for all possible invading challenges of life—and even in some cases to match up with

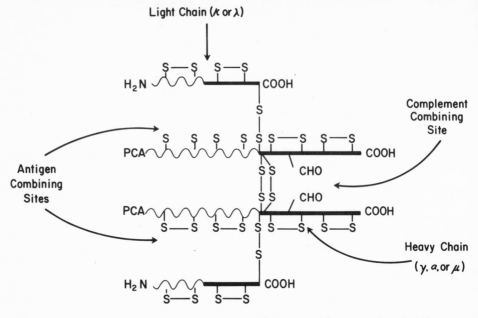

FIGURE 14. In this and the two subsequent figures (Figures 15 and 16) are shown some aspects of immunoglobulin chemistry.

Here is shown an abbreviated chemical model of an immunoglobulin molecule. The molecule has a Y-shape with a single arm pointing to the right in this picture. The heavy chain is shown with the heavy lines, and is about the same in all immunoglobulin molecules. The opening to the right is presumably the site where complement is bound and activated.

To the left are the two sites involving the light chains (shown in light lines), highly variable, and adapted to fit a large number of different antigens.

In this sort of shorthand model the carbon, hydrogen, and nitrogen atoms are not shown; the sulfur atoms are demonstrated to show the cross-linking.

entirely new and unnatural synthetic combinations dreamed up by chemists or drug manufacturers!

A third theory would hold that although a seemingly infinite variety of antigenic substances might threaten the organism, they are not all so different. Possibly they are variants on a finite number of key shapes so that an antibody against one might fit onto several others. This theory would effect a real economy in the number of different immunoglobulins that each person must assemble, and it might explain the phenomenon of cross-reactivity (discussed later). There would still be the necessity for a great variety of immunoglobulin capabilities in each person. Even if antigens do bear some resemblance to each other, there is still a large variety of antigens—proteins, small chains of amino acids, sugarlike substances, and simple molecules such as the commonly used headache drugs.

To consider in greater detail the kinds of molecules that are included in the general category of immunoglobulins, their complexity has been somewhat simplified in the past few years by arranging the immunoglobulins into five major classes based on the five basic types of heavy chains given Greek letter designations. Linked up with these are two types of small light chains. Any given cell appears to make either type of light chain to join up with heavy chains. The characteristic of an immunoglobulin molecule is determined by the nature of its heavy chains.

Designating the heavy chains and the light chains by their symbols, we can then make a sort of code for the immunoglobulins. For example, one molecule has two gamma chains and two kappa chains. This particular one is very widespread in man and animals and is known as immunoglobulin G or IgG. Its particular combination of four chains gives it a molecular weight of about 150,000. This corresponds to a sedimentation coefficient in the ultracentrifuge (another measure of molecular size) of about 7s.* A heavier immunoglobulin, the IgM molecule, contains five heavy chains and ten light chains. As further knowledge accumulates, it is clear that a wide variety of combinations will be identified.

Although some of these immunoglobulins are quite light in weight (as IgG with a molecular weight of about 150,000), others are much heavier, such as IgM with a molecular weight of about 900,000 and a sedimentation coefficient of about 19s. This is one of the immunoglobulins mentioned that has five heavy chains. This identification of

---

* The ultracentrifuge provides data on the weight of molecules by high-speed rotation in a centrifuge, a settling force many times greater than gravity. The heavier molecules then settle (sediment) faster. The familiar proteins of the blood, such as albumin, have a molecular weight of about 75,000. A small molecule like water has a molecular weight of 18, whereas a larger complex such as aspirin has a molecular weight of 162; starches, fats, and proteins are all much larger (molecular weights of 25,000 to 1,000,000). The sedimentation constant (7s, 19s, etc.) indicates this measure of molecular weight as observed by settling in the ultracentrifuge.

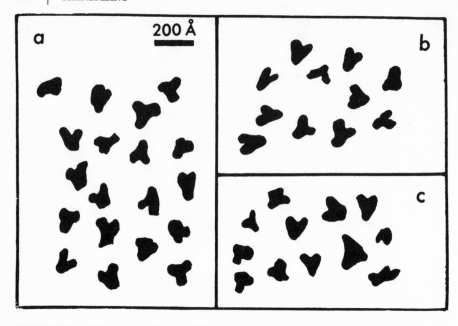

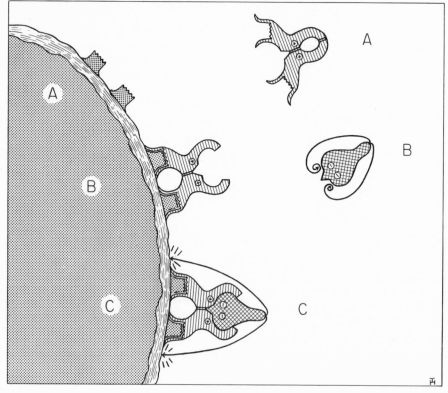

large and small immunoglobulin molecules, and the discovery that each one is in turn composed of numbers of light and heavy chains, led finally to the chemical identification of the precise amino acid sequences and atomic arrangements in these protein molecules.

One of the problems for a chemist trying to analyze immunoglobulins is to obtain enough of the material so that he can have something to work with. The plasma cell (see Chapter 1) is a factory for immunoglobulins. A patient suffering from a malignant tumor of plasma cells (known as multiple myeloma) might have very large amounts of immunoglobulin in the blood and urine. In this disease patients have billions of tumorous plasma cells which secrete huge amounts of one of the immunoglobulin light chains (known for many years as "Bence Jones protein"), which is then excreted in the urine. Dr. Putnam at Indiana University, realized that such a patient could supply the chemist with many grams of such material. From this source he was able to obtain large amounts of one chain, and subject it to chemical analysis. From this he reconstructed the amino acid

---

FIGURE 15.   Immunoglobulin molecules seen under the electron microscope. When an electron microscope is turned up to its maximum magnification (here about 300,000×), it is sometimes possible to glimpse single molecules if they are large enough. These are hand sketched from what was seen under the microscope; they show the Y-shaped configuration which closely resembles the chemical reconstruction shown in Figure 14.

FIGURE 16.   Cartoon demonstrating an imaginary concept of how antigens might link up with antibodies on the surface of a cell, opening up a combining site for complement which is then activated to make holes in the cell.

To the left is shown the cell with its membrane. In "A" above are shown two antigenic sites which protrude from the cell membrane and would presumably be chemical groupings on the cell wall. Nearby there is a circulating Y-shaped antibody molecule (see Figures 14 and 15) that fits this pair of antigenic sites.

In "B" in the center of the figure, the antibody immunoglobulin has latched onto two of the antigenic sites on the cell wall. In so doing, it has changed its configuration slightly so as to open up the attractive binding site for complement. Complement is shown as a blob on the right.

In "C" below, the complement molecule has now been attracted to the combining site of the opened-up immunoglobulin molecule and has been bound where it fits. In so doing, its two-coiled reactive enzymatic processes have been released to drill holes in the cell.

sequence and spatial arrangement of the immunoglobulin molecule. This fascinating picture reveals two slots in the molecule—at the variant end of the chains—where antigens might fit and be bound. The highly variable segment of both the heavy and the light chains point in the same direction and join to form these slots for antigen binding.

Immunoglobulins might be thought of as locks that are circulating in the body and have been made to fit certain keys (the antigens). The outer part of the lock and its strong cylindrical structure are the same for every lock, but the exact combination of inner tumblers is highly variable to fit the endless variety of keys that arrive on the scene. Once the lock finds a key that fits it, the key enters the lock, turns it, and is securely held there by the lock mechanism. It cannot be withdrawn. It is bound or inactivated by being held in the lock.

Whatever model or word-picture we make, the structural model of immunoglobulins reveals much about the immune response that occurs against bacteria, against foreign substances in general, and against the proteins and cell surfaces of transplanted tissue. Still, this model does not answer the first question: does every human being contain a full set of preformed immunoglobulins for every possible antigen, or is there some special system (something like Burnet's theory, noted in Chapter 2) whereby the presence of a specific antigen induces multiplication of those cells that turn out the matching immunoglobulin? Does the introduction of a new key into the lock factory stimulate the production of more locks that fit that particular shape of key? This question is particularly intriguing as it applies to transplanted organs, because the antigens of a foreign kidney are usually quite strange to the new host in the majority of cases.

Even if the lock fits the key, how is the key destroyed? Or, in molecular terms, how does the reaction of an immunoglobulin that binds with an antigenic protein damage that protein? If the antigenic protein is on the surface of a kidney cell, how does the immunoglobulin-binding damage that kidney cell? What is the molecular mechanism of immunologic damage?

Complement and the Mechanism
of Immunologic Damage

Two facts of molecular biology help us understand how molecules become weapons and actually accomplish injury to cells or other molecules.

First is the general chemistry of enzymes, familiar in broad outline for almost seventy-five years. Enzymes are specific proteins that fit onto chemical compounds known as substrates. Once they achieve this fit, which binds the substrates on them, they initiate a reaction in which the substrate is damaged or changed in some way. The enzyme then falls away or is released for another engagement of the same type. It is not used up or consumed in the process, and a small amount of enzyme can go a long way. For example, there is a certain enzyme that fits onto meat proteins present in the intestines after a meal. This enzyme (pepsin) causes proteins to be split (i.e., digested) into smaller pieces which can then be acted on by other enzymes or absorbed and passed along to the liver for further metabolism. These protein-splitting enzymes possess a particular chemical configuration which enables them to attach to their protein substrates and react with them in a way that breaks them up into smaller molecules.

The detailed structure of several of these enzymes is now known as to amino acid sequence, the location of certain heavy metals that are often present in the enzymes, and the three-dimensional arrangement of their thousands of atoms as determined by x-ray crystallography. In several instances molecular models have been made that show precisely how enzymes fit onto their substrates and reveal the twisting or breaking tensions that are introduced to alter the substrate. Each one of these enzymes is a big molecule that has a small area or "active site" where it locks onto its substrate to break it up. Most of the time an enzyme exists in an inactive state. To do its job it must be activated—often by uncovering or opening up the active site—becoming then a potent enzyme that can destroy or modify its substrate.

The second fact, well known to immunologists for many years, is that antibody immunoglobulins do not alone destroy antigens even

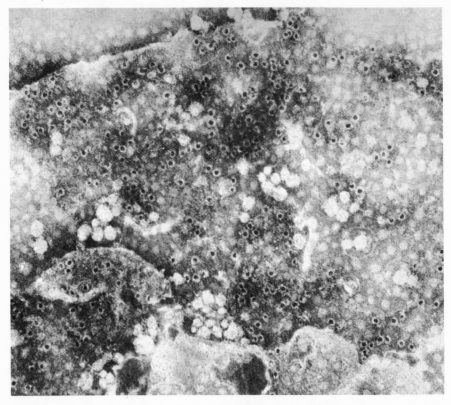

FIGURE 17. Electron micrograph made looking down on the membrane of a red blood cell which has been attacked by antibody and complement. The thousands of tiny holes have been drilled in the membrane by the activating of complement when it is bound to antibody (see Figure 16). This is a specific antigen-antibody reaction resulting in cellular destruction.

Photographs of this type have recently shown for the first time and in detail the actual anatomical results that immunologic damage inflicted on cells when antigen molecules interact with complement and thereby become "weapons."

though they bind them firmly. The antibodies require another substance to be present for the final destructive reaction. This third molecule is needed to *complete* the reaction, and is therefore called complement. It acts as though it were a destructive enzyme, activated by the presence of the antigen-antibody complex. For example, if red blood cells are mixed together in a solution with antibodies against red blood cells, no destruction occurs. If complement is added, then the red cells are drilled with millions of tiny holes (Fig. 17) that allow water to enter. The cell swells up, the membrane is destroyed, and hemoglobin is released into the solution. Blood destruction, or hemolysis, has occurred. The complement that accomplishes this enzymatic job of destruction is now known to involve a series of closely knit chain reactions involving several separate enzyme-proteins. Although antibodies are extremely varied in their detailed structure, as mentioned, complement seems to be pretty much the same throughout the whole animal kingdom. Guinea pig complement, for example, can be used to study human immune reactions in the test tube.

If we think of complement as the enzyme that causes the destructive reaction—an enzyme that is activated only when antibody has caught antigen, trapped it, locked on, and held it—we have a more complete picture. In every person's body there is a great deal of circulating complement, but it does not harm any bacteria or foreign proteins (or grafted organs) until the antibody-antigen junction occurs. The complement is then activated as a destructive enzyme, and destroys, denatures, or breaks up the foreign protein on the grafted cells much as the intestinal enzyme attacks meat.

To elaborate on our analogy of a key in a lock: it is as though when the key fits the lock and turns it, not only is the key captured in the lock so that it can't get out, but a coil spring is then loosened that bends or breaks the key. This spring could be the same type for every lock, no matter what its combination of tumblers, and no matter what the shape of the key, but it would only be released when the key actually fits the lock and turns it. This damaging spring, released when the key makes a perfect fit in the lock, is complement. In keeping with such a picture, we find that the constant or invariant end of the immunoglobulin molecule, opposite to the two antigen-binding sites, has a binding, or activating, site for complement.

Figure 16 illustrates how all this occurs. Once the immunoglobulin has locked onto its antigen, the antigen-antibody complex activates complement to cause damage to the antigen whether it is a protein on a bacterium or the cell of a kidney graft. If the antigen is on the membrane of a unicellular bacterium, such as the body of the diphtheria or the tubercle bacillus, it is so holed or damaged that the white cells can gobble it up and destroy it. If it is a red cell, it is destroyed by hemolysis. If it is the cell of a kidney graft, it is damaged and its structure distorted so that its function ceases. If it is a cell on the lining of a blood vessel, it swells up and closes off the circulation by thrombosis and damages the organ in that way; this may be the primary action of antibody and complement in the rejection of grafted tissue or organs.

All these molecular reactions are so very tiny that it is impossible to see them under the microscope. It would be helpful if there were some way of lighting up antibodies so that we could find them under the microscope, see where they go and where they are deposited. This remarkable feat was accomplished by Dr. Coons who, as a medical student at Harvard in 1935 began work in the laboratory of Dr. Enders (who later received the Nobel Prize for the culture of poliomyelitis virus). Dr. Coons was interested in tracing immune reactions by some sort of a color tracer or dye. After graduation, he traveled to Germany and there in 1939 discussed with organic chemists his idea of making antibodies visible under the microscope by a special visible label or tag. By 1941 he had hit upon the idea of using for this purpose a fluorescent dye—fluoroscein isocyanate. His work was interrupted by the war, but when Dr. Coons came back from his wartime service in the jungles of New Guinea, he returned to his laboratory to perfect the method. Since that time the fluorescent dye method has been used throughout all of immunology, particularly in transplant immunology. Antibody molecules linked with the fluorescent dye can be seen as tiny blobs of fluorescent green stuff when viewed in ultraviolet light under the microscope. The molecules give off an "apple-green" glowing color which is entirely different from anything else seen in the tissue section. Each antibody molecule itself is much too small to be seen, but the location of several in an area can be spotted by their fluorescent glow. It is much like looking down on a city from an airplane at night. You can see where the automobiles and streets are because of the groups of tiny headlights.

This fluorescent staining technique has been remarkably valuable in transplant immunology. For example, it has demonstrated that the IgG and IgM antibodies play an important role in graft rejection, even in early rejection. One can see the glow of the actual molecular combinations of IgG and complement in the capillary blood vessels

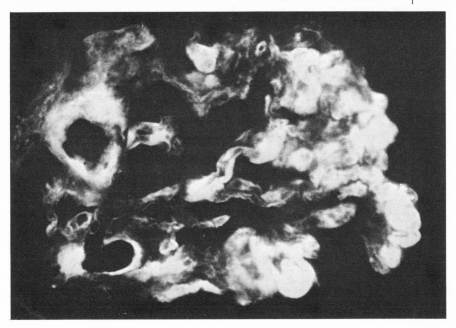

FIGURE 18. Fluorescent antibody staining of a rejected glomerular tuft. In this black-and-white reproduction is shown the fluorescent immune staining of the glomerular tuft of a rejecting kidney.

The convoluted structures ("like a bag of worms") are the blood vessels of the glomerular tuft. Shown in white here are the fluorescent areas that would glow apple green under ultraviolet light. They show that immune proteins have attached themselves to these blood vessels. These are proteins which will cause clotting and finally the shutting off of circulation in this glomerulus, an event that causes cessation of the function of the entire kidney when it involves most of the millions of glomeruli in the kidney. Here the mechanism of immunologic damage favors the formation of clot with scarring rather than drilling small holes in the cell, as shown in Figure 17. This is a very large magnification of a glomerulus seen under the light microscope. Each glomerulus is a tiny dot in the kidney just too small to be seen by the unaided eye.

around kidney tubules in rejecting grafts. Figure 18 is an example of the fluorescent staining technique which, in this case, has been used to demonstrate these antibody-complement complexes in a kidney being rejected.

The fluorescent method has indicated that graft rejection involves several types of immunologic activity at the molecular level and suggests that kidney rejection is sometimes the result of circulating immunoglobulins of the IgG type rather than the result of cellular activity. In all of these reactions antigen and antibody bind together like the key in the lock; if complement is activated, the molecules become weapons and the organ is destroyed.

VARIETIES OF IMMUNE RESPONSE:
IMMEDIATE AND DELAYED RESPONSES;
CELL-BOUND, CIRCULATING, PREFORMED
AND CROSS-REACTING ANTIBODIES

If a person has an allergy to ragweed pollen, exposure to the tiniest traces produces an immediate response in seconds or minutes—there is allergic wheezing, sneezing, or itching. If a person is infected with a streptococcus, there is a rapid response (in minutes or hours), with pain, heat, swelling, and the accumulation of white cells. These are but two examples of immediate immune responses, one to a familiar antigen long known to the sufferer (such as ragweed pollen), and the other a new reaction to an antigen (such as the streptococcus) to which the sufferer himself might not have been exposed before, but to which he develops a rapid response. These immediate types of response seem to be associated with antibodies that are freely circulating in the blood.

By contrast, response to an injection of a protein from the tubercle bacillus (the tuberculin test) is an example of a delayed response. The protein is injected into the skin of the arm, and for the first day or two nothing happens. It may be 36 to 48 hours before there is some redness and soreness. The delayed response requires the appearance of lymphocytes, and does not seem to be associated with circulating antibody. The rejection of a transplant such as a kidney has been considered to be an example of a delayed response, taking three to five days before the first evidences of rejection are visible and requiring the presence of cells. Cellular immunity is evidently able to inflict damage without the presence of antibody. This is shown by the fact that cells that are entirely alone, without plasma, and without the secretion of antibody, are capable of killing other cells. This type of cellular immunity remains unexplained at this time, in terms of our question of "how do molecules become weapons?" It is ironic that we have a better understanding of how molecules become weapons than of how one intact cell can harm another without engulfing it.

Although transplant rejection has appeared to be an immune response of the delayed type involving cells as the primary carrier of antibody, there is recent evidence to suggest that graft rejection can involve some circulating antibody also. The experiments of Professor Medawar (see Chapter 3) indicated that graft rejection could be hastened by exposing the experimental animal to a preliminary graft. Under these circumstances the animal became sensitized and demonstrated the "second set" or hastened response. Recently an experiment has indicated that ordinary "first set" graft rejection can also involve a circulating antibody. In this experiment, blood was taken from a dog rejecting a first kidney graft; the serum was then injected into the renal artery supplying the other kidney of the donor animal. The result was damage to the cells on the inside layer of the blood vessels to that kidney with swelling, blood clotting, and hemorrhage. This was clear evidence for the presence of freely circulating immunoglobulin in unmodified early graft rejection, and favored the idea that a very early event in a kidney graft rejection is a change in the inner lining of the blood vessels.

Working in Australia, Dr. Kincaid-Smith has long suspected that the very first immunologic injury in kidney transplantation might be within the blood vessels themselves, and she has shown that one of the very earliest phases of kidney rejection is the appearance of cells along the capillary blood vessels in the kidney and the deposition there of granular bits of IgG bound to cells and complement, as shown by Dr. Coons' fluorescent staining method. This observation is consistent with the fact that animals can be hypersensitized by several previous grafts (or by previous injections of cell extracts from the donor) to produce a graft rejection that is truly immediate and involves shutting off the capillary blood flow, with death of the graft. This is even more accelerated than the "second set" response of Medawar, and when it occurs in human kidney transplantation the kidney swells and ceases to function within a few minutes, before the eyes of the operating team, who are powerless to prevent it.

Both immediate and delayed responses are important in organ grafting. Prior exposure to antigens can produce an immediate rejec-

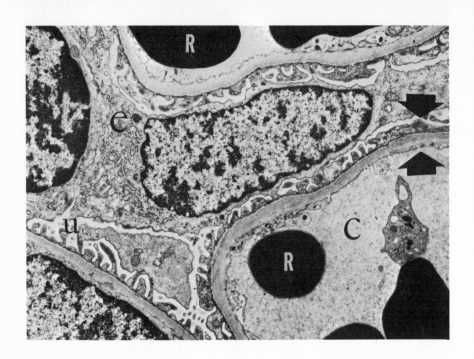

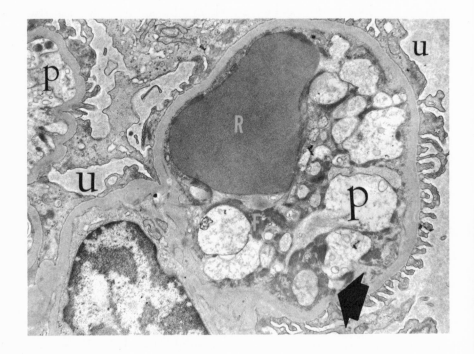

tion of the allergic or hypersensitive type, a reaction in which the molecular weapons are circulating immunoglobulins directed at the blood vessels. The early immunoglobulin damage produces clotting, closing off the circulation and stimulating the growth of scar tissue in the rejected organ.

The question still remains as to whether or not antibodies can be demonstrated against the graft *before* it is put in, and if so, where these could possibly come from in the patient who has had no previous graft.

Dr. Terasaki, working first with Professor Dausset and Professor

---

FIGURE 19.   Blood vessels in a normal human glomerulus as seen under the electron microscope. This picture shows a further huge magnification of one of the blood vessels shown in Figure 18 and provides a basis for comparison with the rejection process shown in Figure 20.

Here the microscopic field consists of small portions of three capillaries. Two of these contain red blood cells, which appear as heavy black round objects labeled "R." The actual lumen, or opening, in the capillary through which the blood plasma flows is labeled "C" in the lower right. In the center of the field there is a cell marked "e" which is in the wall of the blood vessel and is responsible for the regulation of blood flow. The open space around this cell, marked "u," is the urinary space where the filtered urine is first collected. Small footlike extensions of the cell are attached to part of the capillary wall. The upper arrow is in the urinary space, pointing to some of the cellular tissue around the capillary.

The lower arrow points to the thin normal wall of the capillary itself. Magnification is 9800×.

FIGURE 20.   Rejection in the glomerulus as seen under the electron microscope. Here, in contrast with the healthy glomerulus shown in Figure 19, are the electron microscopic appearances of the capillaries in a human kidney graft undergoing acute rejection.

This specimen was taken from the kidney only three hours after opening up the blood vessels at operation, at which time rejection was already evident, as indicated by swelling and pallor of the kidney and cessation of urine output. The right half of this picture is occupied by a capillary which shows obliteration of the lumen due to clotting. The open space is here filled with platelets and clot, marked "p," which have entrapped a red cell "R." The arrow indicates the point of damage in the capillary wall itself where the cellular tissue has been replaced by clot, and platelets are adherent to it. In the middle and to the left of the urinary space, "u," are two additional capillaries showing essentially complete obstruction of their openings with platelet debris, "p." Here, as shown in the immunofluorescent picture (Figure 18) the immune process has caused the formation of a clot as well as damaging cells themselves.

Medawar and then in California with Dr. Longmire, was the first to report that immediate rejection of kidney grafts was associated with preformed antibodies. In a series of over 200 patients tested by cross-matching their serum against the cells of donors prior to the transplant operation, he reported an 80 percent rate of immediate failure when the crossmatch showed preformed antibodies (i.e., a positive crossmatch). This is to be compared with a 4 percent immediate failure rate in donor-recipient pairs with a negative crossmatch test. This critically important observation of Dr. Terasaki has made it possible for transplanters to avoid the use of donors to whom the recipient was hypersensitive, but it only underscores the basic question of where these antibodies came from.

There are several possible answers to the question as to how an individual might already possess antibodies against the kidney about to be transplanted *prior* to the transplant. The first explanation is that people might share antigens* among each other (see Chapter 2), so that if the recipient had received only a blood transfusion from a blood donor (who happened to share antigens with the subsequent kidney donor), then he should have preformed antibodies that would hypersensitize him to the kidney graft. In blood transfusion, it is the blood platelets and the white cells that appear to be especially antigenic, setting the stage for later antibody reactions.

A second explanation for the presence of preformed antibodies in recipients who are about to receive a graft is that the patient may have been on the artificial kidney. Some of the blood put in the kidney coil to prime it might have sensitized him against antigens from human blood much as a transfusion would.

A third possibility, when the patient is a woman, is that a previous pregnancy might have exposed her to antigens from her child, inherited from the father but strange to her. They could elicit an immune response somewhat as the Rh antigens do, which might later make her sensitive to a kidney graft that shared antigens, just by chance, with the tissues of her husband.

A fourth possibility is that prior immune events in the patient's

---

* The term *antigen sharing* merely means that two persons have the same or very similar antigen molecules on their cells.

lifetime—such as his reaction to a bacterial infection—might hypersensitize him to a kidney graft. This could occur only if bacteria and human tissue cells occasionally shared the same antigens. It will be recalled (see page 168) that one answer to the enigma of "an infinite variety of antibodies to meet an infinite variety of antigens" is that the antigens are not so infinite in their variety, and that a patient might have antibodies against some common antigen which happened to fit the antigens of the kidney graft. Such antigens (producing cross-reactivity with human tissues) might even come from infecting bacteria. Dr. Rapaport and his co-workers at New York University have shown that certain streptococcus bacteria produce antigens that will cause the formation of cross-reacting antibodies, producing hypersensitivity against subsequent grafts of skin or kidney. This observation suggests that an individual who had an infection some years previously—and it might even be the very same infection that gave him his glomerulonephritis as a child—could have formed antibodies against the streptococcus at that time. These, by pure chance, are shared by his newly transplanted kidney, rendering him sensitive to the kidney and doomed to reject it rapidly.

Whatever the ultimate explanation for presensitization and preformed antibodies against kidney grafts, the observations of Dr. Terasaki and Dr. Rapaport have made it essential to perform crossmatch tests before grafting—just as one would do a crossmatch test before a blood transfusion.* The serum of the recipient is mixed with white blood cells from the donor in a small well on a plastic plate. If there is a clumping or killing of those cells under the microscope, preformed antibodies are presumed to be present and a graft should not be done. In some cases a long search is required to find good matches and acceptable donors—particularly in cases of patients who have been on the artificial kidney and have been exposed to the blood of many different blood donors in multiple transfusions, or women who have had several pregnancies. In fact, if one tests serum from patients who have been on repeated dialyses against white blood cells from a random group of donors, about 40 percent of these patients will show

---

* Fulfillment, after 40 years, of the wishes and expectations of Dr. Holman and Dr. Williamson (Chapter 4) who foresaw the need for some sort of crossmatch in transplantation.

preformed antibodies against at least one of the donors. This figure is highest among women who have borne children and who are found to have antibodies against certain antigenic components of their husband's tissues. Although this harms neither child nor mother, it may later make a kidney transplant to the mother very difficult to match. It is evident that these crossmatch methods have made kidney grafting much safer and more practical, and yet they have made it a much more demanding search to find an acceptable donor for any given recipient.

CAN WEAPONS PROTECT?
PROTECTIVE AND BLOCKING IMMUNOGLOBULINS;
ENHANCEMENT

Thus far, this chapter has been concerned with the mechanism of immunologic damage, of antibodies reacting with antigens to activate complement and damage the grafted cells of kidney, liver or heart. Many natural phenomena work both ways: enzymes that destroy protein coexist with very similar enzymes that build up protein. There might conceivably be some antibody reactions in which the immunoglobulin is actually protective to tissue rather than destructive. To return to our lock-and-key analogy, there might be some locks (immunoglobulins) which would accept a certain key (antigen) to fit them and bind them, but which did not activate the spring (complement). In this way the lock would block the destructive reaction. The key would be held there, and in a sense protected, unable to fit into a damaging type of lock. When this occurs in immunoglobulin reactions, it is called blocking antibody, and it constitutes a sort of protective coating over the antigenic sites of grafted tissue.

The best way to conceive of this is to relate a typical experiment. An animal, later to be given a kidney graft, is injected a week or two before with a tiny amount of a cell extract from the same donor animal that is to give him the kidney. If this cell extract is injected in the wrong dose or at the wrong time, the kidney rejection is hastened, and there has been presensitization with preformed circulating antibodies as described in the foregoing section. If, however, the extract is injected in the proper quantity at exactly the right time prior to the graft (both the amount and the timing to be discovered only by prolonged experimentation) the graft is not rejected, its acceptance is prolonged, and one can demonstrate the presence of preformed antibodies in the blood.

This phenomenon was first described by Dr. Kaliss working at the Jackson Laboratories in Bar Harbor, Maine. He was transplanting tumors between strains of mice and had shown that by previous injection of certain extracts, the take of the tumor could be enhanced. This turned out to be a way in which tumor grafting could be facilitated. The procedure became known as "enhancement," meaning that the take of the graft was increased or enhanced by these prior injections even though they resulted in the formation of antibodies.

When antibody locks onto an antigen but does not activate complement, it can thus become protective. The phenomenon of enhancement by the formation of blocking antibodies in response to preliminary injection of antigen has not as yet proven useful in everyday clinical kidney grafting. It does indicate one of the future directions for study in transplantation. It raises the possibility that in the future we might make extracts of some tissue from the donor, such as his white blood cells, which are then injected into the prospective recipient, producing blocking antibodies which make a protective coating on the graft. It is for this reason that it is important to consider immunoglobulins as reactive proteins that bind with antigens. It is this *binding* that is important, as well as the destructive reaction that ensues if complement is activated. This sort of enhancement, employing protective antibody, would make it possible to perform organ grafting with less use of toxic drugs or, ideally, none at all.

The Reticuloendothelial System; the Thymus and Lymphocyte Control

Immunoglobulins are manufactured in the cells of a system widely scattered throughout the body (mentioned in Chapter 2), known as the reticuloendothelial system. It consists of the tissues where lymphocytes and their closely related cousins, plasma cells and monocytes, arise by cellular multiplication. It includes lymph nodes, bone marrow, spleen, thymus, parts of the liver, and parts of the gastrointestinal tract.

Lymph nodes vary in size from a pinhead to an almond, and they are scattered throughout the body, clumped in strategic areas where the lymph vessels can filter the lymph fluid through them. They strain out particulate matter, infecting bacteria, foreign proteins, or tumor cells. There is a set of lymph nodes in the groin, for example, filtering the lymph drainage from the leg; there is a set in the armpit doing the same for the arm and the breast; near the liver for the gastrointestinal tract, etc. Viewed under the microscope, these lymph nodes seem to be collections of lymphocytes held in a network of tiny vessels that carry lymph or tissue fluid. There are nests or lymph follicles where the lymphocytes multiply. These lymphocytes, present in such huge numbers in lymph nodes, are chiefly concerned with the production of antibody immunoglobulins which enter the bloodstream via the lymphatic channels.

The studies of Professor Gowans of Oxford have revealed many of the remarkable features of the life history of these cells. He has shown that lymphocytes sometimes circulate in the body for as long as a year before finally dying off. They cross blood vessels directly by migration and by ameboid motion, to get into the tissue fluids. They migrate in and out of lymph nodes and act as sensors of new antigens entering the body as well as warriors gathering to combat them. They are a wandering warning system, attracted to new foreign protein or antigen arriving in the body. They carry some message back to the follicle of the lymph nodes, and evidently stimulate the production there of more lymphocytes to make immunoglobulins against the infecting antigen. More than 90 percent of the many billions of lymphocytes present in the human body are outside the bloodstream at any one moment. Within the bloodstream about one half of the white blood cells are lymphocytes, and those in the bloodstream alone total approximately 500 billion.

In addition to these various organs, the reticuloendothelial system also includes the thymus, an organ about which, until recently, very little was known.

The thymus is a sort of master gland or control center for the reticuloendothelial system during its development. The thymus is in the upper front part of the chest just under the breastbone, or the sternum. In infants it is a large grayish gland and is quite active. In adults it is small, soft, yellow, and appears to be inactive, largely composed of fat. For many years the function of the thymus was unknown. It was a mystery organ, as the spleen had been for centuries, and the pineal gland is even today. A function has now been discovered for the thymus gland that is of great importance in immunity and of great potential importance in tissue transplantation. Much of this knowledge has emanated from the work of Dr. Miller in Australia and Dr. Good and Dr. Varco at the University of Minnesota. Drs. Good and Varco had been interested for several years in a rare disease called agammaglobulinemia. In agammaglobulinemia children are born with an inability to make the immunoglobulin proteins (particularly the gamma globulins), and are therefore lacking any antibody defense against infectious diseases. Their lives are threatened because they are in constant danger of fatal infection. Good and his collaborators demonstrated that these patients could not summon an antibody response to testing antigens and that they did not have any plasma cells in their blood.

Then, turning their attention to transplantation, these scientists showed that allografts of skin could be placed on patients with agammaglobulinemia without any rejection. In their report (published in 1957) one of the skin grafts had persisted satisfactorily for fourteen months and the other one for twenty-three months. This experiment confirmed the suspicion that transplant antibodies were generated by the same system within the body that provides immunoglobulin antibodies for other purposes.

In 1961, the same group working in Minnesota demonstrated that the removal of the thymus in an adult animal had no effect on immunity, but that a similar operation carried out in newly hatched chickens completely prevented the development of normal immunity and produced a state similar to agammaglobulinemia. Dr. Archer and Dr. Pierce, also of Minnesota, then removed the thymus glands from rabbits that were five to seven days old; some months later there was no antibody response in these animals when challenged with a new antigen.

Within a short time these findings were confirmed in many laboratories, and there emerged the concept that the thymus presides over one set of immunologic reactions and that a fraction of the lymphocytes in the body is in a sense controlled by the thymus. These are known as the thymus-dependent lymphocytes. For the previous twenty years there had been but a handful of reports in the scientific literature about the thymus. Now, the thymus, once shown to have a function, became the center of much attention and the principal topic of many publications. All experiments showed that if the thymus was removed in early life, the reticuloendothelial system failed to develop, the production of antibody immunoglobulins was severely impaired, and one major source of lymphocytes was lacking. Such an animal readily accepted allotransplantation of tissue.

Unfortunately for the development of human tissue transplantation, this laboratory animal becomes receptive for a graft of skin or kidney only if the thymus is removed right after birth. Even a few weeks or months later, the thymus has lost much of its "master gland" function, and if it is then removed, there is little effect on graft acceptance. It is for this reason that various surgical attempts to remove the thymus in adult man to promote the take of grafts were unavailing.

No practical method has yet evolved for using our knowledge of the thymus in transplantation treatment. There are some indications as to the direction such practical steps should take. For example, Dr. Miller has shown that the repopulation of lymphocytes after whole body irradiation is dependent upon the thymus. Prior removal of the thymus strengthens the effect of antilymphocyte serum (see next section), prolonging the take of skin grafts. The thymus is necessary to the recovery of lymphocyte activity after the administration of antilymphocyte serum. Several immunologists have made some antithymus serum. Using this it is possible to reproduce some of the effects of thymus removal without the operation itself.

In addition, an extract of thymus containing a thymus hormone called "thymosin" seems to have a special effect, stimulating the production of thymus-dependent lymphocytes from lymph nodes. Dr. Monaco, working at the Harvard Laboratories in the Boston City Hospital, has shown that thymosin given along with antilymphocyte serum prolongs graft takes. Possibly thymosin increases the production of lymphocytes which are then knocked out by antilymphocyte serum.

In each instance, the thymosin must be given slightly before the antilymphocyte serum. Much of this work has been carried out in the mouse, which has a more highly developed lymphocyte system and a more active thymus than in man. These species differences militate against the transfer of thymus experiments to the clinical setting. But despite the shortcomings, further experiments with the thymus or thymus extracts hold great promise for improvement in clinical transplantation.

Lymph Drainage—Biologic Troop Withdrawal

If lymphocytes form immunoglobulin antibodies, and if their physical presence in rejecting grafts is often associated with the loss of the graft, why not just drain off the lymphocytes and get rid of them? This idea has appealed to transplanters for several years. Thanks to a particular anatomical arrangement provided by nature, it has been given a good try, both in the laboratory and in the hospital, and with fair success.

The largest lymphatic system in the body runs all the way from the tip of the toes through the midabdomen to the neck. For most of its length it lies along the spinal column in the thorax and is called the thoracic duct. It is about the size of the lead in a lead pencil, very thin-walled and transparent. It is hard to see and find. It is sometimes seen at operations around the lower part of the thyroid gland because it drains the lymph fluid into the veins of the arm and neck. Sometimes it is injured by bullet wounds or by accident in operations. It drains 4 to 7 liters of milky fluid each day from the abdominal lymph vessels to the veins of the neck, returning the fluid to the heart and back into the circulation.

Among the first to explore the application of thoracic duct lymph fluid drainage (or lymph fistula) to the field of transplantation was Professor Woodruff of Edinburgh. He showed, in rats, that external drainage of lymph fluid from this duct permitted a better acceptance of skin grafts. He also demonstrated that animals who had carried a lymphatic fistula for two or three weeks would accept and keep skin grafts two or three times as long as other animals even though the thoracic duct drainage had ceased or closed up. Other scientists had explored the use of thoracic duct lymph fluid drainage in other diseases, particularly in cancer and in certain diseases of the liver. It had been shown, in man, that a small plastic tube could be placed in this duct and the fluid drained externally without producing any harm.

With this background, in 1964, Dr. Murray and Dr. Wilson began these operations, first in dogs and then in patients having kidney transplantation. If the lymph fluid drained out in large amounts—over 10 liters of fluid containing more than 20 billion lymphocytes—it appeared to make the rejection episodes less frequent and the acceptable dosage lower for the toxic immunosuppressive drugs. Not only did the fluid drain off a great many lymphocytes and remove them from the scene of the action, but the fluid could be spun down in a centrifuge to remove the cells. The fluid itself was reinjected so the patient did not lose the nutritious substances present in it. It was clearly best to drain off the reactive lymphocytes before the graft was placed, and the thoracic duct drainage operation had to be performed several days before the transplantation.

If a kidney graft was to be done with a family donor and a specific date named in advance, the lymph drainage operation could be carried out about five days before the transplant. Such advance planning is impossible if a cadaver is the donor, since no one knows when the tissue-matched cadaver will become available. This is determined at best only a few hours before the transplant. In its very nature, then, the thoracic duct lymph drainage operation was adapted to cases where there were living family donors, thus limiting its usefulness. In our department about one half of the transplants have been done from living family members over the past decade, so that thoracic duct drainage could be used quite liberally. For example, among one group of 40 patients having kidney transplants from living related donors, 73 percent of those with thoracic duct fistulas had excellent results up to five years later; whereas only 50 percent of those without the thoracic duct drainage had good results. There was a significantly lower incidence of rejection crises in patients with the thoracic duct drainage and no significant difference in the rate of serious infections in these patients, although minor infections occurring around the thoracic duct drainage did cause postponement of the transplant operation in four cases. Thus, although thoracic duct drainage has not yet earned a secure place in routine kidney grafting, it has made a contribution to the care of some patients. It may be especially useful when the tissue match is less than satisfactory.

ANTILYMPHOCYTE SERUM AND GLOBULIN

Rather than draining off and removing the lymphocytes, could one eliminate them by a serum, much as horse serum is made against the tetanus toxin? Among the first to explore this method was Professor Woodruff in Edinburgh, and Dr. Mitchell working in our laboratories in 1964, who made a serum against dog lymphocytes by injecting them into a sheep. The blood of the sheep was drawn, the serum separated, and found to contain immunoglobulins against the lymphocytes of the dog. The dog, given a skin graft or kidney graft from another dog, was then less apt to reject it.

In the past six years, there has been an upsurge of interest in the production of antilymphocyte serum (ALS) or its purified immuno-globulin, which is known as antilymphocyte globulin (ALG). This work started up in several centers about the same time (1962–1965), but it has taken several years to reach the bedside. Antilymphocyte serum quickly proved itself effective in animal grafts, and has been transferred to use in man but with less clear-cut proof of effectiveness.

A typical procedure is as follows: Lymphocytes from a number of persons are gathered into a pure suspension of cells by spinning and washing the material. These might be lymphocytes from blood (collected in a special type of centrifuge or separated from a blood donor sample in a special plastic bag); lymphocytes from the spleen removed for some other reason such as accidental rupture; lymphocytes removed from people in the course of thoracic duct lymph fluid drainage; or lymphocytes taken from the lymph nodes of a person who has died of other causes. Whatever the source, this suspension of lymphocytes is then injected into a horse; horses are also used as hosts to produce antiserum against tetanus, diphtheria toxin, or snakebite venom. The horse is immunized and the immune serum is drawn off and purified. The serum is separated, and either the raw ALS (antilymphocyte serum) or the purified ALG (antilymphocyte globulin) is injected into a patient who is about to receive an organ transplant.

Early in the development of these sera ALS and ALG were shown to be effective for the maintenance of allografts, and even in some circumstances for the maintenance of xenografts. Dr. Monaco, for example, working at the Massachusetts General Hospital, carried out skin grafts between normal human volunteers who had been given injections of antilymphocyte serum. He demonstrated that they could maintain skin allografts for prolonged periods of time without any other treatment. In mice, he successfully produced prolonged takes of grafts without any apparent immunologic reaction, using antilympho-cyte serum alone. In some of these mice the graft was held for months at a time without any further treatment—true tolerance or chimerism. Other workers—as, for example, Dr. Birtch of our laboratories—giving antilymphocyte serum (and no other immunosuppressive agent of any type) to a dog with a liver transplant, were able to discontinue the administration of the ALS at six months, and the animal carried on, maintaining his allografted liver without any signs of rejection for more than another year. Thus, by 1966, it was evident that antilym-phocyte serum was capable of improving results in organ grafting and might make an important contribution to the solution of the problem in man. Many laboratories began to produce antilymphocyte serum against human lymphocytes, employing the horse as the protein fac-tory or, to make a serum acceptable for patients sensitive to horse serum, using the rabbit.

It was soon demonstrated that antilymphocyte serum had a re-markable property not exhibited by any other immunosuppressive drug or procedure: it abolished the positivity of long-established skin reactions of the delayed hypersensitivity type—skin reactions that had been positive in the patient for many years. For example, a person who had shown a positive tuberculin test or positive skin reaction against mumps lost this positive skin reaction after he took antilymphocyte serum. These are responses of the cellular type so prominent in allograft rejection, involving the accumulation of lymphocytes in the skin. Abatement of long-established immune reactions could occur after the injection of antilymphocyte serum for only three or four days, indicating a prompt effect on the immune activity of lymphocytes, including the immunologic "memory" of prior exposure to an antigen.

The mechanism was clearly more subtle than merely killing lymphocytes.

Whatever theory ultimately accounts for the action of antilymphocyte serum, its clinical use has come under close scrutiny because of two rather disappointing facts which have emerged after its early success in laboratory animals.

First, while antilymphocyte serum is remarkably successful in prolonging the acceptance of tissue grafts in mice, dogs, and other laboratory animals, it is much more difficult to establish its effectiveness in man. Despite the effort to understand its proper use, we may be using it in the wrong dose or in the wrong strength or with the wrong timing. Whatever the cause, there are only one or two hospitals doing kidney transplants at the present time that can vouch for a clear-cut improvement due to antilymphocyte serum. Few transplants have been done in man with ALS as the sole immunosuppressive agent. A gradual improvement in transplant results is not convincing evidence for the effectiveness of ALS. Transplant management as a whole is evolving all the time, and histocompatibility selection is improving some of the results, as described in the next chapter. Furthermore, individuals on ALS who demonstrate suppression of their own delayed skin hypersensitivity reactions, such as the tuberculin test, may still have severe rejection episodes with typical blood vessel changes in the kidney graft. The action of the material is therefore inconsistent. There is the possibility that patients can become sensitive to the horse serum proteins; some bad reactions have been reported. Because of this, Dr. Najarian at Minnesota has been making antilymphocyte serum, using lymphocytes grown in tissue culture by Dr. Moore of the Roswell Park Hospital in Buffalo, and then desensitizing the patient against horse serum. The ALG when injected is far longer lasting, and Dr. Najarian's clinical results seem to be more convincing than those of any other transplanter.

The second disappointing fact about antilymphocyte serum bears on the fundamental relation between tumor growth and transplantation immunity. An unusually large number of malignant tumors have formed in patients on immunosuppression, many of them tumors of the lymphoid system, in patients on antilymphocyte serum, azathioprine, and steroids. These developments may have revealed a new vista in the cause and treatment of cancer, although they provide a severe blow to clinical transplantation.

TUMOR GROWTH UNDER IMMUNOSUPPRESSION
—A NEW "KICK OF THE GUN"*

Tumors that have developed in transplant patients are traceable to the immunosuppressed state of those patients. In one instance, the tumor actually formed at the very site where the antilymphocyte serum was injected under the skin. This is not a wholly surprising development, since tumors and transplanted organs both represent the establishment of new tissue growth in a host. It might have been suspected that these two aberrations of tissue growth would somehow share a common immunologic basis. To see such a hopeful interpretation in this unfavorable turn of events, one must be willing to turn from transplant science to oncology, the science of tumor growth.

The facts are these: A remarkable number of malignant tumors have now been observed in patients under immunosuppression, tumors not confined to patients under ALS though they appear to be somewhat commoner than in those patients on azathioprine alone. All of these patients had been on high doses of immunosuppressive drugs, many with ALS. Many were tumors of the lymphoid or reticuloendothelial system (such as lymphosarcoma) or reticulum cell sarcoma, tumors of the very system that immunosuppressive drugs inhibit.

An important link to our understanding here is the fact that tumor transplantation is particularly easy when immunosuppression has occurred. There are at least five cases where immunosuppression has permitted cancer cells to grow from a transplanted kidney when their existence in the donor or in the kidney itself had been unsuspected.

---

* A further, entirely unexpected complication or "kick of the gun" from kidney transplantation has been the development of severe bony disease in the hip in a number of patients who have received kidney transplantations and have been treated with azathioprine and cortisone for long periods of time. For a variety of reasons, it is the use of cortisone which is usually singled out as the principal cause of this difficulty, although the drug seems to require the concomitance of poor kidney function and azathioprine administration to produce this complication. The incidence of severe disease of one or both hips is estimated at around 10 percent of patients who have been on cortisone and azathioprine for longer than one year. In some series, the incidence of mild hip symptoms is recorded as high as 25 percent.

These tumors thrived, when the patient was under immunosuppression, to a much greater extent than in a normal person or in a normal animal given transplanted tumor cells. In one case reported by Dr. Wilson, the tumor cells were those of a lung cancer inadvertently transplanted with a kidney. Presently the lung cancer cells began to grow in and around the transplanted kidney. When the immunosuppressive drug (azathioprine) was withdrawn, the patient promptly and completely rejected the transplanted malignant tumor. This was an immunologic cure of a (transplanted) cancer and was therefore a remarkably significant event in itself. Off immunosuppression, the patient went on to reject the kidney. Later he had another kidney graft from a family donor, which was an unqualified success. There was no further tumor growth. This sequence of events showed that human cancer had been easily transplantable in an immunosuppressed patient, and that when immune activity was restored by stopping azathioprine, the tumor was rejected and totally eradicated thereby.

In the same family of facts has been the observation that in liver transplants undertaken specifically for the treatment of cancer, most of the patients have died rapidly from explosive spread of the tumor. Again, it appears as though immunosuppression has permitted the very rapid growth of a tumor, in this case one that previously had grown slowly.

In the light of this background, the new tumors forming under immunosuppression appear especially ominous.

Just how frequent are these tumors in people on immunosuppression? As of April 1969, out of approximately 3000 transplant patients on immunosuppression throughout the world, there had been 20 primary malignant tumors reported. Many of these occurred in patients who had not received ALS or ALG; one half of these tumors were carcinomas or epithelial tumors, and one half of them were sarcomas, including lymphatic tumors of the reticuloendothelial system. This incidence, of about 1 in 150 (or 6 per 1000) is far higher than the incidence of tumors in the general population, and the incidence is highest in patients on ALS. Furthermore, this is the sort of medical statistic that can only rise with the passage of time. Each patient on immunosuppression who has developed a malignant tumor is forever lodged on the roster as a positive case. He can never be removed from the docket. Additional cases can only raise the figure. We can, therefore, say with confidence that the present incidence of malignancy in immunosuppression not only is high but is sure to get higher.

Given these facts, several interpretations are possible. The most important of these is the suspicion that tiny new tumors—maybe only a few cells at a time—are forming in our bodies quite frequently, or all the time. These are recognized by the immune system as being foreign or antigenic in nature because the tumor cells produce some new, foreign, protein. The tumors are therefore killed off by a normal immune rejection response. When this immune response is abated by immunosuppression, tumors are uninhibited and can grow to a large size. Furthermore, they grow very rapidly, as shown by the tumors in liver transplantation.

The evidence suggests that normal control of tumor growth is in part an immune transaction that forms a protection against tumor just as it does against invading bacteria. By reducing immunity, tumor growth is enhanced, and by enhancing immunity after a tumor has started to grow, malignant tumors can sometimes be rejected.

Attempts to isolate antigens from growing tumors go back many years. In a few instances it has been possible to demonstrate identifiable soluble antigens in tumors which will cause antibody reactions against tumor cells. Most of these have been the specialized tumors found in pure strains of experimental animals. Recently, and more encouraging, Dr. Gold of Montreal has found identifiable antigens in tumors of the bowel in man. He can demonstrate antibodies to this antigen in patients who have such tumors.

As this chapter is written, no one can tell how this hazard of tumor growth under immunosuppression will change the practice of clinical transplantation. It will surely lead to increased intensity in the search for tolerance, the production of adaptation, or mechanisms of enhancement. Any one of these three methods, since they constitute little insult to the total immunologic capability of the recipient, should be expected to produce fewer tumors while at the same time permitting acceptance of the graft. For the patient about to have a lifesaving kidney transplantation, the 0.6 percent chance that he might later have a malignant tumor will probably not dissuade him or his doctors from going ahead with the operation. But they are almost certain to advise against such an operation if the patient is suffering from a malignant tumor, and they may hesitate to use ALS or ALG if it is not necessary.

Most important of all, these discoveries about tumor growth when using immunosuppression have already shown an effect on the study of tumor immunity that must be likened to the research explosion touched off by the demonstration of induced tolerance by Billingham, Brent, and Medawar or by the demonstration of DNA structure and the genetic code by Watson, Crick, and Wilkins. It will provide a tremendous impetus to the study of tumor immunity and to improvement in transplant methods. The occurrence of tumors under immunosuppression, and of lymphosarcomas at the site where antilymphocyte serum has been injected, will have a remarkable effect on the entire scientific community, and ultimately on the treatment of cancer.

Adaptation, Tolerance, and Chimerism —Prospects for the Future

Toxicity of immunosuppressive drugs has been a strong driving force toward the development of less toxic and more specific modifications of immunologic behavior, to make graft acceptance possible. The tumor-growth phenomenon makes this search doubly important. At the present time such a search looks toward acquired specific tolerance of some type as the ultimate solution to the transplant problem.

In Chapter 6 was mentioned an example of adaptation—using this term to indicate that an allograft such as that of a kidney, after a long residence in a recipient, appears to be accepted without stimulating any further attempt at rejection. Dr. Murray has shown that the constitution of the graft has not been changed because it will be accepted if replanted in the original donor animal. We know that the recipient animal is still quite able to make antibodies because he can be tested with any standard test of immunity. If ALS or ALG has not been used, he is quite able to produce a normal immune response. Nonetheless, the grafted kidney remains in place and requires less and less immunosuppressive treatment.

For example, Chapter 6 told the story of the fraternal twins and their graft. Many years after this transplant, lymphocytes from the recipient injected back into his brother showed a very marked reaction. This indicated that the recipient's lymphocytes were still capable of a perfectly normal reaction against the donor and were probably hypersensitized. Yet the graft was protected and remained there without difficulty.

This sort of adaptation is frequently seen in animal experiments with kidney, liver, or heart grafts when, after many weeks or months, all immunosuppressive treatment can be stopped, and the graft continues to work. Now, in human transplantation, eight or ten years after the first use of unrelated-donor grafts under azathioprine therapy, we are beginning to witness it in a few kidney transplants. The patient seems to be able to carry the transplant along with less and less immunosuppression. In human kidney grafts, there is not any true security in this adaptation. A number of patients after two or three years of successful graft acceptance have gradually rejected their grafts. Others, in whom the immunosuppressive drugs have been stopped for reasons such as pneumonia or because the patient just got tired of taking the drugs have suddenly rejected their grafts. The phenomenon of adaptation appears easier to produce in the laboratory animal than in man.

Although adaptation has not been completely explained, and there is no clear theory to account for it, it may well be another example of the action of blocking antibodies. The graft has stimulated the production of antibodies which lock onto antigenic sites in the blood vessels without activating complement; these antibodies, then, become protective. By splitting off a part of the antibody molecule that binds complement, it appears possible to make a sort of partial antibody or blocking antibody artificially. This method holds some hope for future use in transplantation.

Tolerance is quite a different type of acceptance of an allograft. Here the graft is accepted without any immunologic transaction whatsoever, and lives on indefinitely, the two genetic types of tissue coexisting peacefully together in a state of chimerism.

In summary, the ideal future setting for the grafting of organs in man would be, first, the achievement of *specific tolerance* so that no immune reaction occurred after the graft was placed even though other defenses were intact. Failing this, the second best would be the production of immunoglobulins that acted as blocking antibodies to provide *enhancement* so that even though there was an immunologic reaction, the graft would be protected. Third, failing to produce either tolerance or enhancement, one could strive to hasten *adaptation* so that the graft, though arousing an earlier immune reaction, quickly became accepted without further immunosuppressive treatment.

Tolerance, enhancement, and adaptation carry the keys to the future of transplantation. Until they are perfected, we will still be dealing with the placing of the graft, its threatened rejection, the prevention of that rejection by lowering of defensive cellular and immunoglobulin activity, making the patient vulnerable to bacterial and viral infections and, by tampering with the reticuloendothelial system, making him prone to tumor growth.

10

DONORS: THE QUICK AND THE DEAD

Is There Life After Death?

What is pomp, rule, reign, but earth and dust?
And live how we can, yet die we must.

— *King Henry VI*, PART III

A MATTER OF HEALTHY TISSUE

If Emerson felt that "In nature nothing can be given, all things are sold," he might well have been thinking of the most painful dilemma in the transplant problem: the procurement of living tissues from healthy people. It is difficult enough to obtain such tissues after death, and even then a price must be paid. But in any event the transplantation of organs from one person to another requires the procurement of healthy tissue from somebody.

Lest some religious person, viewing our subtitle about life after death, should read into it metaphysical or theological meaning, let him be dissuaded at least for a while. The biologist has long known that "I am a body; I have a soul," should be rephrased to "I am a soul, dwelling for a time in a body." Each person's body is a complex machine housing the human mind and soul. When a person dies his mind is stilled, his soul is alleged to depart for other regions, and his body is

200

then consumed by fire or decay. Its many substances are free to enter again into the living cycle of nature. Regardless of what becomes of his soul, each person's body can claim a certain immortality in the recirculation and reutilization of its carbon, minerals, and water, as the endless cycles of nature make use of the elements of the earth and atmosphere to recreate life.

When, immediately after death, some useful portion of that body is placed in another person, this recycling of nature occurs sooner than it otherwise would. There is also an ethical and moral difference: the deceased individual has made better living possible for another person.

Before considering the nature of death which permits some tissues to remain alive while the person is dead, the donor situation must be reviewed again as to its general terminology. The reader will recall that in an *autotransplant* the patient is his own donor. At the other end of the scale, in the *xenotransplant*, an animal of one species is a donor for an animal of another. Between these two extremes are the donors with whom we are chiefly concerned: *isotransplants* and *allotransplants*.

When the donor is an identical twin (*isotransplants*), genetic differences are negligible; it is to assure the continued good health of the twin donor that the main selection effort is directed. In *allotransplants* between individuals who are not identical twins, the matter of donor selection raises a great many issues. Living donors are often used, and family donors are most suitable. These can be classified according to their relationship to the patient. Closest are the fraternal twins, next are the brothers and sisters (the siblings), and then the parent-child or child-parent transplants. Beyond these are blood relatives outside of the immediate family, less closely related but some of them, cousins for example, of potential special importance in tissue matching. Most distant genetically are the transplants from living donors totally unrelated to the patient* or from a cadaver of an unrelated person.

---

* This category of unrelated living donor includes normal volunteers who wish to give an organ, as well as those donors who are having an organ removed for some other reason, an organ that can be reutilized in a new recipient. These are termed "operative donors" and they include those already mentioned in whom a kidney is being removed for some other disease such as hydrocephalus, or persons in whom parathyroid tissue or ovarian tissue is being removed for some other reason.

If a kidney is to be removed for grafting, the health of the donor and the normalcy of the opposite kidney must be established. Even if the donation is to take place from an identical twin and there is no genetic problem, the health of that twin must be assured before the removal of a tissue or organ is undertaken.

Given the most nearly ideal circumstances, the removal of one kidney from a healthy person is an immediate hazard and a potential future deficit. When a small bit of skin is removed, the effects on health are minimal. The same rather minor hazard of donation is associated with the removal of a single parathyroid gland or part of a structure such as an ovary. The operative risk of removing a kidney (nephrectomy) is greater than any of those, and is in the same general class of hazard as the removal of a spleen or a section of the bowel to transplant it into another person.

The potential future deficit also depends upon the organ removed. If the donor of a kidney were later to suffer severe damage to his sole remaining kidney, he would be in serious trouble. This sort of accident was the setting for kidney transplants in Mrs. G. L. and Mr. N. W. who had suffered injury to single kidneys (see Chapter 6). Only the passage of time can reveal how frequently the donor nephrectomy later puts the donor's life or health in real jeopardy. Thus far, all donors who have given a kidney have been informed of this risk and have accepted it. No further trouble has as yet resulted. On the basis of statistical probabilities, this trouble will surely occur someday in some donor, somewhere.

The availability of methods for tissue grouping and crossmatching, as described in the next chapter, adds to the favorable outlook for patients receiving tissue from living donors. In those rare instances where histocompatibility* is excellent, fresh cadaver tissues can be used with a greater likelihood of success than before. No matter how favorable the tissue match, the hard fact is that few organs will be available from living donors. The kidney is paired, so it can be donated. Skin can be given to cover a burn. The spleen, the adrenal

---

* *Histocompatibility,* the compatibility or degree of genetic similarity of tissues as predicted by tissue grouping and matching, and as finally established by the reaction after transplantation.

gland, the parathyroid, an ovary or a testicle, a small blood vessel, or a nerve, or a part of the small intestine about complete the list. In all of these save kidney there is virtually no future hazard to the donor once the immediate dangers of operation are past.

As soon as we move beyond these dispensable tissues and consider the large unpaired internal organs or those others that cannot be sacrificed in the living, such as the lung, then one must consider the use of the body of a recently deceased human being. Then, one must face problems of *definition* and of *viability*—the *death* of a person and the *life* of his organs.

What and When Is Death?

The human organism is dead when the brain has ceased to function and, through deterioration of brain tissue from lack of blood flow and oxygen, this tissue death of brain cells has become irreversible.

Of all the tissues in the body, the brain is most sensitive to a lack of oxygen and sugar, both of which must be brought in a steadily pulsating flow of blood from the heart and lungs. When, at normal temperatures, this lack of blood flow is complete for more than eight minutes, there is absolute cessation of brain function, reflexes cease, the pupils become widely dilated, the electroencephalogram* shows no activity, and the patient is dead. He is dead because the brain is dead and cannot be brought back to life. The machinery has been stopped. It has also been wrecked and ruined.

This cessation of flow of oxygenated blood to the brain can occur, for example, when the heart stops beating, or when the vital blood vessels to the brain are closed off, or when the lungs are filled with water—examples from cardiac arrest, fatal strokes, strangling and drowning. But this same sort of brain death occurs from causes other than cessation of blood flow. Direct injury to the brain kills it by smashing or tearing these delicate tissues and destroying the tiny blood vessels that nourish the brain cells. The passage of a bullet so destroys the brain tissue itself that its function gradually ceases even though blood flow is still normal to some parts of it, and severe bleed-

---

* *Electroencephalogram,* a record of the electrical activity of the living brain.

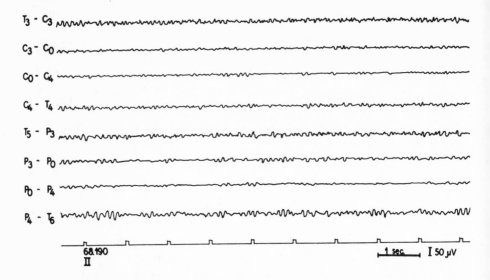

FIGURE 21. Normal electroencephalogram. In this and the next figure (Figure 22) are shown electroencephalograms to contrast the normal finding with that taken from the body of a person recently deceased.

Here are shown eight tracings from electrodes placed in various positions on the scalp. All of them show small wavelike activity which is perfectly normal for a normal awake adult. This tracing took about ten seconds.

ing occurring elsewhere forms clots that cause even more damage by pressure. Diseases of the brain, brain tumors or infections (such as encephalitis), likewise cause complete cessation of function with cell destruction that cannot be reversed.

In milder instances of accidental injury or disease, the brain *appears* to have ceased its function: the patient is deeply unconscious and totally unresponsive to his surroundings. And yet, this damage may be transient. In such cases brain function and consciousness can later return by the processes of normal recovery or by the surgical removal of a tumor or a clot.

In either case there is a pressing question to be answered: is the brain dead? How is the doctor to know, or the patient's family assured,

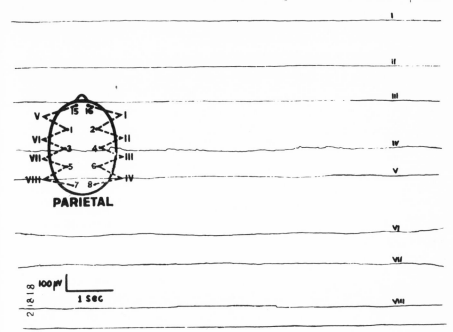

FIGURE 22. Electroencephalogram in death. Here to be contrasted with the wave-like activity shown in Figure 21, are shown the straight lines written from eight leads placed on the scalp of a person who has recently died. To the left is shown a diagram of the scalp, showing the lead positions. With the exception of a small amount of wavelike activity in lead IV, which is due to muscle twitching rather than any real brain activity, this electroencephalogram is perfectly flat. This tracing also took about ten seconds.

that the brain has stopped working completely, its delicate tissues destroyed never to return? How can we say that fruitless efforts should cease or that a time for tissue donation has come?

There was a remarkable change in concept and public under-standing of the definition of death during the years 1966, 1967, and 1968. These were years during which most scientists came to agree that the personal and social meaning of the word "death" applied to irreversible brain death regardless of the state of other tissues and organs. Public accommodation to this concept seemed almost im-mediate.

This was the more remarkable because the moment of death had always been considered to be when the heart ceased its beat or when the patient stopped breathing. These two events were the hallmarks of death. If the heart stops beating for two or three minutes and nothing else is done, the tissues of the brain begin to die from want of blood; if the patient stops breathing for a few minutes, the same thing happens for want of oxygen. If the brain is the primary site of injury or disease, then respiration ceases because the diaphragm is driven by the brain; lacking oxygen from the lungs, the heart then stops. The brain drives the respiratory apparatus that keeps the brain itself alive; central respiratory failure (i.e., failure of respiratory drive) is usually a symptom of brain disease.

The heart will beat without any nervous control from higher centers. In fact, the one function of the brain that is absolutely essential to the maintenance of an oxygen supply for the rest of the body is this function of driving the respiratory muscles and the diaphragm through the two phrenic nerves that run from the spinal cord in the neck down to the diaphragm. Thus, when the immensely complicated functions of the brain are lost, only one component need be restored artificially—that of respiration—to keep the rest of the body viable. If respiration can be driven by a machine, then the heart can go on beating for many hours, days, or even months in the total absence of cerebral function so long as the rest of the body is reasonably healthy.

Clearly, then, some way of judging whether the brain has been irreparably damaged is of paramount importance in considering the removal of an organ or calling a halt to hopeless treatment. If the brain has been lost beyond repair, no humane or social purpose is served by continuance of machine life: if the brain can recover, this machine maintenance can save a life otherwise lost. Intensive care units and special respiratory care wards have been places where countless young people, severely injured or diseased, have been maintained by respiratory assistance until their brains could recover normal function. A young person struck in the head in an automobile accident, with many small hemorrhages throughout the brain, can be kept alive for the two or three months required for these hemorrhages to be reabsorbed and for the brain to recover.

In the presence of critical injury to the brain, a continuous series of decisions are made and remade each day by the doctors in charge. The neurologist, the neurosurgeon, the physiologist, and the chemist must work together to determine whether the maintenance of respiration is justified or is a merciless prolongation of agony for the family. In those cases where the brain is normal but respiration has failed for other reason (as in fractures of the neck) the decision is obvious: keep respiration going and the patient might return to normal life. In other instances, particularly in elderly people with severe hemorrhages in the brain, there is a slow day-by-day change as hope of brain recovery gradually wanes. The machine is keeping alive a body in which a person can no longer return to social existence. In cases of severe brain injury or progressive cerebral disease in younger people, this same subtle change can occur over a week or two. It is this enigma, this gradual change in the meaning of being alive, that has made the understanding of brain death and the definition of irreversible coma so important.

All of these issues were brought into heightened focus by the increasing need for transplantable organs, particularly kidneys. An added impetus for definition was provided by heart transplantation.

In early 1967, doctors in the United States and abroad, lawyers, and clergymen working with them, set forth a number of statements on this subject. Several principles emerged. First, that the death of an individual, a person, a social being, is to be understood only in terms of brain death. Whatever is the soul or vital spark that makes a *person* alive (as opposed to the cellular function of organs), and whatever sort of philosophical framework one wishes to make for the mind or the soul, the irreversible cessation of brain function means the irretrievable loss of the mind and life.

Second, physicians and scientists accepted the principle that a person could be quite dead with a beating heart and with respiration still driven by machine. The change in thinking of experts in this field is seen in the writings or statements of scientists at this time. For example, Dr. Calne at Cambridge stated at the Ciba Symposium in 1965:

Although Dr. Alexandre's criteria [of brain death] are medically persuasive, according to traditional definitions of death, he is, in fact, removing kidneys from live donors. I feel that if a patient has a heartbeat he cannot be regarded as a cadaver. Any modification of the means of diagnosing death to facilitate transplantation will cause the whole procedure to fall into disrepute with the rest of the profession.

Dr. Starzl of Denver, who was taken to task at the Ciba Symposium over the use of convicts as kidney donors, was himself quite hesitant to consider a body as dead if the heart was beating, regardless of the state of the brain.

In the 1963 edition of *Give and Take* it was stated:

Donors for the heart present a very severe problem. Although irreversible damage to the heart by anoxia is slower to occur than it is with the brain, one cannot truly call a patient "dead" until the heart has stopped beating. . . . If such a heart can then be made to resume a beat and to pump blood in a new site, one would inquire why that was not done for and in its original donor!

And yet the answer to this enigma was given in the very next sentence:

The answer will always be that the brain was irreversibly damaged. It is evident that severe problems exist here, soluble only with remarkable sophistication in concept and method.

Within five years, a remarkable change took place in the thinking of all those concerned with this problem.

By 1968, Dr. Calne frequently employed organs from dead bodies in which the heart was still beating.

In 1969, Dr. Starzl wrote:

Initially the fear that the quality of terminal care provided for the donor might be thereby lessened caused us to speak out against the pronouncement of death in the presence of a heartbeat. Our later experience, using the criteria [of brain death] . . . has convinced us that such anxieties were unfounded.

A living kidney is pink and has a live feel about it. Urine issues forth. But it does not show any sure telltale signs or any motion. For fifteen years living kidneys have been removed from the bodies of persons who were quite dead. Life of a kidney has not in any sense signified life of the person. Similarly with the liver, if it is working normally, one cannot see anything particularly remarkable about it except its warmth and color. It has been removed alive for transplantation, and life of the liver has not signified life of the person.

As compared with the kidneys and liver, whose removal while alive we readily accept, the heart differs merely in that its normal cellular function is visible. It moves. Its powerful beat can be seen and felt while the kidney and liver lie quietly, but are equally alive. It is unjustified to single out the heartbeat as a sign of continued life of a person with a dead brain while the continued function of the liver and kidney are not given this significance. The beating of a heart is a sign of continuing cellular function in that particular tissue. Nothing more.

Transplant scientists who had formerly required the cessation of the heartbeat in their definition of death, now abandoned this criterion and were quite content to accept brain death as the indicator, always with the strict proviso that *rigid criteria for assessing brain death could be established.*

When the moment of death occurs through irreversible destruction of the brain, all of the other tissues in the body can still live. So long as circulation and supply of oxygen, provision of nutrients, vitamins, hormones, and removal of the waste continues, their cells will remain alive.

An additional trend of those critical years was increasing public acceptance of this concept. The definition of brain death comes easily to the public mind. This was an interesting example where public acceptance kept pace with changing concepts of medical scientists and doctors. In fact, the public may have been ahead of many doctors who were hesitant to move too fast among these changing and evolving ideas of great emotional content.

Both the public and their physicians have thus agreed that the dead and irreparably damaged brain is the sole sign of death. For such a definition to have any useful meaning, there must be some agreement as to what constitutes irreversible brain disease or irreparable brain damage.

Two sets of criteria must be used for the precise definition of brain death. One is for the *chronically ill patient* who has lain in coma for weeks or months. Here we need a definition of "irreversible coma," the term adopted by the Harvard Committee Report in 1968. The other criterion of brain death is needed for the *acutely injured person* hurt in an automobile accident or by a penetrating wound, for whom a rather different set of criteria is needed because the availability and interpretation of many external or electrical signs are far less reliable.

The criteria for irreversible coma set forth in 1968 by the Harvard Committee* were, in brief summary form, as follows:

1. Unreceptivity and unresponsivity
2. No movements or breathing
3. No reflexes
4. A flat encephalogram, i.e., no electrical activity of the brain. This electrical tracing must be shown to be flat over a period of at least twenty-four hours with no change, in the absence of hypothermia or heavy drugs.

For the second group—namely, brain-damaged persons (patients injured in accidents, or with bullet wounds, fractures, and head injuries)—there is no time for judgments that require two or three days. In patients so badly injured, respiratory maintenance alone will not keep the other organs alive, because of shock from other severe injuries. The brain may be totally destroyed, but in the two days required for those judgments of electrical activity, the rest of the injured body will die. During that time precious anatomical resources needed by other persons would be lost. Other types of judgments are therefore needed for the acute head injury. These include lack of reflexes, lack of reactions in the pupil of the eye, and, if available, a flat encephalogram. But in addition and most important in these acute cases is *direct visual witness of irreparable damage to large areas of the brain itself.* This may be based on the examination done by the physician, on exploratory operation done by the surgeon who hopes to remove a clot (but instead finds a destroyed brain), or on special x-ray methods that demonstrate disruption or loss of circulation to the brain. These special standards, all of which demonstrate gross anatomical

---

* The members of the above committee, in addition to Dr. Henry K. Beecher, as Chairman, were Dr. Raymond D. Adams, Dr. Derek Denny-Brown, Dr. Robert Schwab, and Dr. William H. Sweet, as neurologists or neurosurgeons; Dr. Jordi Folch-Pi as a neurochemist; Dr. William J. Curran from Legal Medicine; Dr. Dana L. Farnsworth, psychiatrist and Head of the Harvard Student Health Department; Dr. Everett I. Mendelsohn, a sociologist; Dr. Ralph Potter, a theologian; and two persons long concerned with the transplant problem both in theory and in practice: Dr. John P. Merrill and Dr. Joseph E. Murray.

destruction of the major centers of the brain, are essential for the declaration of brain death in acutely injured persons. Some unusual cases of severe injury in both civilian and military life have proven that cessation of electrical and reflex activity alone does not always mean irreparable damage to the brain. Respiratory disease, changes in the acidity of the blood, transient cardiac arrest, sudden blows on the head, very low body temperature, and certain heavy drugs all can produce signs simulating a dead brain. A patient may recover from these conditions despite loss of reflexes and electrical activity for short periods of time. Before declaring death in an acutely injured person with a damaged brain, we must therefore insist on the additional rigid standard that gross, visible destruction of the brain must be seen by the unaided eye of the physician.

Prolonged Respiratory Maintenance

It is fitting to end this chapter with a few queries and uncertainties that relate to prolonged machine maintenance of critically ill persons. It was dissatisfaction with the hopeless prolongation of meaningless existence by machine that helped to bring about public realization that death of the brain was death of a person.

Dr. Philip Drinker in 1929 developed a respirator for paralyzed persons. It was a chamber that encased the whole body of a patient except his head and neck. Alternating the air pressure within this chamber caused the diaphragm to move up and down, moving air in and out of the lungs. The Drinker respirator was a bulky, expensive, and immobile device, the first machine to take over the muscular function of the diaphragm. It saved many lives during the polio epidemics.

During the Korean War, 1950–1953, many new kinds of ventilatory devices were developed which could be attached directly to a tube in the patient's trachea. By alternating air pressure in that tube, these devices could ventilate the lungs of an individual whose diaphragmatic muscles no longer moved. These new respirators were much lighter, simpler, and less expensive than the Drinker respirator as a means of providing mechanical assistance to ventilation. Instead of a large tank which enclosed the whole patient, these were merely pressure-changing devices applied to the airway to induce air flow. It became much simpler to maintain respiration in a person whose own diaphragm had ceased to function.

The pacemaker is a device that paces the heartbeat by an electrical impulse led into the heart muscle by a wire. Here the heart's own muscle does the work; the device only triggers it. This cardiac pacemaker is used to regulate the heartbeat of persons whose heart is beating too slowly or with a wrong rhythm. It is only rarely used to provide the trigger mechanism for a heart that is not beating at all. The heart that has stopped completely can be brought back to beat with an electrical shock, but it is unusual to provide prolonged maintenance of the heartbeat *solely* by electrical pacing.

With such effective methods available to keep the body alive without a functioning brain, an acceptable definition of death is especially important. When cellular life of the rest of the body is maintained too long in a dead person, disillusion with this area of hospital medicine is inevitable. The press, the families, and even the clergy are stimulated to statements about "machine life" and the merciless, socially blind inhumanity of doctors in Intensive Care Units.

Unfortunately, it is all too easy to forget the many people with their families around them, or with their lives ahead of them, who owe their lives to these same pieces of machinery in these same units. There is no form of legislation or interhospital inspection that can regulate the use of these devices, anymore than one can legislate or regulate the treatment of diabetes, anemia, or appendicitis. Doctors and medical students must be educated to see the human, economic, emotional, and religious aspects of such problems. With this as a part of their education, and with the knowledge of physiology which makes intensive care effective, the final judgment in each case must be left to the physician. It is one of the responsibilities of the physician caring for a dying patient to explain to the family and his helpers what he is doing and why he is doing it. Although one cannot always be sure of agreement as to the details, he can at least be assured that no person working with the patient will resent the decision to maintain life by machine alone (with the hope that the brain might recover) or to discontinue such existence and make precious organs available to others in need if the brain is dead.

11

TISSUE MATCHING
AND KEEPING

The Grouping of Antigens;
Tissue Donation and Organ Preservation

Nature provides no problems—only solutions.

—ANONYMOUS

With fresh healthy tissue available from a donor either living or dead, there remain three important things to be accomplished before a transplant can occur. These are histocompatibility typing and cross-matching, legal permission to use the tissue, and its preservation until use. These three form the subject of this chapter.

DO TISSUE ANTIGENS COME IN GROUPS?

During the dawn of transplantation, in the 1920's, both Dr. Holman and Dr. Williamson sensed that tissues of various individuals might be of various immunologic types or groupings, and that somehow we should be able to match up these types so that we used tissues from donors who were similar to the recipients. The transplant would thus be more successful. Both Dr. Holman and Dr. Williamson were aware of the possibility of tissue typing or grouping because they were

213

working a mere five years after World War I, when blood transfusion began. It came into being because three scientists, working in three different countries, Dr. Landsteiner, Dr. Moss, and Dr. Jansky, had worked out the blood groups and procedures for identifying them in any donor or recipient. Transfusion crossmatching was perfected. The specter of incompatible transfusion reactions disappeared, and this primal form of tissue transplantation, taking blood from one person and putting it into the veins of another, could be used with increasing success.

It is not surprising that in 1923 workers in transplantation would discern the potential importance of tissue grouping. It is ironic that later transplanters in the 1950's drifted away from this conviction and for a time considered even that blood groups were unimportant in tissue transplantation. Many transplants, carried out as late as 1963 or 1964, were done across incompatible blood group barriers, even at the very time that tissue typing was first being studied. Now it is clear that blood groups must be respected, that blood group compatibility is the first requisite in transplantation, and that tissue compatibility is a major determinant of subsequent success.

What is meant by a "blood group" or a "tissue group"? These terms mean that the cells (red blood cells or tissue cells such as white cells or kidney cells, for example) contain protein antigens that can be recognized or "typed" in categories or groups by specific antisera which contain antibodies against a single type of antigen. When mixed up with the cells in question and viewed under the microscope, these specific antisera cause the cells of that specific type to clump or break, by the same immunologic mechanisms of damage referred to in Chapter 9. In a word, cells of the same group have the same antigens on their surface, and they are identified by the same reactions with the same antiserum. This specific antiserum is called a typing serum.

It is a fortunate circumstance for human blood transfusions that there are only two principal antigens on red blood cells, identified as "A" and "B." Blood cells can, therefore, have neither antigen (type O), both antigens (type AB), or either one (type A or type B). If a person has type A cells, his serum will tend to have antibodies against type B. This simple system of human red blood cell antigens is called the "ABO system" and is the most important system for blood typing.

There are also many minor blood-group antigens, the best known being the Rh antigen, which is responsible for serious reactions in certain types of blood diseases, especially in the newborn if antibodies have been made against the father's Rh antigens by the mother. These are of less importance in ordinary adult transfusion. It is evident that some antigens are very prominent, very antigenic and very widespread, whereas other antigens are weak.

In human tissue types, the predominant antigenic system is identified as HL-A, which means "human leukocyte antigen." Antigens of the HL-A system are of major importance in the histocompatibility aspects of kidney grafting just as the ABO system is important in blood transfusion. At least twelve distinct antigens have been identified in the HL-A grouping of tissue cells, rather than only two as in the ABO antigens of red blood cells. Perfect compatibility of tissue types is therefore much less common than it is for blood types. If an individual carries a specific antigen of the HL-A series, he will not have antibodies against it, but he may have strong antibodies against other HL-A antigens. In tissue typing we therefore seek similarity of the antigens present on cells, using the white cells of blood to perform the test. A direct crossmatch (serum of recipient with cells of donor) is then carried out as a check to be sure that preformed antibodies are absent.

The discovery of these HL-A antigens and of tissue groups based upon them has been one of the most significant advances in transplant immunology since the discovery of drug immunosuppression. It has already revolutionized the practice of donor-recipient pairing, and it has improved the clinical results of transplantation in certain special circumstances. Dr. Terasaki of the University of California at Los Angeles is one of the discoverers and codifiers of the HL-A system of antigens. Let him tell his story:

. . . in 1958, I was fortunate enough to have the opportunity of a one-year post-doctoral fellowship in England with Professor Medawar. We tried then to isolate pure lymphocytes from blood to prove that they were cells which produced the graft-versus-host reaction in chickens. Since we were able finally to isolate lymphocytes, it occurred to me that these cells would be ideal cells to try to type. I, therefore, requested permission to go to Paris to visit Dr. Dausset before returning home to Los Angeles. Dr. Dausset had just published some papers describing leukoagglutination* as a means of detecting antigens on leukocytes. . . . It became evident that unlike typing of red blood cells, only a few lymphocytes could be obtained from blood in a purified suspension and that good serum antibodies would be in scarce supply. A microscopic test was therefore devised to meet this need and has been progressively improved. Once this test was developed, it became possible to test actual transplant patients. Our initial trials were made on patients from Denver and from the Peter Bent Brigham Hospital through the excellent cooperation from the transplant teams at these two hospitals. The bloods were flown out by airplane and often we were unable to type the cells. Almost all of the tests were done late past midnight since the bloods usually arrived on 5 P.M. flights from the east. Soon we found means of sending blood by ordinary air mail special delivery, and methods of fixing the reaction so that readings could be delayed to the next day. But worse than our technical frustrations, many of the answers from tissue typing were not those that we had expected. Patients who were surviving with good kidney transplant function for 1 or 2 years were turning up as being mismatched!

Dr. Terasaki also gives credit to Dr. van Rood of Holland, who was working with tissue typing at the same time, much as the blood group pioneers had worked simultaneously in different countries; Dr. Amos of Duke University was also a major contributor. Dr. Terasaki and Dr. van Rood and several other workers adopted the designation of HL-A numbers to indicate the different antigens. The antisera they used were not pure, and contained antibodies against various antigens, a mathematical problem of great complexity. Dr. Terasaki goes on:

The staff of the UCLA computer facility developed several advanced statistical methods employing modern high speed computers. These methods permitted us to identify 7 antigenic groups initially, and a further 5 or more subgroups later. All 6 of the best defined groups were given international WHO designations—HL-A1, HL-A2, etc. Moreover, antisera were later confirmed to be monospecific by this analysis, and errors in definition played only a minor role. With these refinements, the answer first began to become apparent at the end of 1966 when 196 kidney transplants were analyzed together with a 2 year follow-up. HL-A antigens were found not to be markedly strong antigens; thus mismatching did not result in immediate failure as we had earlier assumed that it would. Rather, the *risk* of failure

---

* *Leukoagglutination,* the immune clumping of white cells (leukocytes).

was higher among mismatched patients, and the risk continued to increase as time went by into the third and fourth years after transplantation.

Future employment of tissue typing must be for cadaver donors, and must be done on a large nation-wide scale, for the variety of tissue types among man would give only a small chance of compatibility. As refined typing becomes commonly available and as organ storage methods improve, national exchange of organs should be possible. Implementation will depend to a large measure on the time necessary to break down the traditional one doctor, one patient relationship to the larger concepts of one dead patient to many other doctors and waiting patients even thousands of miles away.

Within a short time most of the major transplant centers were mailing little test tubes containing lymphocytes from donors and recipients to Dr. Terasaki. He was running a sort of national grouping center based on the UCLA computer, to assist surgeons throughout the United States and Canada and even from countries abroad. As these skills became widespread and the typing sera available to persons taught by Dr. Terasaki, Dr. van Rood, or Dr. Amos, each center began to develop its own laboratory for tissue typing and grouping. Thus, a scientific development anticipated for forty-five years was first used successfully about 1960, was of proven value by 1966, and by 1967 and 1968 was being implemented throughout the world.

The reader should not be confused by the fact that blood cells are used to type tissues. The blood cell used is the lymphocyte itself, in essence a tissue cell found circulating in the blood. It is quite distinct from the red blood cell that is used for grouping and crossmatching blood itself. The lymphocyte contains the important transplant antigens, the histocompatibility antigens, and is used merely as an available cell, to identify those antigens or for crossmatching.

An important question remains as to whether or not the antigens found on the lymphocyte are found also on the kidney cell. If lymphocyte antigens were an entirely different system from the antigenic proteins found in kidney cells, then lymphocyte grouping would mean little for the success of kidney transplantation. It now seems clear that most of the important antigens found on lymphocytes are also found on kidney cells. If lymphocyte grouping shows compatibility and crossmatching is clear, then kidney, liver, lungs, and heart can usually be transplanted with greater certainty. Unfortunately, there is evidence that in some individuals important antigens may be present on the kidney that are not found on the white cells, or at least not identifiable there.

Another element of confusion in public understanding of tissue typing is the fact that the degree of closeness of matching is referred to by letters of the alphabet as an "A" match or a "B" match. This sounds reminiscent of the blood types A and B. There is a similarity of terms with no similarity of meaning. In comparing two persons for HL-A antigens, a donor-recipient pair, for example, they are referred to as an "A" match if they share all of the same antigens. This just means that the match is very good, much as a good examination paper might be marked "A." If they are a little less than perfect they are called a "B" match. Still less perfect, with one unshared antigen, is called a "C" match, whereas the "D" match has several unshared antigens, and the "F" match signifies that the cells and sera of the two persons are incompatible on direct crossmatch.

Like so many other phenomena in biology, the populational distribution favors the middle of the curve. The great majority of matches between random pairs are in the C match category. It is here that rejection occurs in the usual fashion, and where immunosuppression is needed for any degree of success. True A matches are rare except between siblings. They are rarely found in parent-child pairs because the child of a parent always contains strong antigens from the other parent. One would require therefore the coincidence of a husband and wife who happened to share almost exactly the same tissue antigens, for the child to be an A match with either parent. A matches might be more frequent among cousins, and are occasionally encountered in unrelated people. Some of the long survivors of the early kidney transplants and some of the remarkably long survivors of dog experiments in the days before immunosuppression were due to this chance encounter of histocompatibility between unrelated subjects.

In the years 1966, 1967, and 1968 (the same years when the redefinition of death was becoming acceptable and the years when transplantation of the liver, lungs, and heart were first being attempted in man) the selection of donors became more discriminating. A prospective donor, whether living or dead, was now far less likely than before to be acceptable to any specific recipient for donation of liver, kidney, or heart. If your automobile can accept any old carburetor, you can grab the first one on the shelf or in the nearest junk yard; if it takes a very special carburetor, you may have to shop around and look through the stockroom for a long while before you find the one that fits. Worse still, if you don't know how to tell one carburetor from another, you will persist with a series of misfits, and that is the story of transplantation before tissue typing.

The increasing sophistication in donor selection, making the selection of a donor much more difficult (but more effective), led to a drastic reappraisal of donor selection in kidney grafting. It was one of the factors that led to a sharp reduction in the number of heart and liver transplants being done in 1969.

Dr. Patel calculated that there are 2700 identifiable different tissue types in a random population, as based on the number of combinations of the 12 different antigens identified in leukocyte typing sera. Of a total of 3409 matches performed between potential donors and recipients, 161 or 4.7 percent were compatible.*

Dr. Dausset estimated that a pool of 130 recipients of blood-group-compatible persons would be required to expect a compatible match for one *pair* of donor kidneys, a figure close to that of about 150 calculated by Dr. Patel. If we are only going to accept perfect antigen identity—an A match—then the pool as calculated by Dr. Dausset would have to include 500 recipients of randomly distributed blood types to assure a match for both kidneys of any given donor.

Where does this development of histocompatibility testing and crossmatching leave us in the practice of transplantation?

1. If the lymphocytes of a donor and a recipient have all the same antigens and are therefore an A match, the likelihood of success is greatly heightened, rejection is far less vigorous, and less immunosuppressive drugs need be used. This occurrence is commonest among siblings.

2. A negative direct crossmatch (patient's serum against donor cells) is a prerequisite, to rule out preformed antibodies.

3. But even with an almost perfect matching of types, for example

---

* For this study Dr. Patel considered a recipient as compatible when his lymphocytes carried all the antigens found on the donor. An incompatible recipient was a person who lacked one or more of the antigens on the donor lymphocytes.

a B match, there may be a severe rejection, or even preformed antibodies displayed by a positive crossmatch. This anomalous fact is explained by the supposition that there are some antigens, possibly quite weak or rare, that have not yet been discovered, but which exist on lymphocytes or kidney cells. These rare antigens can lead to incompatibility reactions even though the stronger, more familiar antigens are compatible. This would be very similar to the early cases of blood incompatibility between a mother and her child, inexplicable on the basis of the ABO system and not understood until the Rh antigens were discovered.

4. There will occasionally be success with a graft even if the matching up of antigens is not very good. This could occur only in the presence of a negative direct crossmatch, and would signify that even though the recipient did not have some of the antigens of the donor, he had not formed strong antibodies against them.

5. Lastly, if the unshared antigens are in the "right direction"—i.e., the recipient having some that are absent in the donor (rather than vice versa)—the likelihood of significant reaction is reduced.

All of this arithmetic, new to the transplant problem, requires the lining up and organization of recipients on a regional or national scale.

LINING UP RECIPIENTS

Ever since the development of blood banks (at the time of World War II) the idea has appealed to many that tissue banks might also be built up. In grafts where histocompatibility testing is of no importance and preservation a simple matter, as is the case with cornea, bone, and artery, these banks are already in existence. But for the cellular organs in which histocompatibility is important, and tissue preservation a severe challenge, true tissue banking is still a dream; interval preservation even for 6–24 hours is of critical importance, and the "storage unit" is a group of waiting recipients rather than flasks of tissue in a refrigerator.

A blood bank consists essentially of a large refrigerator in which many bottles or bags of blood are kept. When a patient needs some blood, his blood type antigens of the ABO system are determined by typing sera, a crossmatch is done to see which of the bloods in the bank is suitable, and the transfusion is given.

In tissue matching for transplantation the procedure followed, as a cadaver donor becomes available, is exactly the reverse. The lymphocyte antigens of the donor and of several recipients are identified by mixing white cells with the typing serum exactly as Dr. Terasaki first did it. When compatibility of antigens is found between the donor and some of the recipients, a direct crossmatch is carried out using the donor's white cells against the serum of compatible patients on the waiting list. Two recipients are selected: one for each of the donor's kidneys. In blood banking, there is a single recipient and a large number of donors. In transplantation, there is a single donor and a large number of waiting recipients.

When family donors are used, the procedures for grouping and crossmatching are the same, but they can be done in a more leisurely way. The perfect donor is sought and often found in the immediate family.

When a kidney transplant fails, it can be removed and the patient returned to dialysis treatment awaiting another transplant, hopefully from a more compatible donor. There is no such simple solution with a failed transplant of liver or heart, and although some second transplants have been done, they are formidable procedures and none has been successful. Ideally, then, transplantation of the liver, heart, or lung should never be done across a serious incompatibility barrier, and certainly should never be done against a direct crossmatch incompatibility. In the late months of 1968, when the first heart transplants were about a year old, crossmatching capability was sufficiently well developed in most laboratories so that a number of contemplated cardiac transplantations were canceled because of grouping incompatibilities. A year previously, with less knowledge and capability in performing the tests for grouping and crossmatching, these transplants might have been done. In all probability they would have failed by rejection, as so many of the early heart transplants did. Because of the rarity of A matches between random pairs of people, most heart transplants, including several of the long-term survivors, have been C matches; only a few have been B matches.

Tissue grouping and crossmatching have thus brought two

changes in the donor-recipient relationship. First, when donation is imminent from individuals suffering severe brain disease or injury, some hours—enough time for tissue grouping and crossmatching—must pass between the initial identification of the potential donor and the actual use of the tissue. Tissue grouping and crossmatching are an added spur to the development of tissue preservation for this reason.

Second, this new knowledge severely limits the freedom of grafting from cadaver donors that existed for about ten years (1958–1968). Because many potential kidney recipients can be kept alive on the artificial kidney, it is possible to permit the accumulation of groups of potential recipients whose tissue types are known. Groups of recipients may be in the same city or region or, as is the case with the Euro-Transplant System based on Dr. van Rood's laboratory in Holland, in several countries of Europe. When a possible donor is known, the best recipient is found and the organ is shipped by air to his hospital.

In the case of the heart, the gathering together of any significant number of potential recipients is unlikely. More practical is a central clearinghouse which can ascertain from its records the most suitable recipient for any potentially donated heart, to avoid moving patients or cadavers. Cardiac patients awaiting transplantation cannot wait long—life expectancy is short, and there is no artificial device available to keep them alive for more than a day or two. Disease of the sort treated by liver transplantation is sufficiently rare so that no one hospital can accumulate many available patients. Most hospitals concerned with liver transplantation are already faced with the problem of long waiting lists to be evaluated against a potential donor.

TISSUE MATCHING AND THE SUCCESS RATE

Retrospective analysis of kidney transplants carried out with sibling donors shows a fine correlation of tissue match with graft survival. After four years the survival of the transplants stands at 95 percent for A matches and B matches; the figure is 50 percent for C matches and D matches. This is a striking and highly significant difference.

The statistics for a similar analysis of cadaver donors are less clear. With the large variety of antigenic patterns, a few have survived despite the high degrees of tissue mismatch. Probably, the immunosuppression was strong enough to overcome the barrier, and the mismatched antigens were not very strong. Despite the lack of statistical correlation between tissue match and transplant survival in cadaver donors, the fact remains that if one happens to encounter histocompatibility of the A match or B match (to be expected in about 4 percent of random pairs) the survival is longer, the patient's course is smoother, and less immunosuppression is required.

Presensitization as shown by a positive direct crossmatch plays an important role in immediate graft failure (as opposed to gradual rejection). As an example of such data, there was an 80 percent incidence of immediate graft failure in 30 cases studied with preformed antibodies, as demonstrated by a positive crossmatch. By contrast, there were only 4 immediate failures in 195 cases with negative crossmatches (about 2 percent). This again is a highly significant difference and is one of the bits of data indicating that donors should be used only when the crossmatch is negative.

Dr. Hume and Dr. Williams of Richmond, Virginia, have reported immediate rejection of kidneys in which the donor-recipient pair showed no crossmatch incompatibility of white blood cells, whereas when the donor's kidney cells were challenged by the patient's serum, a positive crossmatch did result. The interpretation is offered that some antigens are present on kidney cells that are not present on lymphocytes and can be missed by the lymphocyte crossmatch. Dr. Kountz of San Francisco has been following up this work of Dr. Hume and Dr. Williams. He has been using a suspension of cells from the donor kidney itself, exposing these cells to the serum of the recipient. He has thus been performing a direct crossmatch using kidney cells themselves—the cells of the very organ about to be transplanted. Based on such tests he reports a close correlation between histocompatibility and long-term success of the kidney transplant. This development, reported in January 1970, together with the increasing number of antigens now being detected by typing sera, gives great promise that in the next few years we will see a remarkable improvement in the success of cadaver-kidney grafts, based on histocompatibility testing.

Immediate failure of kidney grafts is more common among women (about 14 percent) than among men (about 6.3 percent). This is probably due to pregnancy sensitization.

In their data, Dr. Patel and Dr. Terasaki report an overall incidence of immediate failure of about 5.3 percent in related donors (247 cases), 15.4 percent in unrelated cadaver donors (143 cases), and about 13 percent in unrelated living donors (23 cases). These figures corroborate the experiences gained before histocompatibility testing was available, that there was about a threefold likelihood of early difficulty with unrelated donors as compared with any sort of related donor. Extending this same concept to a large population of unrelated people, approximately 20 percent of random pairs will demonstrate a positive crossmatch, a slightly higher figure than the figure of around 15 percent for immediate failure of graft. Secondary grafts show the highest incidence of immediate failure, around 40 percent. This indicates that the first kidney transplant has sensitized the patient and that the many blood transfusions often needed in the care of a critically ill patient rejecting a kidney may have further added to the preformed antibodies.

The Postmortem Examination, Tissue Donation, and New Legislation

The advance of medical knowledge in the Western world is indebted to the enlightened scientific tradition of making a careful examination of the human body after death. This postmortem examination, or autopsy, has provided our knowledge of pathology (the scientific description of disease) over the past hundred years. An autopsy is done not merely to satisfy the curiosity of the patient's relatives who wonder why the patient died, what disease he had, or what might have gone wrong with treatment. Nor is it performed merely to satisfy the curiosity of the doctors who have been caring for the patient, who were baffled by the inexorable course of the disease. Even more important than either of these is the role of the postmortem examination in making available for scientific study the cells, tissues, and organs which demonstrate the nature of disease processes and enable their understanding as a basis for prevention and treatment. These have provided the grammar, the spelling, and the very rudiments of clinical surgery and medicine.

It has been standard legal practice in the United States that the body of a deceased person cannot be examined without the permission of the next of kin, unless there is a question of homicide, suicide, negligence, contagion, or accidental death, in which case the death is a medicolegal matter and falls into public domain—the province of the coroner or the medical examiner. In most states this family permission can be neither sought nor granted prior to death. Until recently it could not be given even by the patient himself as part of his last will and testament, the permission of the next of kin still being required after death had occurred. All of these are safeguards established by society to protect the body of a deceased person from unwarranted violation or to preserve it for legal inquiry in the interests either of justice or community health.

In most instances there is no great hurry. Within a few hours after death the next of kin speak with the doctors involved. Sometimes for religious or personal reasons the permission is refused. Sometimes, in questions of homicide, suicide, or accidental death, the autopsy must legally be performed whether or not the relatives concur. Usually the permission is freely granted and the examination carried out accordingly. The frequency with which this step is undertaken is a measure of the excellence of a hospital and the humane concern of both the doctors and their public; it is a barometer of the climate of a culture.

One need not travel far to find other countries with a less humanistic tradition, with antagonistic religious prejudices, or widespread ignorance, in which a postmortem examination is performed in less than 10 percent of patients who die even in the best government-supported hospitals. How can the doctors of such a hospital ever hope to learn? Such doctors cannot be expected to develop so complicated a matter as open-heart surgery or the modern treatment of brain tumors, heart attack, or emphysema if they cannot discover the causes of failure or the clues to success. And as for tissue transplantation, it is totally unacceptable from a moral point of view if postmortem examinations cannot be carried out to find where errors have been made so that procedures can be improved.

The peoples of western Europe, North America, and Australasia, have arrived at this compassionate custom of the autopsy only by the efforts of many. Public education, the assent of the ministry, the overthrow of prejudice and bigotry, and the unselfishness of many families have provided the social background for the passage of enabling legislation.

Now, as the possibilities of tissue transplantation arise, two new dimensions have been added to the matter of autopsy permission. First, permission for postmortem examination and organ donation must be sought very soon after the moment of death. Minutes count, and the more leisurely procedures of the past are no longer effective. Second, it would be most significant should new legislation be passed which would make it possible for previous intentions of the patient himself to be binding on the next of kin so that if he wants his organs donated it can be done immediately. Such new laws should also make it possible for the coroner or the medical examiner to utilize organs from persons killed by accident or violence for whom the next of kin either are unknown or cannot be reached.

Responsive to the need for new legislation in this area, in 1965 the Commission on Uniform State Laws designated a committee to propose a uniform statute for tissue donation and to provide a basis for legislation in various states and regions dealing with the donation of organs and tissues for medical research and treatment. Three years later, on July 30, 1968, the commissioners approved the Uniform Anatomical Gift Act, which has since been endorsed by the American Bar Association. This act has many provisions, dealing with the authority of the individual to donate, the role of the next of kin, possible conflict between the donor and the next of kin, legal problems of the donee (i.e., the hospital, institution, or doctor to whom the gift is made), the use of wills or other written instruments as a mechanism of gift, the drawing up of cards which an individual can carry on his person, telephonic consent, protection from liability, and some aspects dealing with the time of death. By January 1, 1970, forty states had passed laws based on the Uniform Anatomical Gift Act and embodying its various provisions to a greater or lesser extent.

Every effort must be made to facilitate anatomical gifts, yet one cannot expect the impossible. It will require many years and the presence of many millions of persons who have indicated their desires, as shown by certificates they carry with them, before the coincidence of tissue donation based on prior intent is commonplace. Thus far, there have been but one or two transplantations carried out from cadavers as a result of the donor's prior designation based on an Anatomical Gift Act. There have been several instances of premortem wish verbally expressed to others. Several of these donors have been physicians. One, Dr. Zahler of Denver, Colorado, was killed in an automobile accident in October 1968, and became the donor of liver and kidney on the basis of a specific wish expressed to his parents before his death. In the case of living donors, the wishes of the donor are, of course, critical in all cases.

The Postmortem Survival of Tissues: Time-Temperature Curves and the Perfusion Pump

A tissue is defined as living when, returned to normal surroundings and blood supply, it will resume its use of oxygen for the burning of sugar and carry out all its energy-requiring cellular functions in a normal way. In the recently deceased body, the cells and tissues that are still alive are those which are more resistant to lack of blood and oxygen than the brain. The state of liveliness or viability of all these tissues depends upon the length of time they have lacked blood supply and their temperature. The plot of the two—temperature as a function of time—is called the time-temperature curve; such a curve can be drawn for any tissue used in transplantation. The inexorable decay of tissue over a span of time and at any temperature can be modified slightly by providing the tissue with a flow of blood or some blood substitute either during the cooling process or after it has cooled. Prolonged warmth without blood flow is lethal to all living cells.

The contrast of two tissues illustrates this simple point. Consider first the skin, on the outside of the body, always cooler than the interior. After death the skin cools rapidly. It can be removed many hours later for a graft, rolled up in a package and placed in an icebox, kept there for several days or a week, later grafted, and will actually live and grow as a true cellular tissue. But the skin has only a few cells in it—only in the outer layers—and these cells do not have a large requirement for blood or nourishment because they do little metabolic work and no mechanical work. They are a passive cellular covering, cool to begin with, simple in their demands, and easily preserved in the cold state.

The liver, by contrast, is a large central organ constantly working on its many chemical processes, with a large metabolic demand and a large blood supply. It is the furnace of the body, the source of body heat because so much oxidative energy transfer occurs within its cells. Even after the patient dies, the liver goes on for a while doing some metabolic work, generating heat by burning sugar without oxygen. This terminal or agonal metabolic activity of the dying liver is known as anaerobic glycolysis,* a process very injurious to the liver cells because it produces lactic acid that damages cell membranes. It keeps the liver warm for a few minutes after death. If one records the temperature of the skin and various organs in the body of a person recently deceased, it will be noted that all the internal organs remain warm enough to deteriorate rapidly, but the liver is even warmer. Warm, but lacking blood supply, the liver quickly deteriorates. The body as a whole is an excellent insulator; each warm liver cell demands oxygen, blood flow, and sugar. None of these is provided once the circulation has stopped, and in the face of this acute starvation, the liver cells are damaged irretrievably.

If, after death, the body is allowed to remain at room temperature for several hours and the liver is then removed, its cells will be found to be quite dead and it is useless. This degree of damage can be gauged by taking a small slice of the tissue and placing it in a medium enriched with glucose, in the presence of oxygen. If the glucose is "tagged" with radioactive carbon, one can determine the extent to which this liver slice burns the sugar, converting it into carbon dioxide. Healthy liver slices burn glucose rapidly. Liver taken from a body long dead at room temperature will show no evolution of the radioactive carbon dioxide at all.

If, instead, the liver is removed immediately after death, placed in a cold salt solution, and perfused so that it is rapidly cooled to a low temperature (such as 10° C) it will be found by the liver slice test that

---

* *Anaerobic glycolysis,* the breaking up and oxidation of glycogen and sugar (glycolysis) under enzymatic conditions without the supply of new oxygen (anaerobic). This process occurs in any living tissue without adequate blood supply to meet its metabolic demands, and is the source of lactic acid.

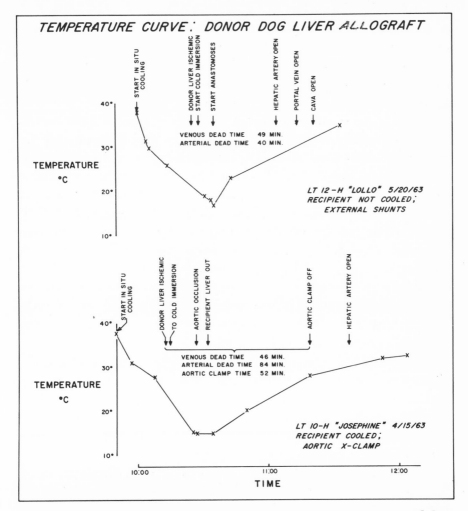

FIGURE 23. Time-temperature curves, illustrating cooling of a transplant and then rewarming in the recipient. Liver is here shown as an example. The two diagrams show the cooling slope as the organ is cooled after removal, and the tendency to rewarm slightly by anaerobic metabolism even before the blood supply is rejoined. When blood flows through the organ it warms to body temperature. In "organ banking" the cold period would be greatly prolonged.

it is very much alive and active many hours later. Such a liver can then be transplanted into another animal and show excellent function. The same is true of heart, kidney, spleen, lung, and many other tissues. Although these other tissues do not have the unique furnace quality that the liver does, they are equally damaged by maintenance of warmth after blood supply has stopped. The two critical factors in preserving tissue for transplantation are time and temperature.

The critical *time* is that which elapses between the cessation of circulation and its re-establishment in the new host. The critical *temperature* is that of the tissue during the ischemic interval.

An important temperature for most tissues appears to be around 15° C. Below this temperature, many tissues can be kept alive for several hours without blood flow. If the temperature is reduced to 5° C, or lower, down to the freezing point, additional preservation is gained, but there is damage to tissues, particularly if freezing is produced and the cells swell and break as a result of ice expansion.

If, while being cooled, the tissue is supplied with continuous circulation of a fluid that removes waste products, however slowly they are produced, and supplies oxygen, however minimal the need, then tissue preservation might be prolonged and the cooling process made safer. The problem of how best to accomplish this, and just how long the tissue can be preserved, is the focus of many laboratories today. It is a quest that has a long history.

Dr. Carrel (see Chapter 2) was a pioneer in this work. During the period between 1925 and 1935, at the Rockefeller Institute in New York, he worked at the design and perfection of small blood-pumps to keep organs alive. He was joined in this work by Dr. Charles Lindbergh who, following his trans-Atlantic flight of 1927, was looking for a scientific effort to use his engineering skills.

Despite a long history and the apparent simplicity of the problem, the cold-pump preservation of tissues has made few basic advances, and the time limitation is still severe. The use of oxygen at high pressures does not seem to be as important as the maintenance of perfusion using a thin watery fluid that contains no blood cells and carries oxygen in the dissolved state to the tissues. The fluid flows easily at low temperatures because it has a low viscosity (the property of resistance to fluid flow). Water is a fluid of very low viscosity. It is easy to pump through small tubes and vessels even when very cold. Blood is thick and viscous because of the protein and red cells in it. The colder the fluid is, the more viscous it becomes. Because of the low temperatures used in cold-pump tissue preservation, low-viscosity fluids are essential.

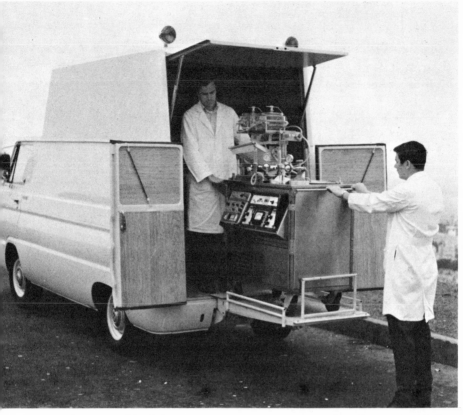

FIGURE 24. Portable kidney preservation apparatus. This shows the "kidney mobile" developed by Dr. Folkert O. Belzer of the University of California.

The apparatus shown is a kidney-preserving unit which keeps the kidney in good condition for 36 to 48 hours by keeping it cold and perfusing it with a solution containing some oxygen. The mobile unit can go to a hospital where cadaver kidneys have become available and transport them, perfused and sterile, to the hospital where they can be used for transplantation.

Among those who have achieved the greatest success with these methods of cold-pump preservation has been Dr. Belzer at the University of California in San Francisco. In the laboratory he has been able to maintain dog kidneys healthy and functioning for periods up to two or three days before putting them back into their original canine hosts to assess the success of his preservation. Two or three days is still far short of anything that one can call "tissue banking." Among the first prolonged preservation records for a human kidney (later successfully used for human transplantation) was one reported by Dr. Belzer in 1968. This kidney was maintained on a cold-pump preservation system for 17 hours. Although it was a record for "kidney banking" at that time, the organ was not perfectly preserved, and its function was not as good as Dr. Belzer and his group had hoped, nor was its function quite as perfect as had been obtained under the controlled conditions of canine kidney cooling in the laboratory. Since that time Dr. Belzer and his team have successfully transplanted human kidneys as long as 36 hours after their removal from the donor, and routinely use a storage interval of 18 to 24 hours.

The kidney is a relatively small organ, and it is easy to cool it by immersing it in a sterile iced saline solution. Until the perfusion-preservation methods are perfected, it is safer to immerse the kidney and avoid any injury to the delicate lining of the blood vessels that might result from forceful perfusion. Using air transport, it is possible to move kidneys about the North American continent or Europe by these simple methods, and with good results. They can be replanted in four to eight hours. Although portable perfusion pumps have been made by Dr. Belzer and others working with these developments, they are heavier and more difficult to move around than a kidney immersed in cold water, and simple immersion cooling still predominates in clinical kidney transplantation today.

By sharp contrast, the liver is a large organ, surface cooling is much less effective, and the effect of anaerobic glycolysis is to maintain the warmth of the liver. These intrinsic processes must be slowed down by cooling. Therefore, in liver preservation, perfusion cooling is essential. All laboratories concerned with liver transplantation have used some form of perfusion cooling to get the liver cold enough so that it can wait those extra two or three hours before the blood supply can be joined again.

The heart is intermediate between the liver and the kidney as to cooling and preservation. It is smaller than the liver and its inside surfaces are readily perfused as cold fluid runs through the heart chambers. The coronary blood vessels are also easily perfused. Furthermore, the heart, being a bundle of muscle rather than a mass of metabolizing cells, has a very low oxygen requirement when the muscle is at rest and not contracting. It is for this reason that cold preservation of the resting heart can successfully be accomplished for many hours at a time with excellent resumption of function when the beat begins again under electrical stimulus. In the laboratory, preservation of the heart for a few minutes or hours is the least of its problems in transplantation. Despite this fact, the cardiac transplants accompanied by the best immediate function, as described in Chapter 13, were those in which the time interval during transfer was kept at a minimum and the very simplest form of interval preservation (or none at all) employed.

What, then, about prolonging this tissue preservation from a few hours to days, weeks, or months? What about the dream of tissue banks with deposit vaults full of frozen organs whose tissue types are known, and whose cellular liveliness can be monitored from day to day? Such things are still far in the future. Most transplanters today would be content with the simple objective of preserving tissues in a very lively state for 24 hours, but with total reliability that the tissues remain alive and ready for replantation. An important feature of tissue preservation is the development of methods to assess the usefulness and viability of an organ when it is cold and in storage. We must have methods of learning the state of the tissue then, and thus predicting its function when transplanted. A variety of methods are now used, none perfect. These include a record of the urine output of preserved kidney, the acidity of the surface of the tissue as measured with an electrode, and microscopic examination of small bits of the tissue. Perfectly reliable storage for 24 hours with a continuous index of the state of the tissue should be the first objective of the tissue banker.

. . . AND THE BEAST

The concept of transplanting organs from one kind of animal to another has appealed to artists and mythologists since the time of the chimera. Even Dr. Ullmann, working in Vienna back in 1902 (Chapter 4), transplanted the kidney from a dog to the neck of a goat.

In the years that have elapsed since that time, it has been shown repeatedly that xenografts are rejected more rapidly and with greater damage to the tissue than are allografts. Furthermore, there has been evidence for some years that the antibodies against xenografts are predominantly circulating immunoglobulins. It has been assumed that xenografting would be very difficult, and that its attempt should wait until the allografting problem has been solved. In addition, there are not many tissues in animals that are very attractive for transplantation into man. The livers and hearts of most animals are too small for man. Skin has too much hair. Possibly kidney would work quite effectively.

Many of the xenografts of the past sixty years have been between animals that were distantly related—dog to goat, rat to rabbit. Xenografts between more closely related species—rabbit to hare, dog to coyote, chicken to turkey—have been less frequently studied. These closely related xenografts might present a somewhat different sort of problem. An example would be transplants within the primate order, such as African monkey to South American monkey, monkey to baboon, or chimpanzee to man.

It was with these considerations in the background that the scientific world greeted with keen interest a report from New Orleans in March 1964 that Dr. Reemtsma and his colleagues, working under the direction of Dr. Creech of the Tulane University School of Medicine in New Orleans, had transplanted the kidneys from a chimpanzee to a man. This was an operation which, regardless of its outcome, was to have an important impact on this rapidly changing field.

The patient had chronic renal failure. He was a man 43 years of age, who had suffered all of the difficulties associated with high blood pressure since he was 37, and had been cared for intermittently in the Veterans Administration Hospital in New Orleans for the previous four years. Like so many other candidates for kidney transplantations, he was suffering from chronic glomerulonephritis. The usual medical means and dietary restrictions of salt made him feel better but did not heal his kidneys. Finally, in June of 1963, he was readmitted to the hospital because his uremia was severe and his heart failure was becoming very pronounced and difficult to treat.

The patient was carried along with repeated peritoneal dialysis, paralleling the case of Mr. M. D., but without providing any lasting solution for his problem. It was impossible to restore him to any sort of useful life. There were no available family donors. After weeks and weeks of waiting, no suitable cadaver became available. Therefore, on

November 4, 1963, a kidney transplantation was done, using both the kidneys from an adult male chimpanzee weighing 41 kg (about 90 pounds). The patient had been placed on immunosuppression for several days prior to the operation, including azathioprine, actinomycin, and the cortisone drugs, and was kept on the drugs after the operation.

On the fourth day, although urine output had initially been good, the patient appeared to be going through an immunologic rejection crisis. He had an increasing fever and a decline in the urinary output. More immunosuppressive drugs were given, and the grafts were treated locally by irradiation. This resulted in enough improvement so that drug dosage could be reduced to normal. At about the third week the patient showed mild symptoms of overdosage of the immunosuppressive drugs so they were stopped for a time. During the fourth week he again appeared to be rejecting the kidneys. The drugs were started again at higher doses, with local irradiation added.

In this particular patient, his own kidneys were not removed, but they were so small and diseased that there was little doubt but that the chimpanzee's kidneys were functioning on their own. Furthermore, by using radioactive isotopes concentrated in the kidney, and going over the region with a scintillation detector, it could be shown that these chimpanzee kidneys were working quite well and had good blood supply.

Immunologic studies in this patient showed that he developed a marked antibody response against chimpanzee tissues. But this response evidently did not reach sufficient intensity to make him reject the chimpanzee kidneys; at least that was one interpretation advanced by these authors. They had tried one previous xenotransplantation of this type, but failure resulted after a few days with a much more rapid rejection.

The patient finally died approximately eight weeks after the transplant, with a high fever and evidence of a severe immunologic crisis. It is possible that rejection of this xenografted kidney was accompanied by a widespread immunologic disease (such as serum sickness) affecting other tissues of his body.

Despite ultimate failure, the study of xenotransplantation was put on an entirely new basis by this experience. Prior to this endeavor, undertaken with strict biologic and chemical controls by Dr. Reemtsma and his colleagues, most scholars would have predicted that the chimpanzee kidneys never would function and would be rejected immediately. Immunosuppression was here shown to be a chemical method for the suppression of antibodies against xenografts, as well as against allografts. A seemingly impractical and visionary operation, denied any likelihood even of temporary success by most who knew of it, had opened up an old field for renewed study.*

Two events that followed this episode demonstrated the ambivalence of scientific growth and some of the difficulties in assimilating new directions into the mainstream of a growing field of biomedical endeavor.

As one side of the coin, transplant laboratories in this country and abroad returned to the problem of xenografting with renewed interest. Among others, Professor Medawar, whose contributions in so many different aspects of transplantation biology have already been noted, was able to make xenografts in the laboratory successful to a greater extent than ever before, using antilymphocyte serum. On the other hand, physicians and surgeons, grasping at straws for sick patients, carried out xenografts of animal tissues to man (using the baboon, chimpanzee, and even in some cases sheep) in ways which left little hope for the patient and cast a general pall of distaste over xenotransplantation of any type, and most certainly of any sort directed toward man.

---

* The current widespread use of pigskin as a temporary graft-dressing in burns, and the cross-circulation of patients in liver failure with baboons, are examples of later "spin-offs" from the chimpanzee kidney transplants.

12

THE LIVER

High Promise for a Few People

A kind of mixture of fools and angels—they rush in and fear to tread at the same time.
—O. Henry, "The Moment of Victory."

The Setting

The liver was the next large organ after the kidney to be considered for allotransplantation in man, to have extensive laboratory study in the dog (1955–1965), to have a few clinical trials (1963–1971), and a *very* few limited successes. It was also the first organ to be transplanted in man that required, of necessity, the use of a cadaver donor because it was unpaired. Liver transplantation began as a natural extension of kidney transplantation, attracted comparatively little scientific or popular notice at the time, and has emerged as the most difficult, most challenging, and least successful of the organ transplants. It is the only hope for a small group of patients who will die of liver disease without it.

In the beginnings of experimental liver transplantation in the mid-1950's, transplant experience was confined to studies of skin and kidney. Blood transfusion, bone marrow transplantation, and the transplantation of those tissues that require neither preservation nor immunosuppression (i.e., cornea and artery) cast only a dim light on the transplantation of functioning cellular organs. Skin had been the model for all those historic and elegant experiments that went back over the years to the treatment of burns and to the early transplant immunology of Drs. Billingham, Brent, and Medawar, their predecessors and followers. Skin had been the tissue most commonly transplanted in man, and most commonly used in small laboratory animals. The kidney had dominated all of the organ experience and virtually all of the thinking on organ transplantation for many years because it was a paired organ with a simple blood supply.

In contrast to these, the liver was a huge mass of tissue ten times as big as the kidney, its blood vessels a complicated crossroads of major blood flow returning from the intestines to the heart. The possibility of transplanting it in man seemed remote, but the immunologic and functional study of its transplantation offered new and significant attractions. The operation itself, even in the experimental animal, looked complex and quite imposing. Ironically, as it turned out, the operative procedure is neither impractical nor impossibly difficult, but the peculiar problems posed by liver disease and liver function have been obstacles to success.

Credit for priority in starting experimental liver transplantation in the dog should go to Dr. Welch of Tufts Medical School and Albany Medical College. For a few years, around 1955, his laboratories worked in this area and published papers dealing with a variety of different types of liver transplantation. In 1957 two laboratories continued the work on a larger scale, work that was to culminate within five years in the first human liver transplants. These were the laboratories of Dr. Starzl, first at Northwestern University in Chicago, and then at the University of Colorado in Denver, and our laboratories in Boston.

We commenced work on this subject with the concept that the liver was such a large mass of tissue that the immunologic defenses of the recipient might be overwhelmed, resulting in immunoparalysis, a remarkable phenomenon signifying the overwhelming of natural defenses by a dose of invading bacteria so huge that the synthesis of immunoglobulin antibodies could not keep up or would even be inhibited.

The initial questions in surgical technique related to the hepatic artery and the portal vein. The hepatic artery is the main artery to the liver. It is small in the dog, and it was not certain that a direct suture-type of anastomosis would provide enough arterial blood flow to support the liver. This problem was solved for the dog, but it has remained a bugbear to clinical work in man. As to the portal vein, the problems had to do with temporary interruption of such a vein returning blood from the intestine to the liver and then to the heart. A further question was whether or not portal blood flow was truly essential to the nourishment of the transplanted liver.

Initial reports from the laboratories demonstrated immediately that the liver could be transferred from one dog to another, and that immune defenses were adequate to produce a rejection phenomenon similar to that seen in kidney. It differed only in its anatomical details. Furthermore, and this was the finding that supplied the impetus and motor power for the tremendous amount of work later devoted to liver transplantation, the new liver functioned for a time with all its normal activities in its new host.

An animal can be maintained alive without a liver for about three or four hours. If special treatments are then instituted, such as the intravenous injection of sugar, protein, or blood, life can be maintained for as long as twelve hours. For those working in liver transplantation, the basic question of liver function was, therefore, answered when animals lived for one, two, three, five, or even up to fifteen days. It was immediately evident that the new liver was functioning in its new host.

Chemical tests that can be done to measure various aspects of liver function are almost legion. There are hundreds of chemical indications to show how each of the various functions of the liver are being performed. In patients with liver disease, these special tests help to define the nature and the progress of the patient's disease. They measure the metabolism of foodstuffs (sugar, fats, and proteins) and of certain toxic substances that the liver can remove. The liver sits squarely in the main channel of blood flow from the intestine to the heart; and as food is absorbed after digestion by enzymes, foodstuffs enter the main channel of liver blood flow, the portal vein. In the portal vein they pass directly to the liver for initial processing before passing to the heart, the lungs, and the general circulation of the body, providing fuel for all the body tissues. The liver excretes some waste products and synthesizes many proteins, particularly albumin for which it is the sole site of production in the body. Many of these functions and synthetic products can be measured and some can even be provided artificially for a while.

By the autumn of 1960, it was evident that a dog's liver could be completely removed and a new one sutured into place. The new liver would perform all of these functions without a flaw—always with the qualification "until it was rejected."

One of the special anatomical or surgical problems involved in these early liver transplants had to do with this portal vein which returns all the blood from the intestinal tract to the heart via the liver. It is divided during transplantation, and for this reason an artificial channel, or a shunt, must be provided temporarily, to let the blood return normally to the heart during the operation. This large shunt could be provided in any one of a number of ways, but it was one of the several factors that made experimental liver transplantation a different, more difficult, and time-consuming surgical challenge than that of the kidney. As far as rejection was concerned, it was evident by 1961 that the immunosuppressive drugs being applied for the first time to human kidney transplantation could also be applied to liver transplantation. Work in the dog showed that some degree of success might be anticipated. Many other laboratories then took up the study of liver transplantation. It was inevitable that sooner or later the first liver transplantation would be tried in man.

In the liver the unequal distribution of the rejection process showed that the connecting parts of the liver, called the "portal triads," were those most attacked by the rejection. These are the millions of tiny areas in the liver where the blood vessels and the bile ducts join as branching twigs before they come together to form the major vessels and bile ducts.

When there is an infiltration of lymphocytes and an intense inflammatory response in those areas, the liver cannot excrete bile normally. There is a bile duct obstruction, but it is of the small bile ducts. It is called "intrahepatic cholestatic jaundice," meaning that it is a jaundice caused by stasis of the bile (chole) inside the liver.

In fact, rejection of the liver (at about the tenth day) closely resembles a disease process seen in other patients with a very rare ailment called cholangiolytic hepatitis. This is also a small-bile-duct intrahepatic cholestatic jaundice, and this striking resemblance of the histologic picture suggests that this type of rare liver disease might also have an immune component, in this case a self-rejection or autoimmunity. Later on, the rejecting liver becomes crowded with lymphocytes. Blood flow stops and parts of the liver become infected. These subtle early changes are swamped or overshadowed by the later massive alterations of advanced rejection.

Where, When, and Why a Liver?

A transplant of liver placed in the normal site, to replace the old one, is called an orthotopic liver transplant. This is rarely done with the kidney. Neither in experimental animals nor in man is the new kidney placed in its normal position next to the aorta in the small of the back. Instead, the new kidney is placed on blood vessels in the pelvis, not originally intended for the kidney at all, but more conveniently situated for the transplant. The ureter is led into the bladder by a new course that is much shorter than the normal. The placing of an organ in a position other than normal is called a heterotopic transplant. When it is done with the liver, the new organ, acting as an auxiliary, is placed somewhere else in the abdomen, leaving the old liver in place.

The three diseases for which liver transplantation might be performed are *cancer, cirrhosis,* and *congenital absence of the bile ducts* in infants. A liver severely injured by a bullet wound or a crushing injury could also be replaced by transplantation. In the treatment of cancer, the patient's own liver must obviously be removed to get rid of the malignant tumor. The same thing is true of injury where removal of the liver is essential because of destruction of liver tissue or bleeding. In both of these an orthotopic transplant would be necessary. For the treatment of cirrhosis or absent bile ducts, an auxiliary liver in a heterotopic position would suffice, leaving the old liver in place.

Many cancers or tumors eventually involve the liver because they spread to the liver (by metastasis) from other areas of the body, particularly from the stomach, the intestine, the ovary, and the breast. So

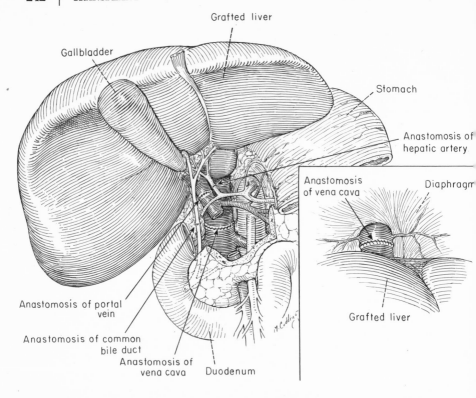

Grafted liver

Gallbladder

Stomach

Anastomosis of
hepatic artery

Anastomosis
of vena cava

Diaphragm

Anastomosis of portal
vein

Grafted liver

Anastomosis of common
bile duct

Anastomosis of
vena cava   Duodenum

FIGURE 25. Sites and sutures: liver allograft. This diagram shows that there are five anastomoses or suture lines required to graft the liver into its new host: the venae cavae above and below the liver, the portal vein, the hepatic artery, and the bile duct. This operation is much more complicated than the heart graft. Its success depends not only on the surgical details, but, as in all other allografts, on the preservation of the organ and the adequacy of the immunosuppressive procedure.

much blood passes through the liver that its network of tiny blood vessels becomes a sieve that strains out cancer cells that grow well there because of the abundance of nourishment. A patient who has a cancer in his liver that has spread from some other site—a secondary liver tumor—would be a fit subject for liver transplantation only on condition that there was no lingering cancer or malignancy present elsewhere in the body. Such presumptions are always hard to prove, since a few tiny cells remaining behind can darken the outlook for any cancer patient. Only the passage of many years, followed by a secon-

cm 2 4 6

FIGURE 26. Surgically removed liver filled with cancer. Here, in contrast to the smooth liver shown in Figure 25, is the photograph of the liver removed from patient J. B., filled with islands ("snowballs") of liver cancer. Each one of the large round white areas is a metastasis from cancer of the intestine. When the liver becomes heavily occupied and replaced by such masses of the uncontrollably growing tumor, the patient succumbs to liver failure. The removal of this kind of a liver, as a surgical specimen sent to the pathologist, is an entirely new feature associated with liver transplantation. Such a liver was never before removed in a living person. Unfortunately, as recounted in the text, immunosuppression permits the rapid growth of tumors, and at the present time liver transplantation is inadvisable for the treatment of most cases of liver cancer.

dary growth in the liver alone, would justify the hope that the liver indeed was the only site of the metastatic deposit. And even then, an exploratory operation would be necessary to prove that cancer was growing nowhere else.

Primary cancer of the liver, hepatoma, is confined to that organ for a considerable time. When hepatoma occurs in young children and young adults, the outlook for survival is hopeless unless the tumor can be completely removed and a new liver provided for the patient. It was, therefore, this group of patients with hepatoma whose problem gave impetus to the early efforts at liver transplantation. Sometimes young people are best able to withstand the surgical operation.

Primary hepatoma grows slowly at first, is painless, and produces almost no symptoms. For this reason, it is rarely discovered in its earliest stages unless by some chance circumstance. In one of our patients this chance arose because of injury incurred in a basketball game, requiring an operation to see if the spleen had been ruptured; at that time it was discovered quite unexpectedly that the young athlete was suffering from an early primary liver tumor, or hepatoma. The painless and insidious onset of hepatoma is one of many factors militating against the success of liver transplantation. By the time the patient knows he has something wrong, the tumor is quite advanced and is often out of bounds for surgical removal.

Although primary hepatoma is a relatively rare tumor in the United States, the situation is different in other countries. There are only a few diseases where regional differences are so striking. Around the bulge of Africa and on the western reaches of the Congo Basin, primary hepatoma is extremely common; 10 to 12 percent of the patients in the few hospitals there suffer from it. The tumor arises throughout the liver, the course is inexorable, nothing can be done for the patients, and they all die. This West African form of hepatoma appears to be the late result of a viral infection or of a food poison; the area is one in which viral hepatitis is very common. In southeast Asia also, in the Malaysian Peninsula and in the area around Singapore, there is a very high incidence of hepatoma. The tumors appear to be a little different from those in the United States or West Africa, and they frequently give an early warning by free bleeding into the patient's belly without any injury. This is rare in other kinds of hepatoma. Here the evidence also suggests that this primary tumor is of dietary origin, caused by a toxic material consumed with certain root tubers, such as the peanut, eaten in large quantities. Whatever its cause, the hepatoma of Malaysia, Singapore, and Indonesia is a local scourge for which no treatment is currently available, and for which liver transplantation, once perfected, would offer new hope.

Turning from these problems of malignant tumors of the liver to cirrhosis, we find a different series of diseases and different sorts of patients, and a situation in which an auxiliary or heterotopic liver can help.

The term "cirrhosis"* is an ancient one referring to the yellow appearance of the liver surface in this disease. The disease process is one in which the cellular substance of the liver becomes replaced by a hard scar, the patient gradually becomes jaundiced, the portal vein develops very high pressure, and there is often fatal bleeding from its branches. The course of the disease, which often takes many years, or even a decade or two, usually ends fatally.

In many cases, cirrhosis of the liver is associated with excessive alcoholic intake. It is a disease either of the chronic alcoholic, of a person who has consumed alcohol to excess in the past but might now be cured of this trait, or of persons who, in conjunction with some tendency to excessive consumption of alcohol, eat a diet that is grossly deficient in dietary essentials. If the old liver could be removed and a new one substituted, letting the portal vein blood drain out through a low-pressure circuit and curing portal hypertension, the problems of the cirrhotic could be ameliorated. Or if the old liver were not too seriously damaged, an auxiliary liver might be supplied. In either case, one would have to insist that the individual himself was cured of his alcoholic habits before devoting precious social resources to such a massive surgical procedure.

Alcoholism is not the only cause of cirrhosis. Young persons who have had hepatitis can later develop a very severe form of cirrhosis known as postnecrotic cirrhosis. This form of cirrhosis, occurring after

---

* *Cirrhosis*, from the Greek *kirrhos*, meaning orange-colored. The cirrhotic liver in very late-stage disease approaches a color that might possibly be called orange. In coining this term, the ancient Greeks slightly overstated the case.

hepatitis, can be treated either by removal of the liver and implanting a new one, or by putting an extra one in, which would drain off the blood and lower the pressure in the portal vein. Acute hepatitis itself, a virus disease often of severe or lethal impact, might on occasion be treated by transplantation. Surprisingly, some such cases have not shown infection of the new liver but, instead, the disappearance of virus from the blood.

High-velocity bullet wounds, mortar shell and artillery fragments produce devastating injuries of the liver that are not immediately fatal. The liver bleeds a great deal, and many blood transfusions are given. Severe infection is almost inevitable and the mortality rate is high. Complete removal of such a shattered liver and replacement by a new one would be a practical step in the treatment of military casualties.

Finally, and most important in this list of persons who might be helped by liver transplantation, there are the infants born with abnormally small and poorly formed bile ducts. Not only does the liver process all the foodstuffs that come to it, but it also elaborates bile—a brownish-yellowish liquid full of salts, cholesterol, and enzymes. When a baby is born with poorly formed bile ducts, it is slightly jaundiced, evidenced by a yellowness of the skin and the whites of the eyes. Suitable study carried out by the pediatrician can demonstrate that this jaundice is a lasting condition, not due to a blood disease in the infant (such as an Rh incompatibility). Congenital atresia (partial absence) of the bile ducts is suspected. To establish this diagnosis beyond a doubt, a surgical operation must be done to determine that the main bile ducts are indeed lacking.

Once this sad finding has been made, there is little that can be done for the infant. The child may live for several months and in some cases for several years. Growth and development are stunted; the child appears deeply jaundiced with yellowish brown skin and eyes. Finally, with no proper pathway to excrete bile, there are malnutrition, bleeding, and a long drawn-out fatal illness.

All the child needs is a few hundred grams of functioning liver cells connected with bile ducts so that bile can be formed and run out into the intestinal tract, cleansing the blood of bile pigment and acid and returning the child to normal. This is the perfect situation where an extra liver, or an auxiliary liver, introduced as a heterotopic transplant, might succeed. More than any other patient offered a liver transplantation, babies could get along with an auxiliary liver in the heterotopic position. From the earliest days of liver transplantation in the dog, the thought was uppermost in doctors' minds that babies with bile duct atresia might possibly be helped by transplantation. But would a liver work if it was not fed on portal blood?

Is Portal Blood the Gateway to Success?

In rearranging anatomy, one sometimes discovers that evolutionary details of arrangement have been arrived at for subtle reasons that are not at all evident and never mentioned in the anatomy books. Nature has fixed things up in a certain way but has neglected to tell us why. The two parts of the adrenal gland, for example, secrete hormones that are entirely different. Only recently has it become evident that these two kinds of hormones have profound interaction and are most effective when coming into the bloodstream together. It is a fortunate circumstance, and a rare example, that the kidney can be moved around so freely and can survive perfectly well on blood vessels never intended for it. Examining the blood flow arrangements for the liver, one might assume that the liver evolved in the midst of the blood coming from the gastrointestinal tract, so that the liver could process foodstuffs efficiently. If it is a processing plant for absorbed foods in the blood, then it obviously should be in the mainstream of that channel, the portal vein.

Liver transplantation has demonstrated that the liver is so situated for another reason: it cannot easily survive without this portal vein blood. Not only does it process this blood, but it seems to thrive on rich and nutritious blood of the intestine. If the liver does not get at this blood first (before other organs have feasted on it) the liver cells suffer. The reasons for this are by no means clear. If the gastrointestinal tract is not being used (as in people who are starving or are maintained on intravenous feeding), the rich nourishment ordinarily found in the portal vein is no longer present, yet the liver does not seem to suffer thereby. Only when weight loss is very severe and prolonged does a sort of fatty degeneration of the liver begin to occur, suggesting that it may not be the nourishment found in the blood that is so important for the liver, but some other chemical substance—possibly an intestinal enzyme or hormone that supports the liver cell.

But take the liver out of an animal and put it in another animal without portal blood flow, leaving that animal's own liver in place, and the new auxiliary allograft will gradually shrivel to a useless nub. Transplanted liver cells wither away without portal blood.* Furthermore, if a new liver is put in place while the old liver is still there, there is competition for portal blood. The liver that gets to it first will thrive. Dr. Starzl and Dr. Marchioro in Denver carried out an ingenious experiment to prove this. The portal vein was divided and half of the animal's own liver was given portal blood, the other half not. This produced selective atrophy of the portion of the liver not receiving portal blood. It seemed as though the liver cell must be the first to get at the portal blood, or if it is rerouted through some other channel, it cannot compete with another portion of liver that is receiving the portal blood first.

In liver transplantation, one solution for the portal blood problem would be to use the portal blood inflow for an auxiliary liver allograft or, failing that, remove the patient's own liver some days or weeks later. This sort of two-stage operation could be done in infants with bile duct atresia. Unfortunately, animal experiments of this type have not been successful. The question of liver atrophy without portal blood and the competition of two livers for some precious portal substance is telling us something about the nature of liver cell function which must be better understood before auxiliary liver allografts can be successful.

THE FIRST LIVER TRANSPLANTS IN MAN

In early 1963 it was evident both in Boston and in Denver that liver transplantation was ready for its first clinical trial. For one thing, kidney transplantation had entered a new era. Patients on azathioprine had now remained in good condition and with kidney transplants

---

* If there is no other liver competing for these substances, it can get along fairly well. This is shown by laboratory experiments called portacaval transpositions in which all of the portal blood is diverted away from a perfectly normal liver, finally reaching it in highly diluted form along with the rest of the body's blood flow. Such a liver is maintained in reasonably good repair.

functioning well for many months, without the hazards that were so severe a problem before the drugs were developed. Although the number of kidney transplantations was few, and performed in only a few centers, organ transplantation was entering a new and more confident era. Animals with liver transplants were now surviving longer than they ever had before; liver function continued to be good, and examination of these livers under the microscope showed few abnormalities.

During 1963, six such attempts were made in man. The first was done by Dr. Starzl, in Denver. None was successful; the stories of these individuals point up the problems in liver transplantation, many of which still remain unsolved.

The first of these patients at our hospital was Mr. J. B. He was a 58-year old construction worker, healthy despite the presence of an enlarging liver mass. He was admitted to the hospital on August 14, 1963, and showed no evidence of any other tumor. He was neither jaundiced nor losing weight. X-rays left few lingering questions: it appeared almost certain to be a case of primary hepatoma, with the tumor widespread throughout the liver, not confined to any single area that could be removed surgically. The patient understood the possibilities of liver transplantation, the minor chance of success, and the hopelessness of his situation should nothing be done.

For several weeks we awaited the identification of a possible donor. Then, on September 16, a policeman (who had been shot in the head by a criminal) was dying. His chances for recovery were considered hopeless by the physicians caring for him at the Massachusetts General Hospital. Because the young man had no other injuries and because the injury was entirely confined to his brain and of unknown extent, every effort was made to restore and maintain life right up to the end. There was a prolonged period of shock, of very poor blood flow, persisting many hours before cerebral function totally ceased and the heartbeat stopped. With the full knowledge that this liver had already suffered a considerable degree of cellular injury due to lack of oxygen, it was removed and transported in sterile iced saline solution, by automobile, across the city, to be placed in the site of the liver removed from Mr. J. B.

Although the operation itself was complicated by the extensive size of the tumor in patient J. B., and its resultant distortion of normal anatomy, the new liver fitted well; its blood flow was excellent. The surgical incision was closed after a complex operation lasting six hours, and the patient returned to his bed in the Intensive Care Unit.

His initial response was encouraging. Early function of the liver was so good that it left little doubt that blood supply was normal. The cells of the new liver were carrying out all their functions. After a day or two of these modestly encouraging appearances, the patient began to develop progressive signs of infection, and his clinical condition deteriorated. The dose of immunosuppressive drugs was high, but did not appear to be excessive; blood group incompatibility added an immunologic burden. On the eleventh day he died with a massive infection in his liver and in his lungs. The autopsy showed the primary reason for failure: a large volume of hepatic tissue was short of oxygen, possibly injured by the poor blood flow in the donor before the liver was removed, and accentuated by the prolonged period of shock before death. In addition, there was revealed a tiny cancer in the intestine, no bigger than a dime, which was the source of this tumor in the liver. The liver tumor was therefore secondary, or metastatic, not a primary hepatoma as had been supposed. Although the tumor in the intestine did not show up by x-ray, it was large enough so that, had the patient lived, it would have caused him a lot of trouble.

Between March and October, 1963, the Denver team of Dr. Starzl, assisted by Dr. Marchioro and Dr. Brettschneider,* carried out five human liver transplantations—all orthotopic transplantations with the liver in its normal position. One of the first was done in a 3-year-old child suffering from biliary atresia. The liver was not well preserved and the infant died of hemorrhage during operation. Three of the patients had hepatoma superimposed on an old cirrhosis. They were 29 to 52 years of age. The final patient had a primary carcinoma of the liver arising from bile ducts rather than from the liver cells.

These four patients lived from 6 to 23 days. The cause of death in two was infection. In another two, clots lodging in the lungs (pulmonary emboli) were a prominent cause of death. If liver tissue is

---

* With the assistance of Dr. Porter of London, who carried out the studies of liver pathology on the basis of continuing collaboration over a distance of 5500 miles.

fading fast at the time of transplant, bleeding rather than clotting is the problem. The fact that blood coagulation was firm enough to make a clot was evidence in these cases that Dr. Starzl's team was using a well-preserved liver.

On the basis of these unsuccessful experiences it was wise not to attempt any more liver transplantations in man until there was greater experience with immunosuppressive drugs, or until there was a better method at hand for the preservation of the liver during its transfer from one person to another. Clinical work lapsed for several years, while laboratory work went on with renewed intensity. Several other laboratories (the Medical College at Richmond, Virginia, and the Universities at Bristol and in Cambridge, England) began working on liver transplantation and joined those in Boston and Denver. With the exception of Paris, Europe had been slow to begin kidney transplantation, but in 1963 or 1964 many European laboratories began to take up liver transplantation almost simultaneously.

The restraint on human transplant experiments, self-imposed by clinicians working in the field of liver transplantation, has often been quoted as a model of how new fields of endeavor should be explored and exploited for the benefit of sick patients, but restrained when the going is poor. Most clinical applications of new drugs or operations go in a stepwise or wavelike progression. In this particular case, more knowledge and experience were obviously needed, both in canine liver transplantation and in clinical kidney transplantation, before it would be in the best interests of the patient, the public, or biologic science to do more liver transplantations.

By 1967, immunosuppressive drugs, particularly azathioprine, had been used in almost 1000 kidney transplantations. The literature was filled with accounts and experiences with this drug and the new operation. Experimental liver grafts had progressed remarkably, and there were several animals that had lived in the laboratory for many months, with a sole allografted liver. Antilymphocyte serum was available, and a simple pump for cold perfusion of the donor liver permitted a few extra hours of surgical preparation.

In the spring of 1967, clinical work started up again. The results from that time until the present constitute our view of liver transplantation throughout the world. This was reviewed at a meeting held

in Cambridge, England, under the Chairmanship of Professor Calne—
the doctor who eight years previously had been the first to apply 6-
mercaptopurine to experimental kidney grafts. To 1969, the world total
was 91 operations for liver transplants. Of these cases about one third
had been done for biliary atresia, one third for cancer, and one third
for a variety of other diseases, including injury and cirrhosis.

The longest survivors in the world experience have been some of
the patients among the 25 operated upon in Denver by Dr. Starzl. His
longest survivor is an infant. The patient was aged two, and was transplanted on February 9, 1968, for the treatment of biliary atresia, and
was still doing well almost two years later. This patient represents the
longest survivor of liver transplantation in man.

As of April 1969, only 10 patients were alive with liver transplants
out of the 91 that had been operated upon up to that time. Only 3 of
these patients were more than 12 months postoperative. Six of Dr.
Starzl's 25 patients lived for a year or more after orthotopic transplantation.

As of October 1970, 133 liver transplants had been done. Twelve
patients survived, the longest living 29 months.

In Dr. Starzl's experience, as in that of all others working in this
field, hepatoma has turned out to be ill-suited to treatment by transplantation. Of his 5 patients with hepatoma (who had posttransplant
survival of two months or more), all developed recurrent cancer which
was directly responsible for death. In most of these patients the
hepatoma appeared to grow with increased ferocity after the operation.
In one case, transplanted more recently, the hepatoma has not recurred
and a long-term survival seems more likely.

Professor Calne reported the second largest series of liver transplants—12 cases, 10 of them orthotopic, and 2 auxiliary livers in an
heterotopic position. Four of his transplantations have been done for
hepatitis in various forms. To these 12 cases have since been added an
additional 2, both done for tumor and both doing well, at home, at
work, and free of disease at 6 and 9 months respectively.

Our group at the Brigham Hospital, now working under the direction of Dr. Birtch and in collaboration with Dr. Filler at the Children's
Hospital Medical Center, has performed 4 liver transplantations: 2 in

adults with tumor, and 2 in children with biliary atresia. There have been no survivors over 7 weeks.

Thus, in liver transplantation we find many early deaths, rapid growth of tumor, and only a scattering of significant long-term survivors. In the first two years of cardiac transplantation, 151 transplantations were carried out. Most of them showed short-term technical success; but there was an equally slim showing on long-term results (see Chapter 13).

Comparing the liver and heart from the point of view of surgical transplantability, the difficulties with the liver are much more severe. The problems are those of blood supply. The arteries to the liver are small. They are difficult to suture together as compared with those leading to the heart which are very large. If a tiny clot, only a few tenths of a millimeter in size, forms on a silk suture in a tiny blood vessel such as the hepatic artery of a child, it immediately and at least partially obstructs it. Blood flow is reduced. The clot then grows, and finally stops blood flow completely. Along the wall of a large blood vessel, such as those around the heart, precisely the same clot is scarcely noticeable. It can grow, be reabsorbed or covered with endothelium. If the tissue is examined weeks or months later, only a tiny scar is left which does not bother blood flow at all.

Of the liver grafts thus far carried out, three quarters have involved complete removal of the patient's liver and suturing the donor liver into the normal position as an orthotopic graft. The remainder have been auxiliary livers, many of them performed in infants or young children with biliary atresia. Of these, there have been about 19 operations with very limited success, the longest survivor being about 4 weeks. Unless a better anatomical situation for the auxiliary liver is discovered, it is unlikely that there will remain much enthusiasm for auxiliary livers even in children with biliary atresia, for whom it is theoretically so appealing.

Complications from liver transplantation (other than rejection) arrange themselves into three categories: infection, bleeding, and thrombosis (or clotting). The infectious complications are more numerous and more troublesome than in kidney transplantation because large areas of infection can occur within the substance of the liver itself.

In kidney grafting the formation of abscesses within the kidney itself is quite rare even though infection around the kidney is a commonplace. The bleeding-clotting dualism of hepatic transplantation presents its most serious enigma: the poorly functioning liver fails to make clotting proteins and severe hemorrhage results. An excess of liver tissue (or healthy liver tissue stimulated by the act of transplantation) appears to make clotting factors in excess, producing a state in which clots are too readily formed. These obstruct the blood vessels or else they form in other veins and pass to the lungs, there to cause severe or fatal difficulty, as pulmonary embolism.

These complications and the low survival rate, especially notable in hepatoma, combine to make liver transplantation a clinical rarity, but it is an operation sorely needed and a project that should not be abandoned either by the scientists working in the field or by the agencies that support research.

For the patient with his primary hepatoma diffused throughout the liver (with no metastases), or with late-stage cirrhosis (with no alcoholism), or a 3-year-old child fated to death from biliary atresia (with no other disease) there is only a liver transplant to offer him.

About two thirds of the liver transplantations thus far performed would be regarded as inadvisable at present, from the point of view of tumor growth. Histocompatibility and even blood compatibility was often short of ideal. In addition, the crossmatch must display the absence of preformed antibodies. Even with these qualifications, liver transplantation is never going to become a commonplace. For those physicians and surgeons involved in transplantation science, the liver remains the ultimate challenge in transplant surgery; for those patients with lethal disease, primary in the liver and which has destroyed their liver tissue, it is truly their only hope.

13

THE HEART

Light with Heat—A Flash in the Pan?

All treasure is surrounded by dragons.

—Old Chinese Proverb

Possible . . . but

Unlike transplantation of other organs, progressing cautiously after a slow laboratory launch, cardiac transplantation leaped into action suddenly, quickly getting off the ground, and basing its meteoric rise on remarkably brief laboratory study. Cardiac transplantation in the laboratory began by posing the question, "Is it possible?" After its first two years in the hospital and 150 cases with but a handful of survivors, it now posits the answer with another question, "Yes, but when is it advisable?"

More than any previous event, cardiac transplantation brought transplantation science to the attention of the widest possible public. Even now, almost twenty years after the beginning of kidney grafting in man, there are many people who believe that cardiac transplants constitute the entire field. By dint of this publicity, cardiac transplantation contributed immensely to the general acceptance of a redefinition of death in terms of the brain and the use of cadaver donors with good visceral function. By sheer coincidence the develop-

255

ment of histocompatibility matching corresponded exactly with the first years of heart transplantation. After its sudden launch, cardiac transplantation has slowed down, stranded by the search for suitably matched donor-recipient pairs. This has grounded the effort for repairs —but in the end may be responsible for whatever success is achieved.

To the transplant scientist, cardiac transplantation offers nothing new. He is not surprised by its many failures, and is unmoved by its occasional remarkable success. To the biologist working in other fields, skeptical, at best, of surgical doings or clinical medicine in its more rampant forms, cardiac transplantation is just another sorry example of the misapplication of human knowledge and the misappropriation of public funds. It is only to the surviving patients and their families, and to the public who had never thought anything about transplantation before, that cardiac transplantation seems to be some sort of a brand-new medical miracle. Despite this attitude of the blasé biologist, the actual sight and sound of a patient carrying a successful heart transplanted from a dead body was a moment of excitement and elation even to the most skeptical and sophisticated. At the Transplant Society Meetings in New York in the autumn of 1968, there were some transplant patients brought from Texas by Dr. Cooley. Several immunologists were there who had long worked in the field of transplant immunology, immunogenetics, and histocompatibility. Men who had read of heart transplants, but who might never have been in an operating room or seen any transplant patients, went to see and talk with these patients, shake them by the hand, see them walk and function as normal human beings. Despite their attitude, almost of boredom, toward this "crass clinical experimentation" as viewed from afar, they could not help but feel excitement at meeting these patients. By the same token, though heart transplantation can be faulted on many scores, it is easy to demonstrate that as a transplantable organ the heart has much to recommend it over the liver. There are thousands or even millions of patients in need. Success, however rare or short-lived, once achieved is very real. It is a field of human endeavor richly deserving close scientific attention and enthusiastic further work.

ANCIENT HISTORY

In 1960, when Dr. Lower and Dr. Shumway of Stanford University reported some of their first work in heart transplantation in the dog, the reaction of many serious workers in the transplant field was one of querulous boredom. Why perform such elaborate, difficult, and expensive experiments merely to look at the rejection of an overgrown blood vessel? Clinical application was dimly perceived, if at all, because the matter of a donor was not grasped nor its implications for a redefinition of death understood. There was some minor scientific interest in the matter because the heart is in fact nothing but a large bundle of muscle such as would be found in an enlarged blood vessel, with few other kinds of tissue present. Its rejection might be expected to be different from that of a cellular tissue, such as the kidney or liver, or a predominantly extracellular tissue, such as the skin.

Some important nerve tissue in the heart integrates the heartbeat, and by organizing its muscular activity into a series of single strong beats instead of a disorganized cacophony of competing minor contractions, impels the blood around the circulation. The heart is lined with a glistening sheet of cells, that same vascular endothelium that appears to be the first site of antigen-antibody transaction in kidney transplantation. In the heart there are no epithelial cells concerned with protein synthesis or enzymatic conversions of foodstuffs as seen in the kidney or the liver. For these various reasons, the heart did present some scientific interest as a purely muscular set of antigens, wholly aside from any potential clinical application.

A further question of scientific interest, not clearly perceived at first, yet adequate to justify an extensive effort in experimental cardiac transplantation, was that of indices of rejection. Some early reports from Dr. Shumway's laboratory raised this question, showed its importance, and indicated a unique feature of the grafted heart that should interest any transplanter: it was possible to judge the degree of rejection on a beat-to-beat basis.

Early reports showed that the electrocardiograph itself (which presents electrical patterns for each heartbeat) would show characteristic changes during rejection of the heart. The electrical potentials generated by the contractile elements of the heart are very small, measured in millivolts, and they generate the flow of a small electric current which can be measured elsewhere in the body as the electrocardiogram. If the cardiac muscle cells are changed in their surface properties (as well might be the case in rejection), then their ability to generate this sort of an electrical gradient should change. Dr. Shumway's work suggested this was the case. Doctors had been struggling over laborious chemical measurements to discern kidney rejection, yet the heart presented the most elegant and frequent index of rejection: an electrical pattern traced with each heartbeat.

New ideas are a rarity, and experimental cardiac transplantation was no exception. Even this was not new in 1961. In 1933, at the Research Laboratories of the Mayo Clinic, Dr. Mann, working with Dr. Priestley, reported on transplantation of the intact mammalian heart. Their interest was in cardiac function when all nervous connections were severed, rather than its effectiveness as an unaided pump or as a problem of graft acceptance. They were studying short-term transplantation of only a few hours, placing the new heart in a new site, as an extra heart in the neck, not essential to survival. Nonetheless, in the course of their work they discerned many aspects of cardiac transplantation that would acquire prominence thirty-five years later.

In 1953, Dr. Luisada and his colleagues in Chicago reported on heart grafts in experimental animals, the same year that Dr. Sinitsin in Russia reported on heart transplantation. Both of these research teams considered the heart as an allograft, and both of them were concerned with its functional capacity, although neither described the changes in electrical voltage or in the muscle itself as a result of rejection. Finally, in 1959 and 1960, Dr. Shumway, Dr. Lower, and their colleagues at Stanford University School of Medicine carried out their classical experiment of cardiac transplantation.

Few people in 1960 visualized the clinical possibility of heart transplantation, for lack of a concept of death that included a viable beating heart as part of the anatomy of a cadaver.

The early animal cardiac transplants demonstrated a number of important points which had been relevant to kidney transplantation twelve years earlier. These were, first, that the heart could be removed from one animal and placed in another with a neat arrangement of

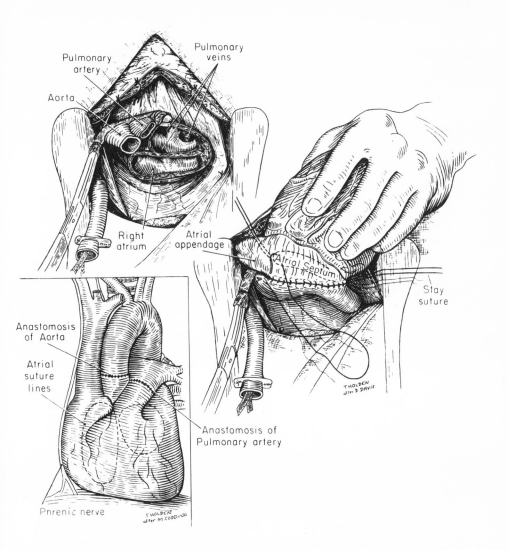

Pulmonary
veins

Pulmonary
artery

Aorta

Right
atrium

Atrial
appendage

Atrial Septum

Stay
suture

T HOLDEN
after D DAVIS

Anastomosis
of Aorta

Atrial
suture
lines

Anastomosis of
Pulmonary artery

Pnrenic nerve

T HOLDEN
after M CODDING

FIGURE 27. Sites and sutures: cardiac allograft. Above and to the left is shown the normal site of the heart with the heart removed. Like the view of a fully removed cancer-ridden liver (Figure 26), this was a sight never seen before in the living, prior to the advent of transplantation.

To the right is shown the new heart being sutured in place, and below to the left is the completed operation, showing the four anastomotic suture lines joining the two atria, and then the two great vessels, aorta and pulmonary artery. The exact position of the suture line of the right atrium, with reference to the vena cava, depends upon the amount of atrium left behind in the operation.

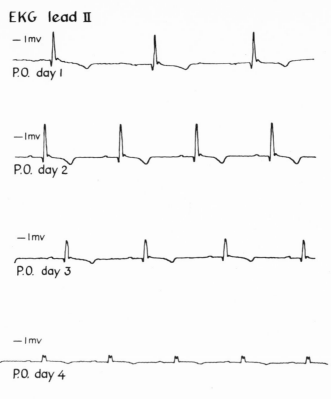

EKG lead II

FIGURE 28. Electrocardiograms in cardiac transplantation. Here are shown the electrocardiographic changes of fatal rejection in the dog after heart transplantation. The height of the electrocardiographic spike (QRS complex) that accompanies each beat of the heart decreases progressively to a very low value on the fourth day, at which time the animal dies. This chart shows unmodified rejection in the laboratory. The object of immunosuppression in cardiac transplantation is to prevent these fatal changes. This tracing shows three or four beats of the heart and therefore occupies about two seconds for each tracing shown.

sutures that presented few local or technical problems. This was in very marked contrast to the liver and was rather similar to the surgical simplicity of kidney transplantation.

Second, they demonstrated that the extracorporeal support methods employed daily for open-heart operations (the pump oxygenator) could be applied directly, and with no essential modifications, to cardiac transplantation, providing the patient with a normal blood

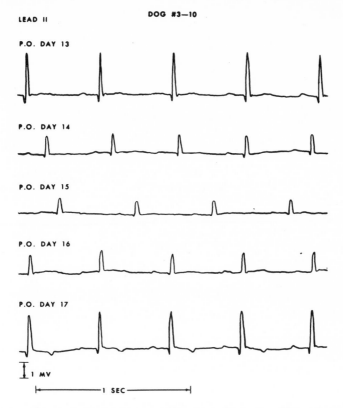

LEAD II   DOG #3—10

P.O. DAY 13

P.O. DAY 14

P.O. DAY 15

P.O. DAY 16

P.O. DAY 17

1 MV

|← 1 SEC →|

FIGURE 29. Electrocardiograms in cardiac transplantation. Here, in contrast to Figure 28, is shown the electrocardiographic tracings from a dog with a heart transplant treated with immunosuppression. Above, starting on the thirteenth postoperative day, there is a progressive lowering in the height of the QRS spike voltage. Starting on the fifteenth day, the animal's treatment was changed by the addition of cortisone and local irradiation treatment of the transplanted heart. The voltage height of the spike of each heartbeat thereafter increases as evidence that the rejection process was reversed. The spike voltage finally returns to normal by the seventeenth day. Again, as in Figure 28, each tracing occupies about two seconds.

flow to brain and vital organs during the period of an hour or more when he is without any heart.

Third, they demonstrated that when the pump oxygenator was turned off and the major vessels opened to blood flow again, the heart in its new host could accept this blood flow and at the very first beat propel it through the great blood vessels to the capillaries of the body with full force and with a normal stroke volume.

CARDIAC TRANSPLANT L.R. ECG LEAD III

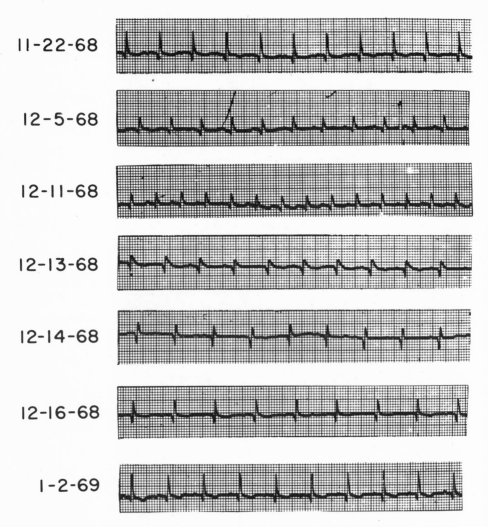

FIGURE 30. The electrocardiogram in cardiac transplantation. Here are shown the tracings over the course of about six weeks in patient L.R., following cardiac transplantation. This patient, operated upon by Dr. Lower and Dr. Hume in Richmond, Virginia, shows progressive lowering of his QRS spike voltage, reaching its lowest point on December 11,·1968. Starting at that time, additional immunosuppression was given, including cortisone and local irradiation, and by January 2, 1969, the spike voltages had returned toward normal and the rejection process had been reversed.

Fourth, the work of Shumway demonstrated that the completely denervated heart—all the connections between its own nerves and the host having been cut when it was removed—will function normally. It will ultimately pick up electrical connections with the nerves of the new host so that the electrical integration of the beat is normal and will finally display all the normal modifications or "overdrive" that are due to changes in the demands of the host. Denervation of the transplanted heart had been a source of concern. The gradual resumption of normal neurologic control of the heartbeat is one of the features of the transplanted heart that requires many months for its completion.

Lastly, the work at Palo Alto indicated that the electrical tracing from the heart would permit an accurate index of rejection. Of all the methods for measuring cardiac rejection developed since that time, none has proven as effective as the altered ECG voltage.

Modern History

By late 1966, only a few laboratories were working in cardiac transplantation. Dr. Lower had gone to Richmond to work with Dr. Hume where he continued his studies on the heart. There was some work being done under Dr. Lillehei and Dr. Varco at Minneapolis. Another such laboratory, abroad, was that in Cape Town where Dr. Christiaan Barnard had been experimenting with cardiac transplantation, but had published very little due to his load of clinical cardiac surgery. In November 1967, he was presented with a patient and a possible donor that led to his initial clinical application of cardiac transplantation. It occurred at least a year before it was expected. The most important impact of this operation was not in transplant science itself, but rather in worldwide attention to a medical event. The publicity was unequaled in two decades of biomedical science, rivaling news devoted to international politics, war, and the exploration of space, and bringing the field of transplantation into every home that had a television set, radio, or a newspaper.

Although Dr. Barnard's first patient did not fare well, and soon died, he was shortly thereafter presented with a second patient, a dentist, named Philip Blaiberg. A donor became available and on December 6, 1967, Dr. Blaiberg was operated on. He demonstrated beyond a doubt that it was possible to achieve long-term survival after cardiac transplantation. Death, when it came, was not due to acute rejection changes in the muscle but instead to a change in the blood vessels closely resembling chronic coronary heart disease.

Dr. Barnard's work was quickly assumed in other centers, leading to a short-lived and self-limited epidemic of heart transplantation in 1968, tapering off in 1969. In this country, Dr. Cooley, of Dr. De-Bakey's Department at Baylor University in Houston, became the most ardent advocate of the operation. Dr. Shumway, best-equipped to undertake the operation as based on a long experience in the laboratory, was another who began clinical work a little sooner than he might have otherwise. Dr. Barnard had broken the ice in moving from the laboratory to the hospital.

Dr. Lillehei in New York, Mr. Ross at the National Heart Hospital in London, surgeons in Paris, Montreal, Sydney, adopted the procedure, looking to its clinical application in many cases before they had done any extensive or inquisitive laboratory work in the dog. Most of these men were expert cardiac surgeons. But only a few of them—Dr. Shumway, Dr. Lower, and their colleagues—had ever done extensive work in the field of transplantation, transplant immunology, histocompatibility phenomena, immunogenetics, and the control of rejection.

On December 6, 1968, exactly one year after the first heart transplant, the 100th heart transplantation operation was performed. More than half of the transplants were done in the United States (53), 14 were done in Canada, and 9 in France. No more than 3 had been done in any one of the other 14 countries involved, including South Africa. Of these first 100 patients, 43 were still surviving at the time that the 100th was done. Two were surviving at 6 months, and 24 at 3 months. Dr. Blaiberg, then at 11 months, was the longest survivor.

A year later, in December 1969, over 150 transplants had been done, including 3 that were second transplants in the same recipient. Of these, 30 were still surviving, giving an overall mortality of 80 percent. By January 1970, the longest surviving patient was a 43-year old man operated upon by Dr. Lower in Virginia on August 24, 1968. He was closely followed by 6 survivors of almost the same duration under the care of Dr. Shumway in Stanford, Dr. DeBakey in Houston, Dr. Bahnson at Pittsburgh, Dr. Zerbini in Sao Paulo, Brazil, Dr. Effler at the Cleveland Clinic, and Dr. Barnard at the Groote Schur Hospital in Cape Town (where his 52-year-old man, transplanted on September 8, 1968, was still surviving). Dr. Blaiberg died 19 months after the operation.

By October 1970, 167 heart transplants had been carried out. There were 23 survivors, the longest (Mr. L. R. of Richmond, Virginia; Fig. 36A) was 26 months at that time.

The peak of enthusiasm for cardiac grafting was between June and November of 1968 when 78 patients were transplanted, and 38 percent of these survived for 3 months or more. Twenty-six operations were done in the single month of November 1968.

Enthusiasm for the operation began to wane by mid-1969 for reasons of histocompatibility typing and a realistic look at results. Between December 1968 and May 1969, only 35 patients were operated on, or less than half the number in the preceding 6 months. Of these, 23 percent achieved survival of 3 months or more.

Just as the number of transplants increased in 1968, so did the number of teams doing the operation—28 in the United States and Canada by the close of 1968. Dr. Crane and Dr. Matthews point out in their review that 10 of the 28 surgical teams were led by graduates of the surgical programs at Johns Hopkins or the University of Minnesota—two hospitals that concentrated on cardiac surgery (rather than transplant science) in the years 1958–1968. Seventeen of the 28 teams doing cardiac transplantations had performed only one such operation. Only 5 had performed more than 5 operations, but there was no apparent tendency to achieve better survival among those teams carrying out more operations, probably because none was using uniquely different techniques or immunosuppressive agents.

No studies have indicated that the heart is any less antigenic than the kidney. As to histocompatibility, there has been no overall correlation of tissue matching with survival, as in the case of kidney with cadaver donors. All of Dr. Shumway's donor-recipient pairs showed negative direct crossmatches. Workers in the field agree that the donor and recipient should have about the same body weight so as to match pump-output capability to bodily needs. In one of the donors available to Dr. Cooley's team, it was possible to measure the cardiac output prior to removing the heart. It was 6.9 liters per minute. The recipient, dying of heart failure, had at that time an output of 2.4 liters per minute, not enough to support life for any length of time. When the heart was removed from the donor and placed in the recipient, it immediately displayed excellent function and within a few minutes demonstrated an output of 6.0 liters per minute.

THE OPERATION

The operation for heart transplantation in man is similar to that evolved in the dog. The history of this operation as an anatomical dissection of the heart dates back to the invention of the extracorporeal pump oxygenator and to the other developments in cardiac surgery which have occurred in the forty years since its inception in the first removal of the diseased pericardium about 1932. The extracorporeal pump oxygenator—the artificial heart-lung machine—in turn traces its development back to the perfection of anticoagulants such as heparin and permeable membranes such as cellophane. In this way the heart-lung apparatus has some of the same historical origins as the artificial kidney.

Once the heart had been invaded for the removal of missile fragments in World War II, and then for repair of heart valves about 1948, the additional step of laying the heart open to fix its interior required some way of keeping the patient alive. The artificial heart-lung machine, or extracorporeal pump oxygenator, satisfies this need for the period of two to six hours required for cardiac surgery. The removal and replacement of the heart is an extension of these techniques.

As a first step the venous blood returning to the heart is siphoned off through two large plastic tubes placed in the right side of the heart. This blood is then returned to the aorta after having been oxygenated. This is done by mixing the blood with oxygen-enriched gas. The blood is then impelled by a forceful pump that perfuses all the arteries and capillaries of the body. The establishment of this circuit takes only fifteen or twenty minutes when everything goes smoothly, and up to an hour if the dissection is difficult.

Having established pumping and oxygenation outside the body, the heart is removed, as shown in Figure 27, dividing the back of the heart across the large vessels and the thin atrial chambers. A similar operation is carried out in the cardiac donor. The donor heart is then sutured in place where the patient's own heart used to be. In most of the operations little time has been lost for perfusion or cooling, and the heart has been transferred while warm and functioning.

In Chapter 12 the complex series of blood vessel anastomoses required for liver transplantation were described. A liver transplantation requires four blood vessel anastomoses, one of them rather small and difficult, and the joining together of the gallbladder with the intestinal tract to make a place for the bile to drain. By contrast, heart transplantation is relatively simple. Only two long suture lines are involved to join together the back walls of the right and left atria or auricles.* Once this is done, the rest of the heart lies in its normal position, and when the patient is taken off the pump oxygenator this new heart will take on its usual work.

The normal pacemaker for the heart is a little bundle of nerves in the wall of the auricle that sends impulses to the rest of the heart after receiving them from the body sensors via the vagus and sympathetic nerves. The transplanted heart has been totally denervated. It has no direct nerve connections with the body of the new host in which it finds itself. Nerves grow quite slowly and one would expect it to take many weeks or months before the connections have grown back together again. Can the heart which has had all its nerves divided function properly and respond to the needs of the patients?

At first, the transplanted heart is completely automatic. It does not have a quick response to the changing needs of the body. In the electrocardiogram you can see the pacemaker of the host firing off, but there is no regular response in the newly transplanted heart which carries on with its automatic function at a fixed rate, and responds only slowly to a need for more output by the patient. When it does so, it is responding to the hormones of the patient rather than to the nerves themselves.

In the dog, where the experimental situation is perfect for making

---

* *Auricle,* the soft low-pressure part of the heart which first receives blood from the body and lungs. The *ventricles* are the two heavy muscle chambers that put the high pressure into blood circulating to the lungs and the body. One might think of the auricles as the two thin-walled reservoirs that receive the blood and let it flow on into the thick-walled heavy pumping ventricles that really do the work.

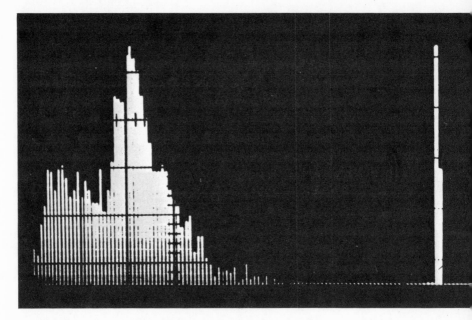

Figure 31. Automaticity of the transplanted heart. These computerized histograms show the distribution of heart rates in a normal heart (to the left) as compared with a transplanted heart (to the right).

The horizontal axis indicates the interval (frequency) between beats and the height of the vertical lines indicates the relative number of beats at each frequency. It is evident that in the normal heart, with a broad tracing, there is a wide variation in the heart rate from minute to minute as the animal comes under a variety of different influences.

By contrast, the freshly transplanted heart, as shown on the right, is almost completely automatic and shows no variation in rate whatsoever.

such an observation, one can demonstrate that over a period of weeks or months the nerves in the auricle of the heart do indeed finally grow back to communicate with the ventricles. They give the heart a beat fully responsive to the needs of its new host. In patients who have had heart transplantations, such regrowth of nerve tissue occurs very slowly. In any event, the newly transplanted heart responds well enough to the hormones if not the nerves of its new owner so that people who have received heart transplants can do their ordinary work, climb stairs, or even run or exert themselves with a heart that delivers most of the required work.

Late Coronary Artery Disease
in Transplanted Hearts;
Some Clinical Results

In the case of any transplanted organ the nature of the rejection process has taught us something about human disease itself. The arteritis or glomerular inflammation in chronic kidney rejection confirms the suggestion that glomerulonephritis might be an autoimmune disease in the first place. The patient seems to be trying to reject his own kidneys, having become sensitized, by some prior disease, to the proteins in the walls of the kidney's blood vessels.

In the case of the liver, the picture of liver rejection somewhat resembles a rare disease called "cholangiolytic hepatitis" and suggests that that particular disease might be somewhat autoimmune in character.

It therefore comes as a revelation to find that disease of the coronary arteries of the sort ordinarily seen in aging is the most prominent late manifestation of chronic rejection of the transplanted human heart. Once the heart has been in place long enough, the allografted organ develops severe disease of the coronary arteries. This was first demonstrated at Stanford University by Dr. Shumway and Dr. Lower when they showed in animals with long-lasting allografted hearts, maintained on immunosuppressive drugs, that there was a change in the small coronary arteries which became increasingly evident after several months. This appeared to be a sign of chronic rejection, resembling the delayed arteritis and glomerulitis seen in some kidney transplants.

If the heart of a young person, with glistening, smooth, widely open arteries, can be changed to the senile heart of an old man in only one year's residence in a hostile host, nature must be telling us something about the aging process itself. In that one year, the youthful arteries have changed to ones that are hardened and closed to little calcified pores, much as they might be in a very elderly person. Is aging a form of self-rejection that takes place over the years, attacking the inner lining of blood vessels—especially those around the heart?

Of more immediate importance to heart transplantation is the fact

URINE VOLUME AFTER SALINE LOAD

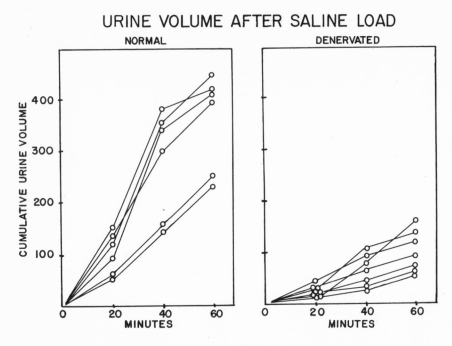

FIGURE 32. Inflexibility of the transplanted heart. This experiment demonstrates the amount of urine secreted after a "load" of saline solution. To the left is shown the fact that the normal animal with a normal heart can put out a large volume of urine when his body water is increased by the saline load. To the right (shown as "denervated") are the findings after a heart transplant. Here the heart is unable to respond to the water load, and there is little if any additional urinary output in response to the same challenge. This demonstrates why, both in heart disease and with heart transplantation, it is so necessary to watch carefully over the amount of salt and water taken in by the patient. Fortunately, it is possible to maintain the living conditions of the patient with a transplanted heart under such close scrutiny that these narrow limits do not bother the patient. Later on, when the heart nerves regrow, these changes revert to normal.

that this late chronic rejection, showing itself as arterial disease, is not easy to reverse (again, a little like aging itself). Dr. Lower has been interested in the use of local x-ray treatment to the heart as a means of reducing the local effects of rejection. This might reduce the extent of coronary artery disease. Dr. Grondin of the Montreal Heart Institute believes that repeated doses of cortisone might be acceptable as a way to reduce coronary disease in transplanted hearts. Against this view is the fact that any patient maintained on high doses of cortisone is quite miserable and develops many other effects of steroid overdosage, including loss of body muscle, loss of bone strength, a red puffy face, and susceptibility to infection.

The most important findings about coronary artery disease in heart transplantation include those discovered in the later course of Dr. Blaiberg. At the time he died (593 days after the transplant) he was by far the longest survivor.

Some details of his story are appropriate here, and the first question is the matter of histocompatibility matching. The donor who provided the heart for Dr. Blaiberg upon subsequent tissue matching, showed the presence of only two unshared antigens. This would place his tissue match as better than average, boding well for a good if not perfect result. Nonetheless, on the 20th day after the transplantation, there was a decrease in the voltage of the electrocardiogram and every evidence of tissue rejection. Dr. Blaiberg was treated with increased dosages of adrenal steroids, and he was discharged home on the 75th day. On the 135th day after the transplant, he again showed evidence of a mild rejection crisis with lowered electrocardiographic voltages. But at this time, on long-term azathioprine therapy, he showed some evidence of liver failure and jaundice; he developed septicemia due to infection with a microorganism known as *Listeria*. These were treated with reasonable success, and the patient recovered sufficiently to go home again.

He did well for this period, 4 to 14 months after the operation. His cardiac output could rise from 5.0 liters per minute to 8.1 liters on exercise, a good exercise response from his heart though not as good as some others who after transplantation have shown rises as high as 15 liters per minute on exercise. To fend off chronic rejection, Dr. Blaiberg was treated with intermittent high doses of cortisone once a week. Shortly before his death he began to show chronic congestive heart failure. His heart failed to move enough blood, yet there was no evidence of a renewed rejection crisis or any focal damage to the heart muscle. It was pure "pump failure" of the type seen in coronary artery disease.

During much of his course, the serum cholesterol value in Dr. Blaiberg was over 300 mg percent, and while this was only a mild elevation, Dr. Barnard regarded it as an unfavorable factor.

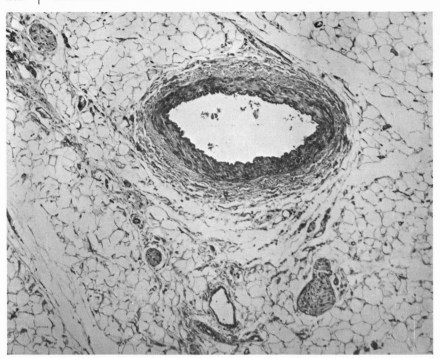

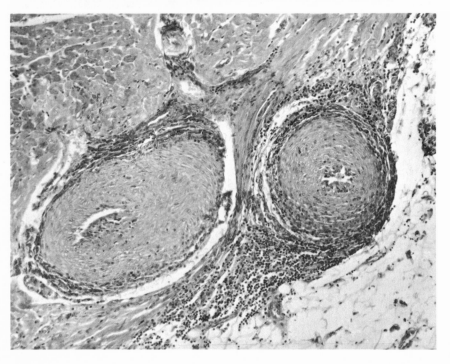

FIGURE 33. Coronary blood vessels in heart transplantation. Here, for purposes of comparison, is shown the cross section of the normal coronary artery of a dog. The artery has been cut across and is seen as a hollow structure, surrounded by the normal fat of the outer lining of the heart. The blood flows through the hollow lumen. The picture shows the heavy lining layers which help the artery to pulsate in response to the blood flow. This is a normal, open coronary artery.

FIGURE 34. Coronary blood vessels in heart transplantation. Here, in contrast to Figure 33, are shown two similar small coronary blood vessels in the heart of a dog, several weeks after transplantation, and demonstrating the filling up of the inside of the artery by the proliferating tissue that is the sign of chronic rejection. Both of these round structures should be hollow to make an opening for blood flow, as in Figure 33. Instead, they are almost obliterated. The one on the left has only a tiny star-shaped opening and the one on the right only a tiny crescentic opening. The many small black dots in the middle of the photograph are lymphocytes which have been involved in this rejection process. It is clear that rejection has reduced the caliber of the coronary arteries to the point where they cannot carry enough blood to give the heart muscle a normal blood supply. These are changes of chronic rejection rather than the acute rejection with electrocardiographic alteration as shown in Figures 28, 29, and 30.

FIGURE 35. Coronary blood vessels in heart transplantation. In this figure are shown the effects of chronic rejection of the heart in man. This is a cross section of a coronary artery illustrating the changes in a case operated on by Dr. Cooley. The particular patient from whom this study was made died 204 days after the graft and was a C-match histocompatibility. This artery looks surprisingly like that shown for the dog with chronic rejection in Figure 34. The round artery is shown filled up with expanded lining layers, hypertrophied as a result of chronic rejection. Only a small slitlike opening in the center of the artery (in a sort of "H" shape) remains for blood flow. A heart with this sort of rejection is struggling along with inadequate blood supply. The patient would have all the symptoms of coronary heart disease as often seen in elderly people, with some breathlessness on exertion and inability of the heart to put out more blood in response to work loads.

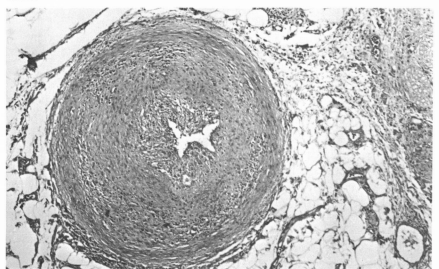

After 19 months, Dr. Blaiberg died of heart failure due to smoldering coronary artery insufficiency traceable in turn to chronic rejection. The autopsy did not show any of the ordinary changes in the heart muscle associated with acute rejection of the heart. Instead, there was marked narrowing and hardening of the coronary arteries, much more so than in the aorta and femoral arteries, the large arteries of the abdomen and the leg. Microscopic pictures of the small arteries in Dr. Blaiberg's case bore a striking resemblance to those demonstrated in long-surviving dogs by Dr. Lower (Fig. 34). The only difference was that there were cholesterol deposits in the arteries of the human patient. This is a feature so characteristically present in the aging patient with arterial disease, especially if he has some tendency to elevated cholesterol in the blood. It is very rare in the dog. Among the other remarkable findings in the postmortem examination of Dr. Blaiberg was the intense arteriosclerotic change in the portion of the transplanted aorta nearest the heart, contrasting markedly with the patient's own aorta just beyond the suture line. This suggested again that chronic rejection of blood vessel structures (such as the aorta and the heart) can take the form of a marked alteration in the smooth, glistening inner lining, with hardening (thickening) and deposits of cholesterol. When this occurs in a major artery such as the aorta, it is not particularly dangerous over the short term, but in tiny arteries such as the coronary arteries these changes produce obstruction. The final result is coronary artery insufficiency with inadequate nourishment to the pumping muscle of the heart, and a death from repeated heart attacks and "pump failure."

Other results of heart transplantation in its first two years demonstrate consistency on two scores: first, that with proficiency and expertise in the operation, early survivorship is regularly obtained, and second, that starting at about a month, there is a rapid decline in survival, usually due to rejection, with coronary disease increasingly prominent as time passes.

As an example, the experience of Dr. Cooley in Texas with his first 20 patients (the first being that patient operated upon in May 1968) showed that only 3 patients lived more than 6 months, only 2 lived more than 8 months. The first patient died of rejection at 7½ months. When these findings were reviewed in the fall of 1969, there was one long-range survivor alive at 11 months, one at 4 months, and one at 2 months.

In one instance, an artificial (mechanical) heart was implanted as a preliminary step. This seemed to have the principal effect of forcing the issue of donor procurement because the outlook for life on the pump alone was absolutely hopeless beyond 3 to 4 days. In the light of this experience, and in the present state of our knowledge about mechanical blood pumps, it does not seem justified to use an artificial heart placed in the chest as a preliminary to cardiac transplantation. Because of imperfections at the biomechanical interface where the blood meets the lining of the pump, there is destruction of blood cells and proteins. There is no hope of survival of the patient beyond a few days. Such an installation therefore presupposes a later transplant. Donors are hard to find, and the patient is apt to be a better subject for transplantation if he has not already had an open-chest operation with its attendant possibilities of infection or pneumonia. Better to await a satisfactory donor, even with all the hazards of waiting, than to decrease the chance of transplant success by subjecting the patient to an extra operation.*

In the face of imminent death and with the prospects for a donor within the next few days, the intermittent use of an extracorporeal pump (i.e., one not requiring a large operation in the chest) to assist rather than replace the heart is a more practical step. Even here the injury to red blood cells is still considerable and the length of permis-

---

* Desperate measures like the interim substitution of a machine heart, or the implantation of a sheep's heart in man, call up for consideration a special ethical question: does the presence of a dying patient justify the doctor's taking *any* conceivable step regardless of its degree of hopelessness? The answer to this question must be negative. Because a man has lost part of his brain, for example, it is unjustified to stitch someone else's brain in place; similarly for the intestinal tract or the spinal cord. There simply is no evidence to suggest that it would be helpful. It raises false hopes for the patient and his family, it calls into discredit all of biomedical science, and it gives the impression that physicians and surgeons are adventurers rather than circumspect persons seeking to help the suffering and dying by the use of hopeful measures. The dying person becomes the object of wildly speculative experiment when he is hopeless and helpless rather than the recipient of discriminating measures carried out in his behalf (Chapter 15). It is only by work in the laboratory and cautious trial in the living animal that "hopeless desperate measures" can become ones that carry with them some promise of reasonable assistance to the patient. The interim substitution of a mechanical heart in the chest, in the location of the normal heart, had not reached this stage for the simple reason that animal survival had never been attained.

sible assist-time is short. There is no device for the heart, such as the artificial kidney, that can reliably serve the patient for months or years.

The series of Dr. Grondin of Montreal included 9 heart transplants carried out after May 1969. Six months later, 7 of these patients were ambulatory, and there had been only one death within 30 days of operation. The excellent functional state of these patients was indicated by the fact that one of them required and withstood an emergency operation for aortic aneurysm* repair during the early postoperative period. In Dr. Grondin's cases the patients who had a good histocompatibility match did seem to get along somewhat better than those with less satisfactory tissue antigen matching. His patients showed late coronary artery disease if they lived long enough to develop this change. Dr. Grondin analyzed the first year's course of 57 patients from various centers as to the timing of rejection crises. He found 54 rejection crises in these 57 patients. In 22 of these rejections the changes were fatal. Most occurred within the first 100 days with a peak between the fifth and the fifteenth day. Since this is the normal time for organ rejection it suggests that immunosuppressive drugs were either ineffective or being used ineffectively. He corroborated the work of Dr. Shumway and Dr. Lower in showing that decreased voltage of the electrocardiogram was by far the earliest and most reliable index of heart rejection. This change appears several days before others of a biochemical or physiologic nature, indicating that the heart is in trouble.

Total survival data are available up to March 1970, through the new Transplant Registry conducted in a collaborative enterprise between the American College of Surgeons and the National Institutes of Health, which operates to cover all organ transplantations and replaces the Kidney Transplant Registry originally started in Boston by Dr. Murray and Dr. Barnes. This Registry reports that there were 24 patients then living after cardiac transplantation, 14 of whom were alive more than a year after the operation, out of 121 done more than a year previously. By August 1971, 175 heart transplants had been done; there were 27 still living.

---

* *Aortic aneurysm,* a dilated weakened area in the wall of the large blood vessel, the aorta, which carries blood under high pressure from the heart to the rest of the body.

Additional information on the race of donors and recipients was also provided when available, answering any lingering questions about racism in the selection of either group. It was shown that the donor was a white person in 106 cases, black in 7, Oriental in 1, Indian or Polynesian in 3, and a Bantu African Negro in 1. The recipients have been white in 107 instances, black in 9, and other races in 1. These data corroborate the earlier figures suggesting that there was no adverse racial selection either in donors or in recipients. Most of the donors (86 percent) were male with a mean age of 29; 59 had sustained a cerebral injury as the cause of death (pointing up the importance of the criterion of gross anatomical damage rather than irreversible coma), and 37 had suffered spontaneous hemorrhages in the brain. In 93 of these instances, a flat electroencephalogram had been helpful in deciding that death had occurred.

This question of the racial and economic status of donors and recipients has been raised by several students of medical sociology. In part because of the origin of this operation in South Africa, and in part because of a rumor that most of the cadaver donors used in the South were Negroes, a sociologic study of the recipients was also carried out by Dr. Crane and Dr. Matthews which demonstrated that the lower socioeconomic classes were under-represented amongst recipients. In their sample, Negroes constituted 15 percent of the recipients, a figure to be compared with the approximately 12 percent prevalence of Negroes in the United States population; 13 percent of the donors were Negroes, and the upper middle class and upper classes constituted 35 percent of the donors. On such a basis, one would have difficulty supporting a contention of adverse social selection either of donors—with its attendant redefinition of death—or of recipients where the accusation of experimental surgery might always be leveled at the surgeon.

Much as was the case in kidney transplantation from cadaver donors, the histocompatibility data were inconclusive. Dr. Terasaki states that as he analyzed the first 48 heart transplants in whom histocompatibility data were available and used survival for 8 months as an index of success, he found that this occurred in 70 percent of those patients who had a B match, and in only 30 percent of those who had a C match or D match. As time went on, however, and more cases were added to this list, there was no statistical difference between those with matches of the B match, C match, or D match categories. As indicated in the discussion of this subject in Chapter 11, there are many possible interpretations of this failure to make good correlation between the nature of the antigen matching from cadaver donors and the clinical outcome of transplantation of any organ. As applied to the heart these are as follows:

1. Factors other than rejection are responsible for some of the deaths, a fact that skews the statistical analysis of histocompatibility data.
2. The tissues themselves contain antigens not found on the leukocytes which are used for the ordinary tissue typing procedure.
3. There may be important antigens in the heart which are not yet being measured at all.

The same conclusions apply to histocompatibility in heart transplantation as they did to liver transplantation: given a patient who needs the organ, and a viable organ in an excellent state of preservation, the transplant should not be done if the preliminary crossmatch is unfavorable, showing the presence of preformed antibodies. If the crossmatch is favorable, a C match or better is a basic requirement. If transplantation is done with a D match, the patient, his family, and all physicians should realize its lesser likelihood of survival. Nonetheless, stray long-term survivors of the transplantations of kidney, liver, and heart with a D match indicate that we cannot use it as a categorical denial of the operation when all other factors are favorable.

While these results of heart transplantation in 1968 and 1969 are very discouraging, the operation was performed in far more patients than in the first two years of kidney transplantation under immunosuppression. Too many and too soon hurt the statistics and wasted effort without indicating the true potential of the operation. The stray long-range survivors continue to suggest the ultimate worth of this procedure. The Richmond patient who at 15 months was on modest doses of immunosuppression, in his regular work, at home, and feeling well discounts the purely statistical evaluation of cardiac transplantation. Early in the days of kidney transplantation, when progress was far more cautious, the stray long-term survivors gave the operation some additional impetus. There are a few other cardiac patients of this type in various countries of the world, each one of whom demonstrates that as transplant science solves some of its current problems, cardiac transplantation will have a place in the treatment of a few patients suffering from any one of the four predominant types of heart disease.

A HEART FOR WHAT?

Which kinds of heart disease could best be treated by removal of the sick pump and insertion of a new one? Such diseases should be those severe enough to have no other effective treatment, occurring in young persons who have arrived at an identifiable "point of no return" in the natural history of their disease.

Heart disease can be categorized into four groups: congenital, valvular, vascular, and muscular—diseases you are born with, diseases of the valves, diseases of the coronary arteries, or diseases of the muscle itself. In each of the four categories certain patients cannot survive without a transplant.

First, *congenital* diseases: Babies born with large defects in the walls between the chambers of the heart, formerly incompatible with life, can have these resutured in their proper alignment, using an open-heart operation of the conventional type. Success is assured only in the hands of those few surgeons particularly talented in the rebuilding of the infant heart. Cardiac transplantation is applicable only to those cases where early repair is impossible and where, if performed in the newborn infant, a perfectly normal heart is available from another newborn in whom other malformations were incompatible with life. Such donors do occur and this is not out of the question. Over the course of years, it is conceivable that the newborn period would be found the best in which to place a new heart. Thus far, none of the cardiac transplantations performed has been in this newborn group with congenital heart disease; 12 have been done for congenital disease at an older age.

Valvular heart disease, usually due to rheumatic fever, has been a common form of heart disease crippling teen-agers and young adults; for many years this has been their commonest cardiac cause of death. The disease is usually of the mitral valve, with narrowing (stenosis) produced by rheumatic fever after streptococcal infection.

The development of surgery of the interior of the heart, about

1948, centered around the surgery of mitral stenosis. The valve consists of two delicate sheets of tissue which close together as the heart beats, preventing the backward flow of blood. These two sheets, cupped together like two hands with closed fingers, resemble the bishop's mitre, giving the valve its name. In rheumatic disease, the mitral valve becomes thickened, immobile, inflexible, and bony hard. Since the turn of the century it had been an attractive possibility that mitral stenosis might be a surgically treatable lesion, using instruments inside the heart. In 1924, Dr. Cutler had attempted mitral operations but without success. Following World War II, and the rapid growth of cardiac operations for missile fragments, the operation was reconsidered, redesigned, and tried anew. In 1948, Dr. Dwight Harken opened up intracardiac surgery by operating successfully on the mitral valve. The principle was firmly established by 1950. By 1955 large series were reported in which mitral stenosis had been corrected by a surgical operation, yet even at that time it was appreciated that some of these valves were so diseased that just opening them wider for a year or two would not provide any lasting cure. Nonetheless, for an extremely ill patient confined to bed, unable to sleep lying down, taking digitalis to the extent of poisoning, and in chronic heart failure, a year or two of complete relief was worthwile even though heart failure later recurred.

Artificial valves were clearly needed, and they, in turn, required the perfection of the pump oxygenator for open-heart surgery. Both became available in 1955, offering a new field of treatment for many critically ill cardiac patients: open-heart surgery for the installation of replacement valves. These new valves were devices that could be placed in a heart when the original valves were beyond repair. Some of these were allografted valves taken from the bodies of other persons. Dr. Barrat-Boyes of Auckland, New Zealand, had been particularly interested in valve transplants, and by 1969 he and his colleagues could report a large series of successfully allografted heart valves, grafts like the cornea that do not require immunosuppression.

This new advance, using pump oxygenator methods and grafted or artificial valves, soon defined a new and more advanced limit of usefulness. There still were patients beyond treatment in whom longstanding valvular disease had produced such deterioration of the heart muscle or of its circulation that placing new valves was far too hazardous. The operation carried a prohibitive mortality because the heart muscle had become so stretched and thinned out that it could not do its work of pumping blood even with new valves.

To the surgeon who has struggled with such difficult cases in patients 30 to 50 years of age, there is nothing more appealing than the vision of total removal of this diseased and worthless heart and its replacement by a fresh, vigorous one. It is so attractive an outlook that it is all to easy to forget the imposing immunologic problems of transplantation! Thus it is that in valvular heart disease, despite all the remarkable advances of 25 years, there still remain patients for whom transplantation would be an ideal solution. Twenty-four of the patients so far treated by a heart transplant have been suffering from valve disease.

The *vascular* diseases of the heart are those involving the arteries which supply the heart muscle itself, the coronary arteries. These are diseases of aging or degeneration: hardening of the arteries or arteriosclerosis. When, because of degeneration of the inner lining of the blood vessels, a clot (thrombosis) occurs, a portion of the heart muscle loses its life-sustaining blood flow. It no longer contracts properly; the muscle dies and is replaced by a scar. The patient goes through a period of pain around the heart, with poor circulation to the rest of his body because of this decrease in the pump function of the heart. This is called coronary thrombosis, coronary occlusion, or myocardial infarct, all three of which are overlapping terms. As far as the patient is concerned, he has had a heart attack. Most people live through their first heart attack. They are prone to have other heart attacks, one of which is ultimately fatal because the clot shuts off blood supply to too much of the heart.

Some patients, even in their early 40's, have had a number of such heart attacks, leaving the heart muscle so flabby and scarred that its beat is ineffective. The patient is limited to a bed-and-chair existence, and must take cardiac support drugs such as digitalis and diuretics; this is the state of heart failure. In cases of repeated heart attacks, heart failure is very difficult to treat because no amount of drugs or chemicals can whip the flabby muscle into a youthful and vigorous heart. As an example, a patient who has had three severe coronary heart attacks, and now is in congestive failure, has an average life expectancy of less than 18 months. Such a patient would be perfect for cardiac transplantation so long as he was not too elderly or a host to degenerative disease too severe to permit normal function of the brain or kidney.

Severe coronary heart disease in young people has been the reason for most of the cardiac transplantations thus far. Coronary heart disease is the most common cardiac cause of death in persons 45 years of age or older. It is much more common in men than in women. It can be severe even in men as young as their middle 30's. It is not difficult to diagnose, but most of the treatments merely enable the patient to live within the restrictions imposed by his disease. None of them—drugs, diets, special ways of life—really affects the disease in the arteries at all. There is really no medicinal treatment for that. It is for this reason that cardiac transplantation offers an entirely new hope to such patients.

The difficulty in selecting patients with coronary disease for transplantation does not lie in the diagnosis, which is usually quite simple, nor in the delineation of the extent of the disease, which can be outlined by special x-rays. Instead, the difficulty lies in precise definition of the patient's life expectancy without the transplant. During the first year of transplantation, it appeared that the outlook for long-range survival after the graft might be as great as 50 percent. One could make an optimistic contrast between this outlook and that of many untreated patients with coronary disease. It was this comparative prognosis with and without transplantation that gave the impetus to most of the cardiac grafts carried out in that hectic first year. Most of these were done for coronary disease.

Of immense importance in this field is the sudden expansion of direct surgical repair of the coronary arteries. The early efforts of Dr. Beck in Cleveland and Dr. Vineberg in Montreal have resulted in operations in which the small arteries inside the chest (internal mammary arteries) were brought into the heart muscle and just left loosely there. This was to bring in some new blood flow where coronary arteries were restricted. These operations were done in large numbers commencing in 1964. In 1968, a new procedure was developed based also on direct anatomical examination of the coronary arteries by new x-ray methods that would show exactly where the block was. An operation was then developed to bring a short new segment of the patient's own vein (borrowed from his leg as an autotransplant) to provide a large flow of blood directly from the aorta through a bypass channel two or three inches long into the side of a coronary artery. This is "direct coronary artery surgery" and is a further expansion of the early attempts made by Dr. Cannon, Dr. Longmire, and others to remove the core of fatty material that obstructs arteries. In this new bypass operation a new blood flow is brought to the artery beyond the constriction, much as an irrigation canal might bring water back to a river beyond the dam. The results of these operations even at this short interval appear to be remarkably good. They can be demonstrated to bring new blood to the heart muscle and thereby provide a whole new range of treatment for patients with severe coronary artery disease. It is too soon to know what fraction of patients who might formerly have been considered transplantable would be returned to normal living by this new direct coronary artery surgery.

When cardiac transplantation can be relied on to provide a better long-term survivorship, and when the late coronary artery disease of rejection is overcome, young patients with severe coronary artery disease will be the most important beneficiaries, particularly those who are not amenable to other forms of treatment. If one considers all the patients with heart disease in this country and groups them into four categories, coronary heart disease leads the list by a comfortable margin, as to total numbers, social salvageability, and a clean bill of health in other organs. At present, 62 of the transplants, or more than one third, have been for coronary disease.

Finally, there are the much rarer *muscular* heart diseases. The heart muscle can develop some diseases of its own which do not arise because of troubles either in the cells or in the blood vessels. Known as myocardiopathies, some are caused by prior infections (such as diphtheria), while others are the manifestations of processes such as rheumatic fever. There is a small group in which the cause of the myocardiopathy is not evident. The disease develops unexpectedly, characteristically in young adults with their useful lives ahead. The disease causes irreversible changes in the heart by which the muscle thins out, the beat becomes weaker, and the heart becomes a dilated and weakened sack. The patient passes into absolutely intractable heart failure and then dies. Here, *par excellence,* would be the disease for cardiac transplantation. There is nothing whatsoever the matter with any other aspect of the patient when the disease begins; its course is inexorable and all that is needed is a new pump. It is the prototype of "pump failure."

But here again, in nature, "nothing is ever given—it is always sold." This disease, myocardiopathy, which is so devastating and is so promising for treatment by transplantation, is evidently an autoimmune process in some cases. These patients seem to have developed immunologic activity against their own tissue antigens.

Although late coronary artery disease is produced in the heart by long-smoldering chronic rejection, it is myocardiopathy that most resembles the acute cardiac rejection process. There has been great difficulty in achieving the proper histocompatibility match in such patients; the course of the disease suggests that one possibility for its cause might be that the patient has developed antibodies against his own heart muscle proteins. This could make it the counterpart, in the heart, of glomerulonephritis in the kidney. Despite these difficulties in matching, 26 transplants have been done for myocardiopathy.

Many persons, in reviewing the large numbers of patients for transplant and comparing them with the scarcity of available donors, have become very gloomy over the likelihood of cardiac transplantation ever developing on a national scale. Such concern, arising purely because of the magnitude of the problem is specious and premature. It is like worrying over the expense of constructing an intensive care unit because it is unlikely that all hospitals can afford one. Each one that is built makes its own contribution. Even though cardiac transplantation will probably never be available for all these patients, we can work toward the ideal and still help a few. If heart grafting can come of age, with gradual perfection of results, good hearts can be provided for some of the thousands of young people with severe heart disease.

The Year of the Heart in Retrospect

The majority of the 150 or so cardiac transplantations done in the world were done during the calendar year 1968. Recent letters from

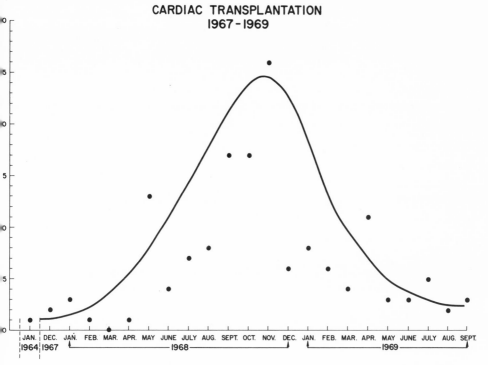

CARDIAC TRANSPLANTATION
1967 - 1969

FIGURE 36. Frequency curve of cardiac transplantation during the years 1967, 1968, and 1969. The wave of enthusiastic trial of this procedure is evident. It reached its peak in November of 1968 when 26 patients were operated upon. With poor results and premature widespread application, enthusiasm waned. At the present time cardiac transplantations are being done at a steady slow rate which enables more careful study of patients and the possibility of a higher success rate.

those colleagues most intimately concerned with this work give us a special insight into the events of that year.

About one year after his first cardiac transplantation, Dr. Barnard, who had done the first two, had still added but a single additional case. Looking back on this period he wrote:

On December 3, 1967, the heart of a girl who died from brain injury was transplanted to a patient suffering from heart disease that, until then, had proved untreatable. This operation, as might be expected, met with reactions ranging from acclaim to condemnation. Of the various criticisms one above all others merits the most careful consideration: the objection that heart transplantation in man is premature.

To refute this criticism, three basic questions need to be considered. First, is there any need for this type of surgery—have we patients who can benefit by this new technic? Second, have we developed this technic sufficiently to use it without undue risk in the treatment of human beings? Third, are we able to detect the complications that may follow this type of procedure, and can we effectively control them when they arise?

Dr. Barnard then answers these questions as best he can, taking a view which he acknowledges is one biased toward the affirmative. As he stated, his bias stemmed from his own experience with two long-term survivors out of three operations carried out. He wrote:

We have shown this operation of human heart transplantation to be eminently feasible, and in these two cases it carried no direct surgical mortality. We are also able to detect and treat possible complications with a high incidence of success, but it is clear that here still lie the major risks and challenges to enduring success.

In the treatment of a sick person, the physician must be free to use the new therapeutic measure if, in his judgment, it offers hope of saving life, restoring health, or alleviating suffering. I think we alleviated the suffering of our first patient although we did not save his life. It is not quite certain yet for how long we have saved the second patient's life, but I have no doubt that we have alleviated his suffering.

In conclusion, I believe that we have dealt with all three questions relating to whether clinical cardiac transplantation in the human is premature. Final judgment of this issue will rest with a growing number of gravely ill patients who are salvaged, and with the testimony of time.

Viewed as a single clinical experience, these three cases of Dr. Barnard arouse differences of opinion in answer to the question, "Was it worthwhile?"

Each reader of this book will form his own answer to this question. Collective opinion on this point will have much to do with the public support of scientific work and the expenditure of public resources for the care of individual patients undergoing operative procedures in clinical research. It is clear that as complicated and expensive a thing as a heart transplantation is not worth it for the individual if it gives him but an added few weeks or months of life, even though the confirmed optimist will point to the renewed hope and the faith kindled in the patient and his family.

With our current awareness of the need for better distribution of medical care, we can no longer regard these personal, social, and humane features as sufficient justification for such a vast outpouring of social resources on a single patient. There must be at least a year during which life is virtually normal before the procedure can be considered worthwhile for him and for society. The period of a year is acceptable, even though a minimum, and has been used as a yardstick in palliation for patients with late cancer. If they have had a year of good living, the palliative operation has done its job. In scoring the individual experience of Dr. Blaiberg, the index of personal value was high, though far from perfect, and the duration was far more than a year.

Beyond these transient judgments about individual cases, the fundamental social question will be answered only by subsequent events in the growth of cardiac transplantation itself. Not a single one of the kidney transplant patients in Dr. Hume's early series lived more than six months, and most of them lived far less than that. But they made possible the first identical twin transplants, and these in turn made possible a new surgical technique for transplantation and the assurance that once the immunogenetic barrier was overcome, the operation could be truly successful for both the individual and society. The transplants attracted little attention or note at the time, save for criticism from conservative medical groups. Now we regard them as having been eminently worthwhile. Possibly they could have been done in some different or better way; possibly more data might have been gleaned from them. There is no research that is wholly free of fault or immune from criticism. The fact remains that all the cases were dismal failures viewed by the same criteria that now lead to harsh judgments about heart transplantation—yet they led directly and almost inevitably to the perfection of kidney transplantation and the present World Series.

Transplantation of the heart is an easier operation to accomplish than that of the liver and appears to have fewer undesirable consequences. It is never carried out for the treatment of malignant tumors and foredoomed to failure by the effect of immunosuppression on

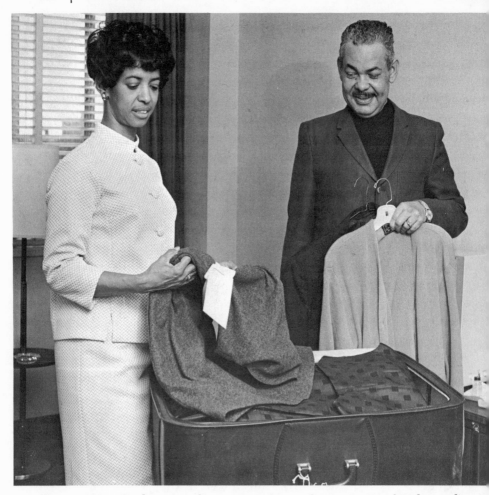

FIGURE 36A. Cardiac transplant patient. Mr. and Mrs. L. R. of Indianapolis, Indiana. Dr. Lower carried out a cardiac transplant for Mr. R. on August 24, 1968, in Richmond, at the Medical College of Virginia, in the Department of Surgery of Dr. David M. Hume. The patient had suffered several severe heart attacks and recurrent bouts of heart failure due to disabling coronary heart disease. The donor was a boy of 17 who had been shot in the head and died in this tragic accident.

Mr. R.'s postoperative electrocardiogram is shown in Figure 30. At present the patient is getting along nicely with a minimum of medication. Although such fine results were rare in the first hectic years of cardiac transplantation, their occurrence indicates clearly the feasibility of the procedure when undertaken under ideal circumstances by experienced personnel in a surgical department long-experienced in immunogenetics, clinical transplantation and immunosuppressive chemotherapy.

tumor growth. There are far more patients in the prime of life who could be helped by cardiac transplantation than by a new liver, and there is the peculiar fact that the beat of the heart indicates the functional integrity of the organ on the basis of simple examination and electrocardiographic study. This is a moment-to-moment evaluation of the viability of an organ for transplantation that is unrivaled in any other transplantable organ, and, as mentioned before, its electrical activity also tells us about rejection.

Whether or not all of these favorable factors can ever overcome the difficulties intrinsic in cardiac transplantation, particularly the late development of coronary artery disease, is still unknown. As the matter now stands, the virtually complete rehabilitation of an almost dead cardiac patient is so impressive, so complete, and so revolutionary in the whole history of human heart disease that the study of cardiac transplantation, if not its daily performance, is here to stay.

14

THE CLOUDED CRYSTAL BALL

New Tissues for Old . . . But Which?

In 1933, four years before his death, Rutherford said, firmly and explicitly, that he didn't believe the energy of the nucleus would ever be released—and nine years later in Chicago, the first pile began to run. That was the only major bloomer in scientific judgment that Rutherford ever made. It is interesting that it should be at the point where pure science turned into applied.
—C. P. SNOW, "THE TWO CULTURES AND THE
SCIENTIFIC REVOLUTION."
THE REDE LECTURE, 1959, CAMBRIDGE.

ARE ALL TISSUES CREATED EQUAL?

Twice in the past twenty years there have been surprisingly false predictions by experts in biology. In the early 1950's, a satisfactory device to replace the heart and lungs, pumping and oxygenating the blood outside the body, was regarded as an impossibility; allotransplantation of tissues in man was regarded merely as a visionary dream. In this short span of time, both have been shown to be possible and both have come into practical daily reality.

A tacit assumption of much transplantation research has been that when the transplant barrier is broken, all tissues can equally be transplanted. This assumption neglects many anatomical, surgical, and functional features of various tissues (some of which are superficial problems easily solved), but it points up the central question of whether or not all tissues are created antigenically equal—i.e., do they share the same antigens? Does the body throw off or reject a graft of skin with the same gusto with which it rejects a graft of kidney or liver? Are all tissues equally annoying and provocative in arousing an antagonistic antibody response?

It appears that the tissues studied fall into three groups. Firstly, there are one or two privileged tissues which do not seem to arouse much of an antagonistic response, at least in certain experimental animals. Ovary is one. This tissue, necessary for the production of estrogen as well as for the production of the ova or eggs, survives at least to some extent in a totally unprotected environment in certain animals.* There may be other endocrine glands (parathyroid, for example) which occupy a similarly privileged position. Some animal experiments suggest that certain tissues are privileged and easily functional, whereas the few human experiences suggest that rejection is unfortunately quite normal.

Secondly, a large group of organs (including kidney, liver, lung, heart, adrenal, thyroid) are in the mid range of antigenicity. They can be allografted, but only with the help of immunosuppression. Again, species vary, as witness the remarkable survival of liver transplants in the pig.

And finally, there is skin. This tissue appears to be more antigenic than most other tissues, a finding that may have its counterpart in the fact that certain kinds of sensitivity or immunity tests (for example, the tuberculin test and tests done to study hay fever and asthma

---

* It has already been mentioned in Chapter 1 that certain structural grafts such as artery and bone are, as usually employed, not cellular grafts at all because they are equally effective if the tissue is dead. Cornea is also exceptional because most of it is intercellular tissue, and the few cells that do survive are placed in a privileged site, the anterior chamber of the eye. Here the rejecting cells of the blood cannot get at it. In addition, the special cells of the cornea appear to be able to take up oxygen directly from the air in front of the eye, a most remarkable property not shared by any other tissue.

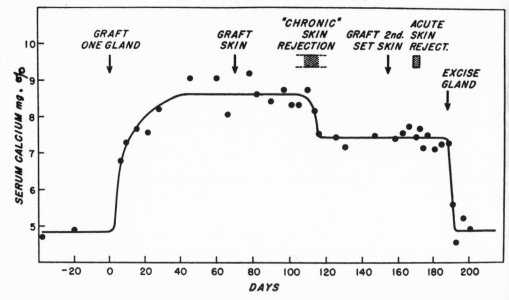

FIGURE 37. Antigenic differences. Studies of Russell and Gittes (1959). Here is another example of the use of a chemical method to follow the life of a graft (see also Figure 7). The parathyroid homograft in the parathyroidectomized rat supports the blood calcium concentration upward toward normal ("graft one gland").

Later, when a skin graft is taken from the same donor strain, even though there be rejection, the calcium level falls only slightly. That the parathyroid graft was still working is shown by the abrupt fall when it was removed.

The diagram demonstrates the different antigenic compositions of skin and parathyroid; while one is lost, the other is held. This suggests that as tissue transplantation is gradually perfected, some organs and tissues will be found easier to transplant than others.

allergies) are most provocative of an allergic response if they are injected within the skin itself (i.e., intradermally).

The question of varying antigenicity and antigenic contrasts between two different tissues was nicely shown by Dr. Russell and Dr. Gittes. They transplanted parathyroid tissue in rats and found that, despite some genetic diversity between related strains, the parathyroid glands would live and function indefinitely even without protection from rejection (Fig. 37). Then, if such a rat, carrying a parathyroid graft and doing quite well, was given a skin graft from the same donor, a sickness developed and the skin was rejected. At the time of skin rejection, the parathyroid gland itself was disturbed or rejected. This was interpreted as indicating that skin had antigens that aroused a response much stronger than that from the parathyroids. Once stimulated, this response then directed its antibodies against any foreign tissue in its path, including the formerly accepted parathyroids.

These experiments also find reflection in some work done by Dr. Pierce in Minnesota on dogs with kidney grafts and by Dr. Murray in our laboratories. Both have shown that an animal carrying a kidney may at the same time reject skin transplanted from the same donor. In addition (as with Dr. Russell's rats) such dogs will, at the time of rejecting that skin, frequently make an effort to reject the kidney; the kidney can be maintained in place only by increasing the dose of immunosuppressive drugs.

Recently, and more conclusively, Dr. Hume and Dr. Williams in Richmond, Virginia, have shown by analysis using antisera that there are antigens on kidney cells that are not found on lymphocytes (see page 217). They have used this finding to explain why some patients who appear to have good histocompatibility by matching of lymphocytes can still have a hyperacute rejection of the kidney. These scientists believe that the visceral organs share most of the same antigens (that is, they were unable to demonstrate antigenic differences between kidney and heart), while the lymphocyte, a freely circulating specialized cell generally used as a basis for tissue matching, lacks some of the antigens found in the organs. This is a very important observation and may well modify our procedure for matching donors and recipients. It will be necessary to test the reaction of the recipient's serum against donor cells of several tissues as well as his lymphocytes.

To one side of this array of antigenic tissues are those that act against their new host by the graft-versus-host reaction. These are immunologically competent grafts of the antibody-producing reticuloendothelial system itself, such as lymph nodes, spleen, and bone marrow. The most commonly grafted example is bone marrow (see Chapter 6). A successful take of bone marrow in mice induces graft-versus-host reaction, a curious wasting process with loss of weight and roughening of the fur known as "runting" or "runt disease." Dr. Uphoff (page 134), using amethopterin, made one of the first observations on drug immunosuppression in abating this runt disease in mice.

All tissues are not created equal. Immunosuppression adequate for one may not be adequate for another. Tolerance or acceptance of one set of cells may not connote acceptance of another; the absence of preformed antibodies against one is no guarantee of another's acceptance. In some tissues, immunosuppressive drugs must be used to protect the host as well as the graft. Each tissue must be considered on its own merits and involves its own problems.

This chapter will concern itself with a list of organs and tissues, for each of which there will be described one or two of the *diseases* that appear most in need of transplantation for treatment; then the matter of *donors; surgical* or operative considerations; and finally the biologic and clinical *evaluation* of the function of the graft. Kidney, liver, and heart have been described in such detail that they will not be listed here again.

BRAIN

Treatment by allotransplantation is needed particularly for destructive brain tumors occurring in childhood. Degenerative vascular diseases of the brain such as strokes would likewise be suitable for treatment if they occurred as isolated instances in young people. This is frequently the case in those strokes known as subarachnoid hemorrhage which encase a young and active brain in a useless mass of blood clot.

Donors of brain present insuperable problems. A person is not dead until the brain is dead, in which case it would be no good for transplantation. If cut or severed, tissues of the nervous system are slow to regenerate, and many do not regenerate at all.

Surgical considerations appear equally difficult. The blood supply to the brain spreads from several blood vessels small enough to be a challenge to surgical anastomosis. The spinal cord also has a diffuse segmental small-vessel blood supply.

Evaluation of function would depend on consciousness, neurologic examination, and electrical activity.

Comment: Allotransplantation of whole brain into a normal functioning site is idle chatter; there is no way of accomplishing a hookup. This master computer of the body must have its input and output connected to all the thousands of nerves and that great cord of nerves running down the back, the spinal cord itself. Without these connections an isolated brain perfused with blood is merely a laboratory experiment. Possibly allotransplantation of portions of the central nervous system or of the peripheral nerves offers more practical and scientifically attractive possibilities.

Dr. White, working in the research laboratories of the Mayo Clinic, has made preparations of isolated animal brain, using circulation from the heart of another animal or from a pump oxygenator. In a sense this is an allotransplanted brain, and has been so interpreted in the public press. But the nerves of this brain are not reconnected to any other sensory structures, and as a brain transplantation it is quite meaningless. In Dr. White's view, this is a preparation for the study of brain function and of brain circulation.

Some Russian investigators twenty years ago transplanted the head of a dog onto the blood vessels of the neck of another dog. That brain was kept alive by the blood supply of the recipient. The only nerve disconnection was in the spinal cord where the neck was cut across; the new head could see, hear, and taste. But there was no regeneration of nerve-muscle power to the limbs or diaphragm of the recipient dog from the new brain, or feeling from the limbs to the grafted brain. The animal's own brain was still in place with all its own connections. The Russian press suggested that this was transplantation of the brain (or of the head), when in point of fact it was a short-term blood perfusion of the head and neck of one dog from the circulation of a recipient animal with no immunosuppression and no attempt to establish any connection whatever between the nervous systems, muscles, or bones of the two animals.

LUNG

Treatment by allotransplantation is needed especially for chronic progressive pulmonary fibrosis and insufficiency in young people. Persons in their 40's and 50's develop a kind of chronic pulmonary insuffi-

ciency associated with difficulty in breathing, chronic cyanosis*
(shown by blueness of lips and fingers), getting out of breath easily,
and also developing changes by x-ray that are called emphysema (or
overdistention of the lung air sacs). The almost universal cause of
emphysema is prolonged heavy cigarette smoking. Most lung special-
ists state that they have rarely seen the disease in a nonsmoker, although it is similar to the lung dust lesions seen in miners, especially
miners of asbestos and other powdery material. Emphysema is a crippling and ultimately fatal disease for which only one treatment could
be successful: new lung tissue (Figure 38). It is a clear example of a
nontumorous or benign destruction of tissue by an outside agency in
which a new organ, protected from that outside agency, should be
expected to function well.

It is remarkable that there is virtually no form of tumor which
would require treatment by transplantation of new lung tissue. If the
whole lung can be removed it need not be replaced; the other lung is
sufficient if it is normal. If the tumor is in both lungs, it is almost surely
so spread elsewhere as to make transplantation inadvisable, and in any
event the experience from both kidney and liver has shown the futility
of treating any sort of tumor or cancer by transplantation under the
current methods of immunosuppression.

Donors should present little problem. If healthy liver, kidney,
heart, or intestinal tract can be procured from a recently deceased
person, then lung tissue should theoretically be obtainable likewise.
Lung transplantation has already been tried in this country (Hardy,
Barnes, Beall, Blumenstock), and has shown that the initial procurement and the necessary time-temperature curve can be achieved in
man. The tissue itself is far more vulnerable to infection and fluid
accumulation than any of the other organs of the body.

Repeatedly in this book reference has been made to the occasional
or stray success of remarkable duration, in transplantation of various
organs. The present interpretation of such stray successes is the finding
of unusual histocompatibility between donor and recipient. The pres-

---

* *Cyanosis*, from the Greek *kyanos*, meaning "a blue substance"; blueness of skin and lips
due to the presence in arteries of dark blue nonoxygenated hemoglobin pigment normally
found only in veins: the true blueblood. A dangerous sign of anoxia.

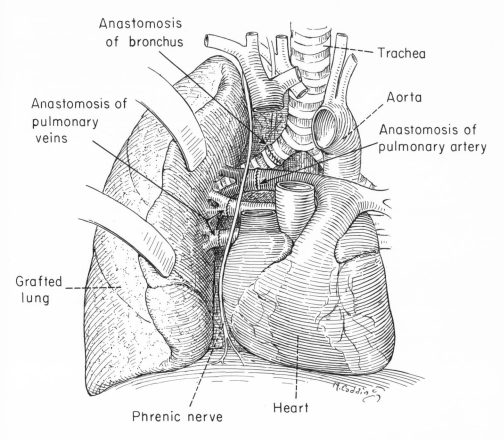

Anastomosis of bronchus

Trachea

Anastomosis of pulmonary veins

Aorta

Anastomosis of pulmonary artery

Grafted lung

Phrenic nerve

Heart

FIGURE 38. Sites and sutures: lung allograft. This diagram shows the right lung grafted onto the bronchus to let air in and out, and the pulmonary artery and vein for its circulation.

ent status of lung transplantation illustrates this point, as will be described.

Surgical considerations are simple enough to be appealing. Several large vessel anastomoses and the bronchial anastomosis are all that need be done. Experience has shown, however, that the resistance to flow of blood and air is very critical in the function of a transplanted lung. So long as the opposite lung is favored, for flow of either blood or air, producing a disproportion in ventilation and perfusion in the transplant, it will not function well. This has turned out to be a problem in several of the lung transplants that have been done. One lung takes all the air (usually the host's own lung) while the transplant has taken the blood. One of the basic principles of pulmonary function is even distribution of blood flow and air flow; this is so difficult with a transplant as to become a severe obstacle to success.

Evaluation of function and especially maintenance of function are also problems here. A lung that is not properly expanded with air is a lung vulnerable to bronchopneumonia. A lung that has too much fluid collecting in it, or without proper venous drainage, is also a wet lung and therefore a dangerous lung. The problem in lung transplantation will surely be this question of adequate ventilation, adequate drainage, and adequate fluid removal from the air sacs. A denervated lung does not communicate normal reflexes to the diaphragm, but this is evidently not a limiting factor. Whether or not the lung transplant is working satisfactorily can easily be determined by blood analyses, by x-ray, and by special new tests with radioctive isotopes. These tell precisely which parts of the lung have blood going through them and which parts are ventilating normally.

Comment: Up to the fall of 1970,* 25 human lung grafts had been carried out. The first was carried out by Dr. Hardy and his associates of Jackson, Mississippi, on June 11, 1963, about the same time that the first liver grafts were performed. To date, only two to six lung transplants have been carried out each year. There is none surviving (long-term) at present.

Dr. Hardy's first patient, who survived 18 days after the operation, turned out to be a longer survivor than most. Of all the attempts to transplant lung, approximately 16 have involved the entire lung, and the remainder a single lobe of the lung. With but a single exception, all of these patients have died or the transplant has been removed within four weeks. In one case the lung transplant was removed and the patient survived.

The one long-term survivor of lung transplantation remains noteworthy, not only because he lived for almost a year, but also because

---

* We are indebted to Dr. Arthur C. Beall, Jr., of Baylor College of Medicine in Houston, Texas, for the summary of the world experience in lung transplantation. Dr. Beall has carried out two transplants, both of which demonstrated problems in distribution of ventilation and perfusion.

he epitomizes the rare success hoped for in the transplantation of any organ. Lung grafts are so imposing that far fewer have been undertaken than is the case with either liver or heart. One long-term survivor, living entirely on a transplanted lung, was unique.

This was the case of a Belgian steelworker operated upon by Dr. Derom at the University of Ghent Hospital on November 14, 1968. The patient was a victim of silicosis, a form of lung scarring found among miners or industrial workers exposed to inhalation of certain dusts. Prior to the operation he had become severely short of breath with a marked reduction in all his respiratory measurements and with a marked loss of weight, as is so common in chronic pulmonary failure.

The cadaver donor was a B match on histocompatibility testing, a 40-year-old woman suffering brain hemorrhage. The operation was a transplant of one entire lung. The total dead time for the tissue was about fifty minutes. Pulmonary function immediately commenced and improved remarkably over that present preoperatively. The unremoved left lung of the recipient finally became completely obliterated; the pulmonary artery clotted and was completely ineffective. This sort of change occurring in both lungs would be fatal.

The new lung showed two rejection crises, one rather early and the other at about five months. During these rejection crises the patient showed a drop in his arterial oxygen saturation. A higher dose of immunosuppressive drugs was prescribed. Antilymphocyte globulin was also provided. The patient recovered from each rejection crisis; the operative lung was working at about 70 percent of normal function. The patient returned to normal living, but the unremoved collapsed lung was chronically infected. Finally, in the autumn of 1969, almost one year after the operation, the patient died of a chronic infection.

From the perspective of the 1970's lung transplants seem much farther from clinical usefulness than those of liver or heart. The problem of pneumonia, pulmonary infections superimposed on disorders of ventilation and blood perfusion seem almost insurmountable until specific tolerance, enhancement, or adaptation has controlled the patient's rejection potential without damaging his immunity to microorganisms. The solution of this problem will come, but who can put a year on it? Or a price? For the 20,000 patients dying each year of emphysema it is a need here and now, and without monetary value.*

By contrast, an artificial lung, adequate to support ventilation for periods of several days or a week, is imminent. Using such a mechanical lung, the patient can have ventilation with minor surgery (only a small incision made in the groin to tap the circulation into the artificial lung). Such a substitute will not equal the artificial kidney because the support time will inevitably be shorter and the perfusion will have to be almost continuous rather than once or twice a week. This development will assist in the problem of lung transplantation. When other aspects of transplantation science have made lung transplants more feasible, the artificial lung, or extracorporeal membrane oxygenator, will be useful to assist the patients either before, during, or after operation.

Spleen

Treatment by allotransplantation of the spleen would be helpful for at least two diseases: agammaglobulinemia (page 187) and hemophilia.† Dr. Starzl has attempted splenic transplantation in agammaglobulinemia; Dr. Norman of the Boston City Hospital has attempted grafting of the spleen into animals that have a congenital form of hemophilia that resembles the human disease. In both instances the spleen should supply something that is lacking: in agammaglobulinemia normal lymphocytes, and in hemophilia the antihemophilic factor, or AHF. Up to the present no human being with hemophilia has been treated by splenic grafting, although the possibility is attractive.

Donors would present the same selection problem as they would for a kidney. The living donor could be used because the spleen is a dispensable organ in a normal person.

---

* The vast majority of patients with severe and fatal emphysema are heavy cigarette smokers. Their habituation is almost as pernicious as that of opiate users. They *cannot* stop even when they know it is killing them! A psychiatric or public health approach might be useful; most legislative assaults on this problem have been ineffective.

† *Hemophilia,* a familial disease carried in the female line but manifesting itself only in the male—the scourge of royal dynasties. There is inability of the blood to clot, and a trivial injury will sometimes initiate a fatal hemorrhage.

Surgical details have been worked out and are quite simple. A direct anastomosis of the artery and vein is all that is needed.

Evaluation of function of the spleen for both of these diseases would be direct and simple. Standard methods of blood analysis for proteins would indicate whether or not immunoglobulins were being synthesized. In hemophilia, the levels of antihemophilic globulin in the blood can be measured by standard methods.

Comment: Here is a transplant where graft-versus-host disease would be a potential problem. If the patient could make no antibodies of his own, as in agammaglobulinemia, then he could not reject the spleen. The spleen would be accepted without further immunosuppression. The patient's body would then have living within it a very active spleen, making strong antibodies against the antigens of the new host. In the case of hemophilia, the patient's immune process is normal, and an attempt to reject the spleen would doubtless be seen, competing, as it were, with the graft-versus-host response emanating from the spleen itself. In experimental splenic transplantation the initial reaction is graft-versus-host (the spleen reacting against the new host), followed then by rejection of the spleen in a typical host-versus-graft reaction. But this latter was often much delayed (up to 60 or 70 days), as if the initial graft-versus-host reaction had slowed down the rejection process.

BONE MARROW

Treatment by allotransplantation is needed for a variety of blood diseases, including aplastic anemia (in which the bone marrow is virtually absent) and certain kinds of cancers or tumors of the blood such as leukemia in which the patient's bone marrow must intentionally be destroyed if the tumor is to be cured. Some of the diseases involving failure to form antibodies or leukocytes, mentioned in the previous section on spleen, might also be treated by transplantation of marrow.

Donors present no problem. The procurement of bone marrow by needle aspiration from human volunteers has already been successfully accomplished.

Surgical problems appear to be minimal. The marrow is injected intravenously. It may lodge in a number of tissues in the body, but for the most part it seems to settle in the marrow cavity of the bones, where it belongs.

Evaluation of function would not be difficult if a marrow transplant was done for aplastic anemia or thrombocytopenia (a lack of blood platelets). The count of cells in the blood would be the basic measure of success. In addition there are subtle immunologic methods of determining whether these cells appearing in the blood are actually the product of the transplant or some new product from the host himself.

Comment: Just as with spleen, the graft-versus-host reaction could be a problem here. The new and immunologically potent bone marrow can react against the host, as indeed it does in about 25 percent of cases.

Up to October 1970, 90 bone marrow transplants had been reported, more than half done for leukemia or immune deficiency states. Of these about one third survived more than 30 days. There were 18 survivors in October 1970, the longest, 27 months.

BLOOD

Ordinary blood transfusion, used liberally for the past fifty years, is a cellular allotransplantation because blood is a mixture of cells and plasma.

The survival of allografted cells in blood transfusion is often thought of only in terms of the red cells. The red cell antigenic system (see page 214) is so simple (the A, B, and Rh antigens being the only important antigens in about 98 percent of blood transfusions) that red cell compatibility and survival can be assured if the blood has been well preserved, properly grouped, and crossmatched.

From the point of view of tissue transplantation, other cells in the blood are more important than the red cells. There are instances where blood transfusion is given to provide the patient not only with the plasma fluid and red cells but with other formed elements he lacks in his blood: leukocytes, lymphocytes, or platelets. If blood is used for this purpose, it must be very fresh and transferred in plastic bags because the white cells are nucleated (unlike the red cell); they must respire and will die in ordinary blood bank storage. These cells constitute a true allograft. In recent years it has become possible to fractionate donor blood in a blood bank to separate these special white cells and platelets in concentrated form for patients who need them. Even though they do not persist, and can be used only to tide the patient over some emergency, the transfusion of these nucleated cells and platelets brings in its wake all the typical problems of allografting. This is true for any transfusion of fresh whole blood.

For many years this transfusion-allograft of white cells and platelets did not seem to be a very important aspect of transplantation. It has now emerged as a matter of great importance, especially in kidney transplantation, because prior blood transfusions can presensitize the recipient against subsequent organ grafts, by arousing antibodies against lymphocytes and platelets.

Examples of this are most notable in the kidney, where prior blood transfusions (given to bolster up the failing patient or as a feature of dialysis) have been a principal source of presensitization against antigens of the HL-A system. This can produce preformed antibodies, a positive crossmatch, and hyperacute rejection. Knowledge of the importance of this factor has grown up only in the past few years (see page 182); the avoidance of transfusion of white cells in patients with renal failure has become a widespread practice. If red cells must be transfused to build up the patient's blood counts, then washed red cells free of the antigenically sensitizing white cells and platelets should be used.

Blood transfusion is therefore to be included on any list of allotransplantation of tissues even though it is a very special tissue, and only a tiny fraction of any blood transfusion contains nucleated cells that are antigenic. Sometimes these white cells and platelets are useful in treatment, but always they present the hazard of sensitization should an allotransplantation of some other tissue or organ later become necessary.

INTESTINAL TRACT

Treatment by allotransplantation is most urgently needed for only one ailment: absence of the small bowel. Each year we see one or two young people who have lost most of their small intestine through an injury to its blood supply, from an embolus (a small clot) thrown off from the heart, a twisting accident known as volvulus, or injury due to a bullet or a knife wound. The patients waste away and finally die from progressive starvation, a slow and miserable process. In such cases, even if it were possible to transplant but two or three feet of small intestine, nourishment would be more normal, and there would be a prospect of survival to a normal life. This is an urgent problem because these patients are usually free of other diseases; yet they are irretrievable except by continuous intravenous feeding, rarely possible at home and never permitting them a normal life or a transplant of the intestine.

The matter of *donors* needs much more careful research than it has received in the past. Living donors would be feasible because people can get along quite well after the loss of three, four, five, or even six feet of their small bowel. It is conceivable that the family donor might be used as he is for kidney donation. The recently deceased cadaver might also be considered, though the gastrointestinal tract deteriorates very rapidly after death.

Surgical aspects are difficult. The small bowel has many small blood vessels. The anastomosis of the arteries presents little difficulty, but the small venous anastomoses are treacherous and tend to clot. At present, these surgical considerations are paramount. They must be solved in dogs before it is worth attempting bowel transplants under immunosuppression in man. Preliminary experiments done by Dr. Preston in Chicago and Dr. Lillehei in Minneapolis have shown that small bowel transplantation has real potential. This would be done using histocompatibility matching among family donors, avoiding high doses of immunosuppression, and placing the small bowel under the skin or in some location where difficulty with its blood supply would not produce peritonitis.

Evaluation of function can be done by weight and nutrition or by selective studies of the absorption of foods. There are several radioactive substances that can be given, and by simple external counting techniques or studies of the blood it is possible to determine whether or not they are being absorbed from the food.

Skin, Bones, and Limbs

Treatment by allotransplantation of whole limbs has been explored only in one or two isolated examples. Its greatest urgency would be in military surgery or in children who are born with bilateral deformities of the arm, so that they have no useful arm or hand on either side. Such children usually have normal blood vessels and nerves at the upper part of the arm. Were it possible to obtain satisfactory tissue from a recently deceased person, the transplantation might be accomplished. Immunosuppression in such an event offers remarkable problems because a limb involves so many different tissues that the spectrum of antigenicities would all be exhibited in one offering of a mixed tissue. Success for the patient would hinge on a proper evaluation of this mixed antigenicity.

It is difficult to conceive of a situation where the transplant of a leg would be useful enough to justify the hazards. This is something that has fascinated Russian investigators for several years. Much of their transplantation research on whole limbs has involved transplantation of the leg in dogs. The regrowth of the nerves of limbs takes many months, and even years. Recent instances of young persons whose arms were cut off in accidents and were then sutured in place (as autotransplants) illustrate the intriguing possibilities in this field and the length of time required for nerve regeneration. These experiences show that allotransplantation of a limb would be feasible, but there would be a long wait for return of normal function.

The treatment of burns by massive cadaver allografting of skin is a commonplace today. It is rarely done with immunosuppression, the patients being far too sick and infected to tolerate the drugs. The skin is therefore soon lost, but it is an effective wound covering. Long-lasting skin allografts are a much-needed advance in burn treatment. Burned patients are so sick, that some nontoxic method of immunosuppression would have to be found, or a means of producing tolerance or adaptation of a specific sort.

Donors for whole limbs would be recently deceased cadavers. The matter of skin donors has already been discussed. The family can be used; histocompatibility matching among siblings might make it possible to use fresh skin allografts to cover burns. If done with a perfect match, it would be possible to avoid immunosuppression entirely. This offers a new horizon in burn therapy that has not yet been explored.

Surgical details of limb transplants would involve very accurate suturing of arteries, veins, and nerves, with fixation of the bone. These problems have repeatedly been solved in wound surgery. They have also been solved in the replant patients mentioned above, and would be quite simple as compared with some of the surgical problems mentioned elsewhere in this list.

Evaluation of function would be obvious; nerve regeneration would be slow.

Comment: Grafts of bone itself (as small pieces) do not require viability, i.e., they work well if the cells are dead. The allotransplantation of an entire bone in its full anatomical dimension and as fresh tissue with cellular viability has never been done. This might be used for fractures of the hip in older people, in certain types of wounds, or as a source of bone marrow. The vascular anastomoses involved would be quite forbidding.

ENDOCRINE GLANDS*

General Comment: The endocrine glands as a group are structures that could be transplanted without direct vascular anastomosis. Bits and pieces or minced preparations of the endocrine glands could be placed in a bed in which they would grow. They are, therefore, somewhat different from many of the tissues previously discussed (though bone marrow has this same property) in that they can be placed in the body without the direct suture-anastomosis of blood vessels.

PITUITARY GLAND

Treatment by allotransplantation is needed in two types of situations: children who have developed pituitary insufficiency and adults with the type of acute pituitary insufficiency that occasionally develops in

---

* The author is indebted to Dr. John R. Brooks for this review of recent endocrine transplantation.

women after childbearing. Although many hormones are available to help such patients, hormone treatment is grossly unsatisfactory. Normal growth is rarely achieved in children. Normal sexual function is never obtained. The treatment is expensive, never-ending, and involves innumerable pills or injections. Allotransplantation would indeed be a viable alternative.

Donors would have to be recently deceased cadavers. Time temperature curves must be worked out. Practically nothing is known about the time-temperature requirements for pituitary transplantation.

Surgical management would not be difficult. The pituitary gland is easily removed after death; presumably it could be made to function in some new position as a preparation of pituitary cells, were it possible to avoid rejection of these cells, by immunosuppression. The pituitary has a very special local blood supply, bringing to it blood that has already passed through special cells in the brain. Whether the pituitary would function in a different kind of vascular setting is not well understood at this time.

Evaluation of function would be a delight to any practicing endocrinologist. All of the delicate tests carried out in blood and urine, for function of the target organs, would now have a direct application in determining whether or not the new "master gland" transplant was functioning well.

Comment: Allotransplantation of the pituitary, amongst all the endocrine glands, is the most urgently needed.

THYROID

Treatment by allotransplantation is not needed. Thyroid hormone replacement is so simple, easy, and inexpensive that thyroid transplantation is not an urgent problem and is largely of experimental interest.

Donors could be living volunteers, since a person gets along well with half or more of the thyroid removed.

Surgical considerations would be very difficult if direct vascular anastomosis had to be carried out. However, using transplants of total gland from stillborn infants, it would be possible to join the larger vessels. The thyroid would presumably function as a cellular suspension, if immunosuppression were adequate.

Evaluation of function would depend on the many rather delicate measures of thyroid function now available, such as the blood levels of thyroid hormone.

Comment: Much work has already been done on thyroid transplantation (Brooks, 1962) because it is an excellent model for endocrine transplants in general, even though it is seldom needed clinically. Dr. Lemaire and his group in Paris have reported on survival of thyroid and parathyroid grafts. It appears at the present time, based on the studies done in 1967 and 1968, that the thyroid grafts will not survive no matter how they are protected, within the framework of present methods.

PARATHYROID

Treatment by allotransplantation is severely needed for the condition arising from lack of parathyroid tissue—hypoparathyroidism. In this condition blood calcium is low and the patient is severely bothered by muscle spasms. The need for parathyroids is therefore in sharp contrast to the situation as regards the thyroid. The normal parathyroids are four tiny glands, each about the size of a wheat seed, situated behind the thyroid. Occasionally they are absent due to natural causes, but all too frequently are completely absent because a surgeon has inadvertently removed them, particularly in the course of radical surgery for cancer of the thyroid.

Donors present no problem. Several parathyroid transplantations have been done at this hospital, using living family donors and removing only one parathyroid. Benign parathyroid tumors can also be used.

Surgical considerations in either type of graft (normal glands or tumors) consist of mincing the tissue and placing it in the new recipient. The millipore filter chamber* has been extensively used here just as it has for thyroid. The results have been disappointing; immunosuppression is more promising.

---

* *Millipore filter chamber,* a special little chamber, about the size of a dime or a nickel, consisting of two faces glued together. The two facing parts are slightly porous, permitting nourishment and water to soak through, but preventing the entry of those lymphocytes and plasma cells that would reject the tissue. Here is an example of tissue transplantation done in a "privileged or protected site."

Evaluation of function is quite simple. The effect of hypoparathyroidism is to lower the amount of calcium in the blood. If the transplant functions successfully, the calcium level will be well supported. Even in the unsuccessful transplants there was an immediate rise in serum calcium for the first few days after the transplant, as passive transfer of hormone into the new host occurred.

Comment: Of all the transplants of endocrine glands, that of the parathyroid seems the closest to realization. A normal full-sized human the size of a professional football player can be kept in good health (as regards calcium metabolism) by a single tiny parathyroid gland! One would think that such a tiny bit of tissue would behave itself in the new host, and the new host behave himself so as to permit this small friendly invader to stay put. Thus far, this mutual acceptability has not been achieved. Dr. Filatov, a Russian physician, reported a series of 58 cases in 1969 using parathyroid glands joined by blood vessel anastomosis. He reports 28 functioning grafts at 7 years! He does not discuss what sort of immunosuppression (if any) was given. No one else, in Russia or elsewhere, has reported such success. In this country and in Europe there is little enthusiasm for parathyroid grafts at this time.

PANCREAS

Treatment by allotransplantation is needed chiefly for diabetes. Small islets of special cells in the pancreas are the insulin-producing cells of the body. It is for this reason that the pancreas is listed with the endocrine organs rather than with the other organs (such as liver or bowel) that supply digestive juices for the gastrointestinal tract. The lack of pancreas produced by total pancreatectomy does indeed produce some nutritional difficulties in the patient, but they can be largely repaired by giving pancreas pills. The lack of insulin, especially in young people who are "total" diabetics, is not satisfactorily made up by giving insulin by injections.

Donors would be a severe problem because of the tendency of the pancreas to digest itself after death. As every medical student knows, it was the solution of this problem that led to the initial discovery of insulin by Banting and Best. It is likewise difficult to make the pancreas survive in a new site. The active digestive ferments tend to digest the tissue within the pancreas, including the islet cells that make insulin, even after grafting.

Surgical considerations are difficult, as indicated above. The blood vessels are small; the minced pancreas does not function; it is difficult to tease out the islets from the rest of the pancreatic tissue.

Evaluation of function of pancreatic islet cells is not difficult because of the readily determined effect on the blood sugar.

Comment: One occasionally encounters patients with islet cell tumors of the pancreas. Here is islet cell tissue *par excellence* available in large amounts and free from the encumbrance of other pancreatic cells. Were it possible to make pancreatic islet cell allotransplants remain in a patient, then a benign islet cell tumor would be a most acceptable source of tissue, and might supply enough tissue for a whole family of diabetics!

In the past several years there has been renewed enthusiasm for pancreatic transplantation. Most of the work is based on animal studies such as those reported by Dr. Brooks, indicating that the entire pancreas should be transplanted along with the bowel to which it is attached (the duodenum). Dr. Lillehei in Minnesota has reported doing pancreatic allografts in man. Immunosuppressive agents—including antilymphocyte serum, cortisone, and azathioprine—have been used, but it is evident that the diabetic is a poor subject in whom to use azathioprine. Up to the present time, there have been 21 pancreatic allografts done in man; of these, 10 have been done by Dr. Lillehei and his group in Minnesota. One patient lived 10 months with some function. The other grafts have been rejected.

ADRENALS

Treatment by allotransplantation is not urgently needed for any adrenal diseases. Thanks to the pioneering efforts of such physicians as Dr. Thorn and Dr. Kendall it is now possible to treat Addison's disease (lack of normal adrenals) by various hormone pills or injections. Nonetheless, if transplantation were ever to be achieved the treatment of Addison's disease would best be accomplished by adrenal transplantation.

Donors would not present a problem. The adrenals are paired organs, and a family donor could be used. Recently deceased cadavers would also be acceptable.

Surgical management would be virtually impossible if direct suture-anastomosis were required. The vessels are very small and fragile. As with the other endocrine organs, one would hope that the tissue could function as a minced preparation of cells without direct blood-vessel anastomosis.

Evaluation of function, as with so many of the endocrine glands, would again be a delight to the endocrinologist. Daily measurements of blood or urine hormones would reveal the extent of function of the transplant to a remarkable degree of accuracy.

Comment: Like thyroid, adrenal transplants in animals have been a "model" for study in this field, even though the necessity for transplantation in man is neither very great nor very frequent. Dr. Kohlenbrener and his group attempted in 1963 to allograft fetal adrenal glands to some very young children who had adrenocortical insufficiency. The authors felt that they did have some functional take of these grafts, which were placed in the abdominal muscles, but there was no proof of function.

As mentioned, the use of the hormones is very effective, and there does not seem to be much of a place for adrenal grafts at this time.

GONADS—THE SEX GLANDS

Treatment by allotransplantation of the ovaries in the female or the testicles in the male is needed chiefly for reproductive purposes. Both glands make a steroid hormone (estrogen in the female and androgen in the male) that is responsible for the female or male qualities of the individual. In most circumstances these hormones can be provided quite readily by pills or injections.

Some young women are born with congenital absence of ovarian function; they do not grow or mature normally. In such women an ovarian transplantation, even if it did not release eggs for reproductive purposes, would make for a much more normal life. The similar condition in the male is known as eunuchoidism. It is quite rare. But here again, transplantation of testicular tissue would have significance.

There is a curious philosophical problem in regard to the reproductive potential. If someone else's ovaries were put into a woman so that she could bear children, the children would be hers only in the sense of growing in her womb and being borne by her. But they would not be her children genetically; instead they would be one-half the genetic product of the individual donating the ovaries. The same considerations would be true for functioning testicle transplants.

Donors here could again be among the living because both organs are paired. In addition, for the endocrine transplant of ovary—an ovarian transplantation that secretes estrogen even if it doesn't release eggs—the partial transplant of ovary from a normal woman has occasionally been used.

Surgical anastomoses are very difficult for such tiny vessels as nourish the ovary and testicle. But they can be done, either by hand under the microscope or by the suture machine. The egg-releasing function of the ovary requires a normal, intact ovary in its normal position next to the fallopian tube leading to the uterus. If the millipore filter chamber is used for ovary transplants, the egg-releasing function is lost, but the endocrine function is gained.

Evaluation of function, endocrinologically, of both these glands would be quite simple because there are precise chemical methods for measuring the amount of androgen or estrogen secreted. Evaluation of the reproductive function would be quite a different matter. If there were no other gonad present, and successful reproduction was actually achieved, there would surely be no doubt about success!

15

THE DOCTORS' DILEMMAS

How Far and How Fast to Venture
on the Transplant Voyage—
and How to Pay for It—
Is It Ethical—and What to Say About It . . .

Thus when I shun Scylla, your father, I fall into Charybdis, your mother.

—*The Merchant of Venice*

PRINCIPLES IN REVERSE—
SURGERY IN AN AGE OF NUCLEAR CHEMISTRY

Tissue transplantation is a unique field of surgery. It flaunts the ancient principles upon which medical and surgical care are based: do no harm, and help the patient to help himself. The welfare of a healthy person, heretofore never sacrificed in humane medicine, is now jeopardized when tissue is obtained from the healthy donor. The patient's own immune defenses are flouted and battered, if not destroyed.

Some transplanters, disturbed over injury to the donor, have been so strongly opposed to the use of living donors that they have employed cadavers only. For the past ten years it has been evident that cadaver kidneys are far less satisfactory than those from living family

313

donors, preferably siblings. The new histocompatibility data add the final proof. Until cadaver tissues become as useful as those of a sibling, there is no single or general solution to this ethical problem. If a suitable and willing brother or sister is available as donor, this is the best solution for the patient. Each case must be decided on its own merits and virtues, and each donor—living or dead—must be carefully screened for histocompatibility, genetic relationship, and the state of his own health prior to donation. Should animal tissues prove suitable in some cases, this would ease the donor problem; but even at that, only a few of the internal organs of animals would ever be suitable for use in man for obvious reasons of size and blood supply.

Sidestepping the living donor, one incurs two ethical and humane problems in using cadaver donors. The first relates to the definition of death (discussed in Chapter 10). The second bears on the doctors of the transplant team as they rub elbows with the doctors taking care of the dying donor. There is universal respect for the admonition that these two teams of doctors should be entirely independent. There is also universal recognition among doctors (though not among the clergy or the public) that few hospitals make a practice of needless prolongation of useless or hopeless life. The ultimate care for each patient could therefore be threatened by cadaver donor procurement, and every precaution must be taken to avoid any possibility of interference with the patient's welfare or any shadow or semblance of such interference.

Another ancient principle challenged by transplantation is that of "help the patient to help himself"—assist the patient's own defenses and responses, and above all, do no harm. The abrogation of immunologic processes to achieve success of a transplant is a drastic departure from this maxim.

Over the millennia, surgery, possibly more than any other field of medicine, has relied on the built-in responses of the patient for its success. No surgical operation, however simple, could be safe or effective were it not for the fact that blood clots, wounds heal, and bacterial contamination is overcome by normal immunologic processes.

A historic example of overcoming a normal response to achieve a surgical result was the introduction of anesthesia. Pain had long been regarded as the price that woman had to pay for childbirth, and that

THE DOCTORS' DILEMMAS | 315

mankind had to pay for surgical invasion of the human body. Deadening of that pain was considered dangerous and even immoral. The controversy that raged in the 1850's over the use of anesthesia in childbirth centered on this concept that pain was a God-given penance that had to be paid.

The analogy between anesthesia and immunosuppression ends right there. Within a few weeks of the first successful public demonstration of the use of ether, it was obvious that removal of pain did not interfere with healing or convalescence, and within a few years even the most ardent quasi-religious opponents of anesthesia for surgery or childbirth withdrew their opposition. *

The more that is learned, however, and the more experience there is with immunosuppression—irradiation, azathioprine, cortisone, actinomycin, azaserine, lymph fistula, or antilymphocyte serum—the more it becomes evident that there is no escape: removal of normal bodily defenses imposes a severe hazard to the patient's survival. A successful kidney transplant at four years, doing well and with no reason to fear the future, represents a double triumph: first, that histocompatibility has not imposed a burdensome need for excessive immunosuppression, and second, that the suppression of immunity necessary to avoid rejection of the transplant has struck the precarious balance and has not brought illness or death from infection. Conversely, the cardiac transplant patient who began to reject at six months and was given large doses of steroids only to die of a fungal abscess of the brain represents an example of a double defeat even though there was no further rejection. Histoincompatibility had imposed an excessive burden for immunosuppression. The balance of survival had not been found.

No matter what further course tissue transplantation takes in the years to come, it must continue to go through a long period of evolution and innovation, exploring new treatments as alternatives to

---

* It is an historic turnabout that eighty years later, about 1930, obstetricians began to be aware of the adverse effects of deep obstetrical anesthesia on the respiration and early development of the lungs in the infant. Modern methods of mild sedation together with instruction of the mother have combined to remove deep anesthesia from the obstetrical scene, save for those special or difficult cases involving operative delivery.

present-day immunosuppression, so that transplantation can follow the ancient surgical maxim of "do no harm."

THE ETHICS OF THERAPEUTIC INNOVATION

Whatever the nature of the donor, no matter how the bodily defenses are accommodated or reduced, there always remains the ethical and humane problem involved in the exploration of any new field of medical or surgical treatment. This is one of the most widespread but poorly understood ethical problems in all of modern-day medicine. The first use of insulin, the first operation for removal of the lung, the first administration of polio vaccine, the first open-heart operation—all had the same character of initial patient trial. This is called human experimentation by those who oppose any particular step in question, but accepted as an inevitable feature of therapeutic innovation by those who favor it. The steps we take, the drugs we use, the surgical operations or special procedures must at some time have gone through a period of therapeutic innovation when some patient, or patients, were given a new treatment.

Many critics of transplantation argue that a new operation should not be performed on a patient until it has been removed from the area of human experimentation and become truly "therapeutic." Such a view neglects an important aspect in the growth of clinical science: that there is no way of moving from tentative to final without passing through the experience of individual patients who are necessarily the first. It is only those first patients, and it may take a hundred before the "firstness" has worn off, whose treatment makes it acceptable for others. And it is the laboratory background itself that makes it scientifically and ethically acceptable for those first patients.

The critic who states that it is human experimentation and unethical until it is truly therapeutic predicates a false dichotomy. The line between a new treatment (therapeutic innovation) and something tentative and insecure (human experimentation) is never a sharp one. It is a wide gray area including even the initial use of established treatments for the first time in a new patient. Many things that are done every day in surgery, medicine, pediatrics, and psychiatry carry an important element of experiment. That is why every young doctor must learn the nature of the experimental method and its limitations. Only by personal experience in the laboratory can he appreciate the nature of the experimental method and know its strengths, its virtues, its hazards, its weaknesses. When he gives digitalis to a patient who has never received the drug before, it is a critical experiment. The response of that particular heart to this drug requires experimental design and careful recording of results, done with as devoted care to detail as if it were done in the purest laboratory setting. The same thing applies to the initial dose of insulin in a brittle diabetic, and, of course, it is true for any surgical operation whether it is a simple operation like an appendectomy or something complicated like a transplant: the surgeon must prepare, plan, search, solve, and document if the operation is to be ethical and effective.

Any transplant done during the next decade, whether of a kidney, liver, heart, lung, adrenals, spleen, pancreas, or any other tissue or organ, represents therapeutic innovation. The ethical surroundings are acceptable only if they fall within certain guidelines which bear on four aspects: the man, the laboratory, the institution, and the patient.

As to the *man* entrusted with this kind of innovative work, there must be one person ultimately responsible (even though he may be surrounded by a team of many helpers), and he should have certain special qualifications. He should be a person who has studied the disease in depth. He must have the ability to see through the sheen of newness to the realities of clinical results. This can only come from experience with the disease itself. The man carrying out these new treatments should be the same man who is primarily responsible for the welfare of the patient. Science and compassion should not be separated.

The *laboratory* background he can bring to bear separates ethical innovation from precarious unsupported adventure. This laboratory background should include personal involvement with several experimental features of the new treatment or procedure: synthetic organic chemistry (new drugs), experiments in small animals (notable in the cancer field), experimental operations in large animals (especially in many surgical developments), or attention to the phenomena of human illness through clinical study of many patients.

It is the unification of this laboratory background (the laboratories, the people, the support, and the clinician) in the hospital itself that characterizes the uniquely American *institution* in advancing medical science. These institutions provide ethical stability in therapeutic innovation and the safety harness for the patient in the application of new procedures. They provide an environment that protects the patient through freedom of consultation, a tradition of openness about new things, and free discussion amongst young students and senior faculty. The institution also provides the expensive engineering and scientific backup that protect the patient with every safety device: the blood banks, the laboratories, the intensive care units, able anesthetists, well-trained nurses, and the young interns or residents who are up all night the first few nights to be sure each little detail is going well. The hospital provides the checks and balances that the brilliant investigator often needs, and surround the patient with safety.

Fourth, and possibly the most important in the ethical guidelines for therapeutic innovation, are those that relate to the *patient* himself. The concept of "informed consent" is rarely applicable in a literal sense. How can a patient who has never received a medical education possibly hope to understand all the complicated pros and cons of a transplant or any other new procedure? He should never have this burden thrust upon him. But all his questions must be answered and the background laid before him as clearly as possible. How can the scientist, who himself does not know all the answers, help the patient to understand? If the doctor knew what was most likely to happen, then it would no longer be a new procedure or therapeutic innovation. The uncertainty of the doctor and the strangeness of the patient make "informed consent" an unattainable ideal, but not a false doctrine. The approach to informed consent cannot reside in a single conversation, but must be a continuing personal contact over many days and weeks between the patient and his family and the scientists working with him.

SOCIAL INVESTMENT AND WELFARE DIVIDENDS

In its simplest form medical care is a charitable act. The fundamental act of medical care is the assumption of responsibility for the welfare of the patient. The great medical foundations of Europe, as epitomized in their ancient charitable hospitals with traditions going back a thousand years, provided the fundament upon which American medicine was based. The welfare of the patient is assumed to justify the cost, to society, of his treatment. In the light of their cost we must analyze the social investment involved in organ transplantations and compare it with the welfare dividends gained for the individual patient.

If a well-matched young cardiac patient who would die without transplantation were to be given an ideally preserved and well-matched histocompatible heart and gain two years of useful pain-free life, the judgment might be that the patient's welfare more than outweighed the social investment. The cost of the procedure might be as high as $75,000 to $100,000. The full-time efforts of a few doctors would be involved for several weeks, with part-time efforts of many doctors and nurses, stretching out long after that, plus extensive utilization of hospital facilities. Intuitive acceptance of any such procedure must be based on the assumption that the experience in that patient will enable many others to be treated with a greater likelihood of success.

There have been several surveys made to examine the dollar cost of a kidney transplantation. An average figure appears to be about $15,000, though under some circumstances it is as low as $3000. If the course is complicated with multiple operations, procedures, transfusions, antibiotics, laboratory tests, and x-rays, as well as two or three additional transplants over the course of several months or years, then the cost is probably closer to the figure given above, namely $75,000 to $100,000.

Here we define cost as the actual dollar investment made in the care of the patient, including not only the familiar cost items that all hospital accountants are so expert at listing, but also the more subtle ones such as the time of ancillary personnel and the physicians and surgeons involved. But still we are not counting the cost of educating the doctors and nurses; we are projecting their future usefulness, enhanced by this experience, to other patients. This cost figure must be balanced against four other cost figures about which we know very little: the cost to society of maintaining a cripple for years until he dies, the cost to the family of having no mother or no father for the rest of their natural lifetime, the cost to people everywhere of taking away hope, and finally the cost to medicine of a loss of public trust because treatment was refused on fiscal grounds.

Then, over and against these estimates of cost must come some sort of estimate of the dividends which can only be measured as the patient's welfare, the ultimate criterion regardless of any possible future benefits to others.

With all signals "go" and all conditions ideal for a kidney transplantation, the welfare dividend has now reached a point comparable with complex treatment for any other severe disease such as cancer, heart disease, or diabetes. Life expectancy is not normal, but a good life for some years is assured. Where signs are not so favorable, the patient's welfare dividend is less reliable and is surely of a lesser magnitude. For liver transplantation, the patient's welfare dividends are still unreliable at best, and for heart equally questionable. Further scientific study and clinical trial will enhance these results. There is the intangible in social return from any new treatment: the experience gained is applicable to other future patients. No matter how glowing this future possibility, it can never justify the individual effort unless there is a reasonable likelihood for longer life and relief of suffering for the individual patient.

Scientific Competition for the Tax Dollar

Government support enters the field of transplantation at two levels: federal support for basic science, and federal support for dialysis and transplant programs, meeting the cost of patient care.

In 1946, the National Institutes of Health initiated a broad program of support for biomedical research in universities and foundations, to increase the store of human knowledge basic to medicine. This was the peacetime extension of the work of the Office of Scientific Research and Development during World War II, which had demonstrated again—as in other wars since 1860—that government support flowing freely to civilian institutions can be very productive of new knowledge, leading to new techniques for the care of the sick. Professor Hastings, a leading biochemist of the period, stated it succinctly: "There is nothing as practical as sound basic research." He had seen and contributed to the development of modern biomedical science over a period that stretched from liver extracts to the atomic bomb and radioactive isotopes. He could attest to the practical effectiveness of the scientific method when pursued in the rigorous discipline of the laboratory.

By 1956, the program of the National Institutes of Health in grant-supported research (largely in the universities) had more than doubled; and by 1966 it was at its peak of expenditure ($1.4 billion), an expenditure made so generously as sometimes to call into serious question the ability of the scientific establishment to spend the money wisely.

Then, a reaction among the public and Congress resulted, in 1968, for the first time, in a cutback in government support for biomedical research. This negative reaction arose because of bioscience competition with the space program and the military for the tax dollar—rather obvious reasons—and for one much more subtle reason: understanding science.

The obvious relationship of the biomedical sciences' cutback to the Vietnam War needs no further elaboration here. The relationship to the space program is a little harder to rationalize. In 1968, the space program was the largest nonessential government expenditure taking funds away from public programs, including the biomedical sciences and many other social projects such as education and urban renewal. The space program had increased by leaps and launches, each successful space shot increasing the confidence of the public and its Congress in this method of expending money for engineering projects readily understood by everybody. This competition is difficult for basic biomedical science to overcome, not only because of a difference in popular priorities, but for the more subtle reason that the public and the Senate can understand engineering undertakings much more easily than they can understand primary or inductive science.

In an engineering program, the objective is known and the general methods to be used in meeting that objective are outlined. The problem is to assemble the parts and put together the details. The strategy is given. Only the tactics remain to be mastered. In the space program, the objective was to get to the moon, and means to that end, such as rocket propulsion, weightlessness, prolonged maintenance in a small artificial oxygen-enriched environment, and space navigation, were relatively well known if not totally mastered. The main thing to be done was a typical engineering problem: the assemblage of these pieces into a coordinated whole. Whatever additional research was needed to perfect the process could be accomplished during assembly. The engineer need not be a discoverer of new principles to perform such a task. Congressional committees can check on a month-to-month basis the motion toward the achievement of the moon trip.

Contrast this with a biomedical science problem such as the underlying discoveries that make possible the conquest of poliomyelitis, the perfection of open-heart surgery, or transplantation. Here, although a very general objective—better health care—is easily defined, no one knew the best means to approach any one of these objectives. Primary inductive science is not amenable to an engineering or task-force approach. Its support requires the long-range financing of institutions and people, the maintenance of many promising individuals in institutions congenial for their intellectual development, hoping that some of them turn out to be geniuses and that some of the data they uncover in their search for truth will be applicable to the problem at hand. Polio vaccine became possible because Dr. Enders conceived the growth of the virus in cultured primate kidney cells. No congressional committee or appeal to popular objectives could possibly have voted specific funds for primate kidney cultures in 1945. They had never been thought of. Open-heart surgery was developed because of the perfection of heparin and cellophane. Heparin was an anticoagulant made from animal tissues, and no one would have predicted that it was fundamental to any sort of open-heart surgery. Cellophane was invented as a commercial wrapping for packages; it turned out to be a dialysis membrane useful also for an oxygenator. As to transplantation, it is hard to know which critical discovery was most important, but certainly the description of immunosuppression with 6-mercaptopurine was basic to all that we do at this time, and this advance came about in a laboratory that was not concerned with transplantation, but was looking at certain immune processes in relation to anemia. *Basic science cannot be supported on the basis of applied objectives; it must be allowed to grow by itself.**

For the growth of transplant science to continue and for therapeutic innovation in the field to be ethical, funding must be returned by the Congress to the National Institutes of Health and its sister agencies such as the National Science Foundation, to support our biomedical scientific community.

The other feature of governmental support in transplantation is for patient care. Federal support for clinical patient care should be initiated on a national scale, identifying fifteen or twenty clinical centers in which transplantation can be financed for the patient, using federal funds to supplement local or insurance-derived support. A step has already been made in this direction with federal support of regional dialysis programs and cadaver donor procurement. The collection of third-party payments from insurance sources should be maintained. For those patients who have no insurance or who cannot afford the remainder of the bill, some agency of government (state, local, or federal) should provide for the difference. It is wrong to put this red ink into the account books of each charitable hospital which then, in turn, must increase the cost for all the other patients in that hospital.

As to welfare payments in transplantation for the indigent or underprivileged, there should be some limitation on charges to limited local welfare sources so that individual patients, particularly those from small communities, do not sop up too much of the available funds from that community. It is for a small community, trying to pay the cost of some one transplantation operation, that the social investment becomes much too great to be balanced by patient welfare dividends. When the total resource is small, these bills become excessive. Here again, the extra costs should be picked up by some larger agency of government, either state or federal. The generous donor to private charitable hospitals will always have plenty of other hospital costs to

---

* The diversion of large amounts of public funds to some categorical disease-oriented objective such as "cancer research" may actually have the effect of *diverting* support from the very institutions which would give the ultimate discoverer his start in some entirely different field such as color vision or morphogenesis.

meet. Charitable giving should not be tapped to support the care of individual patients of this type; local, state, or federal subsidy is absolutely essential.

PUBLICITY VERSUS PUBLIC INFORMATION

Since World War II there has been an increasing tendency for newspapers to publish accounts of medical developments that are still in formative stages, even before scientific publication has taken place, and in some cases before the patient is awake from the anesthesia. These articles make good headlines. Overstatement is hard to disprove. Such articles can become a source of false hope to patients and involve inaccurate publicity about the doctors who participate in surgical operations such as transplants. Publicity of this type is damaging, not only to the reputation of individual doctors but to the cause of medicine as a whole because it raises false hopes and invades privacy. Nothing is more cruel to the desperately ill than an empty promise of help. Tissue transplantation is particularly prey to this sort of maltreatment by publicity because of the unusual "human interest" associated with a healthy person giving tissue to assist an ill or dying patient.

A seeming disregard for modesty and privacy characterized some of the publicity about operations done for cardiac transplantation in 1968. The worst of these included planned television appearances by teams of surgeons in the operating room or on the steps of the hospital, and others involved the public display of scenes from the operation itself. The names of the patients or of the donors were freely given. One might like to excuse such things as a part of a fund-raising campaign for the heart society or some other worthy purpose. But they were not, and even had some fund-raising been tied to this publicity, it would have been a gross distortion of the private relationship between a patient and his doctor. One must conclude either that personal publicity, or publicity for the hospital, was sought, or that the press mishandled the more modest data they had been given. In at least one instance the publicity about heart transplantation seemed almost to be a matter of international prestige, seeking a public display when a country first entered the lists of those performing cardiac transplantations, an episode very reminiscent of the space race.

In contrast to this publicity is the need for essential public information on medical matters. Many writers for the newspapers and magazines make a consistent effort to avoid premature and spectacular acclaim and concentrate on public information. They combine good background information with accurate scientific reporting, checked before publication. Such articles are helpful to the public and to the medical profession. It is up to doctors to provide such information whenever they can be confident that it will be well handled. Writers in the mass media should overcome their tendency to claim that everything they write about is the "first," "best," or the "most." Superlatives rarely have a place in scientific reporting. They are usually inaccurate and therefore embarrassing to the doctors and researchers involved, producing a severe type of stubbornness when those same doctors and researchers are later approached for more information. If such overstatement is avoided, and the story of new medical developments told as a rational explanation of scientific history (with the significance of the new finding, and how it came about), then public information is served without the imbalance of excessive publicity. This high standard is frequently met by the finest medical writers in our public media.

Sound public information on medical matters represents a process that occurs at the interface between medical institutions and medical writers. This process is deserving of more analysis than it has received. It takes time and effort, as well as a particular skill, to nourish the interface between the doctor and the press so that the net product is elevating rather than depressing.

Conservative reporting will help assimilate science into our culture. As Dr. Conant so fervently hoped, it will bridge the gap between the scientist and the humanist; it will help to unify the "two cultures." It is to the unity of science and the humanities that public information is devoted, and this has been one justification for a book such as this.

C. P. Snow, in "The Two Cultures and the Scientific Revolution," made the point:

A good many times I have been present at gatherings of people who, by the standards of the traditional culture, are thought highly educated and who have with considerable gusto been expressing their incredulity at the illiteracy of scientists. Once or twice I have been provoked, and have asked the company how many of them could describe the Second Law of Thermodynamics. The response was cold: it was also negative. Yet I was asking something which is about the scientific equivalent of: have you read a work of Shakespeare's?

Acquired tolerance and transplant rejection may not be quite as fundamental as the Second Law of Thermodynamics or quite as important as Shakespeare. But such biology has become a part of the scientific language of our age. If articles carefully written by science reporters, or this book, bring about a better understanding of clinical science and laboratory study, they have fulfilled their mission.

Bibliography

327

N. Cadaver Laws; Donor Procurement; Donor Legality; Supply of Tissues; Definitions of Death; Transplantation Ethics
O. General Literature of Science and History of Science
P. General Texts or Review Articles on Transplantation

A. Classical Transplant Immunology

Billingham, R. E., Brent, L., and Medawar, P. B.: Actively acquired tolerance of foreign cells. Nature *172:* 603–606. 1953.

Burnet, F. M.: A modification of Jern's theory of antibody production using the concept of clonal selection. Aust. J. Sci. *20:* 67–70. 1957.

Burnet, F. M.: The Clonal Selection Theory of Acquired Immunity. Nashville, Tenn., Vanderbilt University Press, 1959 (The Abraham Flexner Lectures, 1958).

Burnet, F. M.: The Integrity of the Body: A Discussion of Modern Immunological Ideas. Harvard Books in Biology, No. 3, Cambridge, Harvard University Press, 1962.

Dunsford, I., Bowley, C. C., Hutchison, A. M., Thompson, J. S., Snager, R., and Race, R. R.: A human blood-group chimera. Brit. Med. J. *2:* 81, 1953.

Lillie, F. R.: The theory of the free-martin. Science *43:* 611–613, 1916.

Medawar, P. B.: Tests by tissue culture methods on the nature of immunity to transplanted skin. Quart. J. Micr. Sci. *89:* 239–252, 1948.

Owen, R. D.: Immunogenetic consequences of vascular anastomoses between bovine twins. Science *102:* 400–401, 1945.

B. Classical Experimental Transplantation

Bauer, K. H.: Homoiotransplantation von Epidermis bei einigen Zwillingen. Beitr. klin. Chir. *141:* 442–447. 1927.

Blandford, S. E., Jr., and Garcia, F. A.: Case report: unsuccessful homogeneous skin graft in a severe burn using identical twin as donor. Plast. Reconstr. Surg. *11:* 31–35. 1953.

Brown, J. B.: Homografting of skin: with report of success in identical twins. Surgery *1:* 558–563, 1937.

Cannon, J. A., and Longmire, W. P., Jr.: Studies of successful skin homografts in the chicken. Description of a method of grafting and its application as a technic of investigation. Ann. Surg. *135:* 60–68, 1952.

Carrel, A.: La Technique opératoire des anastomoses vasculaires et la transplantation des viscères. Lyon Méd. *98:* 859–864, 1902.

CARREL, A.: The transplantation of organs. A preliminary communication. J.A.M.A. *45:* 1645–1646, 1905.

CARREL, A.: Transplantation in mass of the kidneys. J. Exp. Med. *10:* 98–140, 1908.

CARREL, A.: Results of the transplantation of blood vessels, organs, and limbs. J.A.M.A. *51:* 1662–1667, 1908.

CARREL, A.: Remote results of the replantation of the kidney and the spleen. J. Exp. Med. *12:* 146–150, 1910.

CARREL, A., and GUTHRIE, C. C.: Successful transplantation of both kidneys from a dog into a bitch with removal of both normal kidneys from the latter. Science *23:* 394–395, 1906.

DANFORTH, C. H., and FOSTER, F.: Skin transplantation as a means of studying genetic and endocrine factors in the fowl. J. Exp. Zool. *52:* 443–470, 1928–1929.

DEMPSTER, W. J.: Kidney homotransplantation. Brit. J. Surg. *40:* 447–465, 1952–1953.

GIBSON, T., and MEDAWAR, P. B.: The fate of skin homografts in man. J. Anat. *77:* 299–310, 1942–43.

HOLMAN, E.: Protein sensitization in isoskingrafting. Is the latter of practical value? Surg. Gynec. Obstet. *38:* 100–106. 1924.

JABOULAY, M.: Greffe de reins au pli du coude par soudures artérielles et veineuses. Lyon Méd. *107:* 575–577, 1906.

MANNICK, J. A., LOCHTE, H. L., JR., ASHLEY, C. A., THOMAS, E. D., and FERREBEE, J. W.: A functioning kidney homotransplant in the dog. Surgery *46:* 821–828, 1959.

MEDAWAR, P. B.: The behavior and fate of skin autografts and skin homografts in rabbits. (A report to the War Wounds Committee of the Medical Research Council). J. Anat. *78:* 176–199, 1944.

MEDAWAR, P. B.: A second study of the behavior and fate of skin homografts in rabbits. (A report to the War Wounds Committee of the Medical Research Council). J. Anat. *79:* 157–176, 1945.

MEDAWAR, P. B.: Skin transplants. Sci. Amer. *196* (4): 62–66, 1957.

NEUHOF, H.: The Transplantation of Tissues. New York, Appleton-Century-Crofts, 1923.

PADGETT, E. C.: Is iso-skin grafting practicable? Southern Med. J. *25:* 895–900, 1932.

PRINCETEAU, M.: Greffe rénale, *in* Société d'Anatomie et de Physiologie de Bordeaux. Séance du 16 Octobre 1905. Gaz. Hebd. Sci. Méd. Bordeaux *26:* 548–549, 1905.

SIMONSEN, M.: Biological incompatibility in kidney transplantation in dogs. II. Serological investigations. Acta Path. Microbiol. Scand. *32:* 36–84, 1953.

SIMONSEN, M., DUEMANN, J., GAMMELTOFT, A., JENSEN, F., and JORGENSEN, K.: Biological incompatibility in kidney transplantation in dogs. I. Experimental and morphological investigations. Acta Path. Microbiol. Scand. *32:* 1–35, 1953.

ULLMANN, E.: Experimentelle Nierentransplantation. Wien. klin. Wschr. *15:* 281–282, 1902.

ULLMANN, E. *in* "Offizielles Protokoll der k. k. Geselschaft der Aerzte in Wien," Sitzung am 27. Juni 1902. Wien, klin. Wschr. *15:* 707–708, 1902.

UNGER, E.: Nierentransplantationen. Berl. klin. Wschr. *47:* 573–578, 1910.

WILLIAMSON, C. S.: Some observations on the length of survival and function of homogeneous kidney transplants. Preliminary report. J. Urol. *10:* 275–287, 1923.

WILLIAMSON, C. S.: Further studies on the transplantation of the kidney. J. Urol. *16:* 231–253, 1926.

C. MOLECULAR IMMUNOLOGY

CHIPMAN, D. M., and SHARON, N.: Mechanism of lysozyme action. Lysozyme is the first enzyme for which the relation between structure and function has become clear. Science *165:* 454–465, 1969.

COONS, A. H.: The beginnings of immunofluorescence. J. Immun. *87:* 499–503, 1961.

DIXON, F. J., and KUNKEL, H. G. (eds.): Advances in Immunology. New York and London, Academic Press, 1959–1969, vol. 11.

GREEN, N. M.: Electron microscopy of the immunoglobulins. Advances Immun. *11:* 1–30, 1969.

HUMPHREY, J. H., and DOURMASHKIN, R. R.: The lesions in cell membranes caused by complement. Advances Immun. *11:* 75–115, 1969.

LEDERBERG, J.: Genes and antibodies. Science *129:* 1649–1953, 1959.

PUTNAM, F. W.: Immunoglobulin structure: variability and homology. Amino acid sequences of immunoglobulins reflect evolutionary change and may explain antibody variability. Science *163:* 633–644, 1969.

TOMASI, T. B., JR.: Human immunoglobulin A. New Eng. J. Med. *279:* 1327–1330, 1968.

D. MODERN TRANSPLANT IMMUNOLOGY, IMMUNOGENETICS, AND LYMPHOCYTOLOGY

DUBERNARD, J. M., CARPENTER, C. B., BUSCH, G. J., DIETHELM, A. G., and MURRAY, J. E.: Rejection of canine renal allografts by passive transfer of sensitized serum. Surgery *64:* 752–760, 1968.

GOWANS, J. L.: Immunobiology of the small lymphocyte. Hospital Practice (March): 34–46, 1968.

GOWANS, J. L., and KNIGHT, E. J.: The route of re-circulation of lymphocytes in the rat. Proc. Roy. Soc. (Series B) *159:* 257–282, 1964.

LINDQUIST, R. R., GUTTMAN, R. D., and MERRILL, J. P.: Renal transplantation in the inbred rat. VI. Electron microscopic study of acute allograft rejection. Amer. J. Path. Transplantation *8,* 19, 169.

MOWBRAY, J. F.: Methods of suppression of immune responses, *in* Integration in Internal Medicine, Proceedings of the Ninth International Congress of Internal Medicine, A. J. Dunning (ed.). International Congress Series No. 137. Amsterdam: Excerpta Medica, 1967, pp. 106–110.

PAYNE, R., and ROLFS, M. R.: Fetomaternal leucocyte incompatibility. J. Clin. Invest. *37:* 1756–1763, 1958.

PERLMANN, P., and HOLM, G.: Cytotoxic effects of lymphoid cells *in vitro.* Advances Immun. *2:* 117–193, 1969.

RAPAPORT, F. T., and CHASE, R. M., JR.: Homograft sensitivity induction by group A streptococci. Science *145:* 407–408, 1964.

RAPAPORT, F. T., and MARKOWITZ, A. S.: Streptococcal antigens and antibodies in transplantation. Transplantation Proc. *1:* 638–644, 1969.

WILLIAMS, G. M., HUME, D. M., HUDSON, R. P., JR., MORRIS, P. J., KANO, K., and MILGROM, F.: "Hyperacute" renal-homograft rejection in man. New Eng. J. Med. *279:* 611–618, 1968.

WOODRUFF, M.F.A.: Can tolerance to homologous skin be induced in the human infant at birth? Transplantation Bull. *4:* 26–28, 1957.

WOODRUFF, M.F.A.: Evidence of adaptation in homografts of normal tissue, *in* Symposium on Biological Problems of Grafting. Springfield, Illinois: Charles C Thomas, 1959, pp. 83–90.

WOODRUFF, M.F.A., and LENNOX, B.: Reciprocal skin grafts in a pair of twins showing blood chimerism. Lancet *2:* 476–478, 1959.

WOODRUFF, M.F.A., and SIMPSON, L. O.: Induction of tolerance to skin homografts in rats by injection of cells from the prospective donor soon after birth. Brit. J. Exp. Path. *36:* 494–499, 1955.

E. DRUG IMMUNOSUPPRESSION

ALEXANDRE, G.P.J., and MURRAY, J. E.: Further studies of renal homotransplantation in dogs treated by combined Imuran therapy. Surg. Forum *13:* 64–67, 1962.

BAKER, R., GORDON, R., HUFFER, J., and MILLER, G. H., JR.: Experimental renal transplantation. I. Effect of nitrogen mustard, cortisone and splenectomy. Arch. Surg. *65:* 702–705, 1952.

BUCHANAN, J. M.: The enzymatic synthesis of the purine nucleotides. Harvey Lect. *54:* 104–130, 1958–59.

CALNE, R. Y.: The rejection of renal homograft: inhibition in dogs by 6-mercaptopurine. Lancet *1:* 417–418, 1960.

CALNE, R. Y., and MURRAY, J. E.: Inhibition of the rejection of renal homografts in dogs by BW 57–322. Surg. Forum *12:* 118–120, 1961.

DAWID, I. B., FRENCH, T. C., and BUCHANAN, J. M.: Azaserine-reactive sulfhydryl group of 2-formamido-*N*-ribosylacetamide 5-phosphate: *L*-glutamine amido-lipase (adenosine diphosphate). II. Degradation of azaserine-C^{14}-labeled enzyme. J. Biol. Chem. *238:* 2178–2185, 1963.

GOLDBERG, I. H., and RABINOWITZ, M.: Actinomycin D inhibition of deoxyribonucleic acid–dependent synthesis of ribonucleic acid. Science *136:* 315–316, 1962.

HAMILTON, L. D., FULLER, W., and REICH, E.: X-ray diffraction and molecular model building studies of the interaction of actinomycin with nucleic acids. Nature *198:* 538–540, 1963.

HEKTOEN, L.: The effect of benzene on the production of antibodies. J. Infect. Dis. *19:* 69–84, 1916.

HEKTOEN, L: The effect of toluene on the production of antibodies. J. Infect. Dis. *19:* 737–745, 1916.

HEKTOEN, L., and CORPER, H. J.: The effect of mustard gas (dichlorethyl-sulphide) on antibody formation. J. Infect. Dis. *28:* 279–285, 1921.

HITCHINGS, G. H., and ELION, G. B.: Chemical suppression of the immune response. Pharmacol. Rev. *15:* 365–405, 1963.

MONTAGUE, A.C.W., GREENBERG, J. B., DAMMIN, G. J., and MOORE, F. D.: The effect of nitrogen mustard in altering the histocompatibility rejection sequence in splenic homotransplantation in the dog. J. Surg. Res. *2:* 130–135, 1962.

MONTAGUE, A.C.W., HALGRIMSON, C., DIXON, J., DAMMIN, G. J., and MOORE, F. D.: The maintenance of prolonged reticuloendothelial system depression in dogs using nitrogen mustard. J. Surg. Res. *2:* 124–129, 1962.

PHILIPS, F. S., STERNBERG, S. S., HAMILTON, L., and CLARKE, D. A.: The toxic effects of 6-mercaptopurine and related compounds. Ann. N.Y. Acad. Sci. *60:* 283–296, 1954.

PIERCE, J. C., and VARCO, R. L.: Induction of tolerance to a canine renal homotransplant with 6-mercaptopurine. Lancet *1:* 781–782, 1962.

PIERCE, J. C., VARCO, R. L., and GOOD, R. A.: Prolonged survival of a renal homograft in a dog treated with 6-mercaptopurine. Surgery *50:* 186–195, 1961.

SCHWARTZ, R. S.: Immunosuppressive drug therapy, *in* Rapaport, F. T., and Dausset, J. (eds.), Human Transplantation. New York, Grune and Stratton, 1968, pp. 440–471.

SCHWARTZ, R., and DAMESHEK, W.: Drug-induced immunological tolerance. Nature *183:* 1682–1683, 1959.

SCHWARTZ, R., DAMESHEK, W., and DONOVAN, J.: The effects of 6-mercaptopurine on homograft reactions. J. Clin. Invest. *39:* 952–958, 1960.

SCHWARTZ, R., EISNER, A., and DAMESHEK, W.: The effect of 6-mercaptopurine on primary and secondary immune responses. J. Clin. Invest. *38:* 1394–1403, 1959.

SCHWARTZ, R., STACK, J., and DAMESHEK, W.: Effect of 6-mercaptopurine on antibody production. Proc. Soc. Exp. Biol. Med. *99:* 164–167, 1958.

UPHOFF, D. E.: Alteration of homograft reaction by A-methopterin in lethally irradiated mice treated with homologous marrow. Proc. Soc. Exp. Biol. Med. *99:* 651–653, 1958.

ZUKOSKI, C. F., LEE, H. M., and HUME, D. M.: The effect of 6-mercaptopurine on renal homograft survival in the dog. Surg. Gynec. Obstet. *112:* 707–714, 1961.

F. ANTILYMPHOCYTE PROCEDURES, ANTILYMPHOCYTE SERUM, THYMUS, SPLEEN, AND THORACIC DUCT FISTULA

BIRTCH, A. G., ORR, W. McN., and DUQUELLA, J.: Evaluation of horse anti-dog antilymphocyte globulin in the treatment of hepatic allografts. Surg. Forum *19:* 186–190, 1968.

Ciba Foundation Study Group No. 29: Antilymphocytic Serum, G.E.W. Wolstenholme and M. O'Connor (eds.). Boston, Little, Brown & Company, 1967.

DIETHELM, A. G., BUSCH, G. J., DUBERNARD, J. M., ORR, W. McN., GLASSOCK, R. J., BIRTCH, A. G., and MURRAY, J. E.: Prolongation of canine renal allografts by horse anti-dog lymphocyte serum and globulin. Ann. Surg. *169:* 569–577, 1969.

FLOERSHEIM, G. L., and RUSZKIEWICS, M.: Bone-marrow transplantation after antilymphocyte serum and lethal chemotherapy. Nature *222:* 854–857, 1969.

GESNER, B. M., and GOWANS, J. L.: The output of lymphocytes from the thoracic duct of unanesthetized mice. Brit. J. Exp. Path. *43:* 424–430, 1962.

HOWARD, R. J., DOUGHERTY, S. F., MERGANHAGEN, S. E., and SCHERP, H. W.: Enhanced prolongation of skin homografts by rabbit anti-mouse lymphocyte serum (ALS) in mice rendered tolerant to rabbit gamma globulin (RGG). Fed. Proc. *27:* 431, 1968.

LEVEY, R. H., and MEDAWAR, P. B.: Nature and mode of action of antilymphocytic antiserum. Proc. Nat. Acad. Sci. 56: 1130–1137, 1966.

LEVEY, R. H., and MEDAWAR, P. B.: The Mode of action of antilymphocytic serum, in Ciba Foundation Study Group No. 29: Antilymphocytic Serum, G.E.W. Wolstenholme and M. O'Connor (eds.). Boston, Little, Brown & Company, 1967, pp. 72–80.

McGREGOR, D. D., and GOWANS, J. L.: Survival of homografts of skin in rats depleted of lymphocytes by chronic drainage from the thoracic duct. Lancet 1: 629–632, 1964.

MEDAWAR, P. B.: Biological effects of heterologous antilymphocyte sera, in Rapaport, F. T., and Dausset, J. (eds.), Human Transplantation. New York, Grune and Stratton, 1968, pp. 501–509.

MILLER, J.F.A.P.: Immunologic function of the thymus. Lancet 2: 748–749, 1961.

MILLER, J.F.A.P.: Immunologic significance of thymus of the adult mouse. Nature 195: 1318–1319, 1962.

MILLER, J.F.A.P.: Role of the thymus in transplantation immunity. Ann. N.Y. Acad. Sci. 99: 340–354, 1962.

MITCHELL, R. M., SHEIL, A. G. R., SLAFSKY, S. F., and MURRAY, F. E.: The effect of heterologous immune serum on canine renal homografts. Transplantation 4: 323–329, 1966.

MONACO, A. P., WOOD, M. L., VANDER WERF, B. A., and RUSSELL, P. S.: Effects of antilymphocyte serum in mice, dogs, and man, in Ciba Foundation Study Group No. 29, Antilymphocytic Serum, Wolstenholme, G.E.W. and O'Connor, M. (eds.). Boston, Little, Brown & Company, 1967, pp. 111–134.

NAJARIAN, J. S., MERKE, F. K., SIMMONS, R. L., and MOORE, G. E.: Studies of anti-lymphoblast globulin in clinical organ transplantation. Brit. J. Surg. 56: 616, 1969.

SELL, S.: Antilymphocytic antibody: effects in experimental animals and problems in human use. Ann. Int. Med. 71: 177–196, 1969.

STARZL, T. E.: Heterologous antilymphocyte globulin. New Eng. J. Med. 279: 700–703, 1968.

STARZL, T. E., GROTH, C. G., TERASAKI, P. I., PUTNAM, C. W., BRETTSCHNEIDER, L., and MARCHIORO, T. L.: Heterologous antilymphocyte globulin, histoincompatibility matching and human renal homotransplantation. Surg. Gynec. Obstet. 126: 1023–1035.

STEVENS, L. E., FREEMAN, J. S., KEUTEL, H., and REEMTSMA, K.: Preparation and clinical use of antilymphocyte globulin. Amer. J. Surg. 116: 795–799, 1968.

TILNEY, N. L., and MURRAY, J. E.: The thoracic duct fistula as an adjunct to immunosuppression in human renal transplantation. Transplantation 5: 1204–1208, 1967.

TILNEY, N. L., and MURRAY, J. E.: Chronic thoracic duct fistula: operative technique and physiologic effects in man. Ann. Surg. 167: 1–8, 1968.

WILSON, D. B., and BILLINGHAM, R. E.: Lymphocytes and transplantation immunity. Advances Immunol. 7: 189–273, 1967.

WOODRUFF, M. F. A., and ANDERSON, N. F.: The effect of lymphocyte depletion by thoracic duct fistulae and administration of anti-lymphocyte serum on the survival of skin homografts. Ann. New York Acad. Sci. 120: 119, 1964.

G. MISCELLANEOUS TRANSPLANTATION IMMUNOBIOLOGY;
WHOLE BODY IRRADIATION; AGAMMAGLOBULINEMIA;
TUMORS IN IMMUNOSUPPRESSED PATIENTS

BARNES, D. W. H., CORP, M. J., LOUTIT, J. F., and NEAL, F. E.: Treatment of murine leukemia with x-rays and homologous bone marrow; preliminary communication. Brit. Med. J. 2: 626–627, 1956.

CARPENTER, C. B., and MERRILL, J. P.: Modification of renal allograft rejection in man. Arch. Int. Med. 123: 501–513, 1969.

CAVINS, J. A., SCHEER, S. C., THOMAS, E. D. and FERREBEE, J. W.: The recovery of lethally irradiated dogs given infusions of autologous leukocytes preserved at −80 C. Blood 23: 38–42, 1964.

DEALY, J. B., JR., DAMMIN, G. J., MURRAY, J. E., and MERRILL, J. P.: Total body irradiation in man: tissue patterns observed in attempts to increase the receptivity of renal homografts. Ann. N.Y. Acad. Sci. 87: 572–582, 1960.

DEODHAR, S. D., KUKLINCA, A. G., VIDT, D. G., ROBERTSON, A. L., and HAZARD, J. B.: Development of reticulum-cell sarcoma at the site of antilymphocyte globulin injection in a patient with renal transplant. New Eng. J. Med. 280: 1104–1106, 1969.

GOOD, R. A., VARCO, R. L., AUST, J. B., and ZAK, S. J.: Transplantation studies in patients with agammaglobulinemia. Ann. N.Y. Acad. Sci. 64: 882–928, 1956–1957.

HAMBURGER, J., VAYSSE, J., CROSNIER, J., AUVERT, J., LALANNE, C.–M., and HOPPER, J., JR.: Renal homotransplantation in man after radiation of the recipient. Experience with six patients since 1959. Amer. J. Med. 32: 854–857, 1962.

HAMBURGER, J., VAYSSE, J., CROSNIER, J., TUBIANA, M., LALANNE, C.–M., ANTOINE, B., AUVERT, J., SOULIER, J.–P., DORMONT, J., SALMON, CH., MAISONNET, M., and AMIEL, J.–L.: Transplantation d'un rein entre jumeaux non monozygotes après irradiation du receveur; bon fonctionnement au quatrième mois. Presse Med. 67: 1771–1775, 1959.

HECHTMAN, H. B., BLUMENSTOCK, D. A., THOMAS, E. D., and FERREBEE,

J. W.: Organ transplants in dogs after cross-circulation, chemotherapy, and radiation. Surgery 52: 810 818, 1962.

HELLSTROM, I. E., HELLSTROM, K. E., EVANS, C. A., et al.: Serum mediated protection of neoplastic cells from inhibition by lymphocytes immune to their tumor-specific antigens. Proc. Nat. Acad. Sci. U.S.A. 62: 362–368, 1969.

KRUPEY, J., GOLD, P., and FREEDMAN, S. O.: Physicochemical studies of the carcinoembryonic antigens of the human digestive system. J. Exp. Med. 128: 387–398, 1968.

KÜSS, R., LEGRAIN, M., MATHE, G., NEDEY, R., TUBIANA, M., LALANNE, C.–M., CAMEY, M., LARRIEU, M.–J., SCHWARZENBERG, L., VOURC'H, C., DESAR-MENIEN, J., MAISONNET, M., and ATALLAH, F.: Prémices d'une homo-transplantation rénale de sœur a frère non jumeaux; après nephrectomie bilatérale et irradiation du receveur. Presse Med. 68: 755–760, 1960.

KÜSS, R., LEGRAIN, M., MATHE, G., NEDEY, R., TUBIANA, M., LALANNE, C.–M., SCHWARZENBERG, L., LARRIEU, M.–J., MAISONNET, M., BASSET, F., and DELAVEAU, P.: Etude de quatre cas d'irradiation totale par le cobalt radioactif. (A des doses respectives de 250, 400 et 600 rads). Préalable à une transplantation rénale allogénique. Rev. Franc. Etud. Clin. Biol. 7: 1028–1047, 1962.

MAIN, J. M., and PREHN, R. T.: Successful skin homografts after administration of high dosage x-radiation and homologous bone marrow. J. Nat. Cancer Inst. 15: 1023–1028, 1955.

McKHANN, C. F.: Immunobiology of cancer, in Najarian, J. S., and Simmons, R. L. (eds.). Transplantation. Philadelphia, Lea and Febiger. In press.

MURRAY, J. E., MERRILL, J. P., DAMMIN, G. J., DEALY, J. B., JR., WALTER, C. W., BROOKE, M. S., and WILSON, R. E.: Study on transplantation immunity after total body irradiation: clinical and experimental investigation. Surgery 48: 272–284, 1960.

PENN, I., HAMMOND, W., BRETTSCHNEIDER, L., and STARZL, T. E.: Malignant lymphomas in transplantation patients. Transplantation Proc. 1: 106–112, 1969.

STARZL, T. E.: Discussion of Murray, J. E., Wilson, R. E., Tilney, N. L., et al.: Five years' experience in renal transplantation with immunosuppressive drugs: survival, function, complications, and the role of lymphocyte depletion by thoracic duct fistula. Ann. Surg. 168: 416, 1968.

THOMAS, E. D., COLLINS, J. A., KASAKURA, S., and FERREBEE, J. W.: Lethally irradiated dogs given infusions of fetal and adult hematopoietic tissue. Transplantation 1: 514–520, 1963.

THOMAS, E. D., KASAKURA, S., CAVINS, J. A., and FERREBEE, J. W.: Marrow transplants in lethally irradiated dogs: the effect of methotrexate on survival of the host and the homograft. Transplantation 1: 571–574, 1963.

WILSON, R. E., DEALY, J. B., JR., SADOWSKY, N. L., CORSON, J. M., and

MURRAY, J. E.: Transplantation of homologous bone marrow and skin from common multiple donors following total body irradiation. Surgery *46:* 261–276, 1959.

WILSON, R. E., HAGER, E. B., HAMPERS, C. L., et al.: Immunologic rejection of human cancer transplanted with renal allograft. New Eng. J. Med. *278:* 479–483, 1968.

WILSON, R. E., HAGER, E. B., MERRILL, J. P., CORSON, J. M., and MURRAY, J. E.: Cancer as an allograft in man: transplantation of epidermoid carcinoma of the bronchus, incidental to a cadaver renal transplant, *in* Dausset, J., Hamburger, J., and Mathé, G. (eds.). Advance in Transplantation. Copenhagen, Munksgaard, 1968, pp. 777–779.

H. KIDNEY DISEASE AND DIALYSIS

ABEL, J. J., ROWNTREE, L. G., and TURNER, B. B.: On the removal of diffusible substances from the circulating blood of living animals by dialysis. J. Pharmacol. Exp. Ther. *5:* 275–316, 1913–1914.

ADDIS, T.: Glomerular Nephritis: Diagnosis and Treatment. New York, The Macmillan Company, 1948.

BYWATERS, E.G.L.: Ischemic muscle necrosis. Crushing injury, traumatic edema, the crush syndrome, traumatic anuria, compression syndrome: a type of injury seen in air raid casualties following burial beneath debris. J.A.M.A. *124:* 1103, 1944.

ESCHBACH, J. W., JR., BARNETT, B. M. S., DALY, S., COLE, J. J., and SCRIBNER, B. H.: Hemodialysis in the home. A new approach to the treatment of chronic uremia. Ann. Intern. Med. *67:* 1149–1162, 1967.

KOLFF, W. J.: New Ways of Treating Uraemia: The Artificial Kidney, Peritoneal Lavage, Intestinal Lavage. London, W. & M. Churchill, 1947.

KOLFF, W. J., and BERK, H. TH, J.: The artificial kidney: a dialyser with a great area. Acta Med. Scand. *117:* 121–134, 1944.

McEWEN, W., and MOORE, F. D.: Attempted canine hemodialysis using celloidin membranes without anticoagulation. Total failure of method. Jour. Neg. Results *12:* 34, 1936.

MERRILL, J. P., THORN, G. W., WALTER, C. W., CALLAHAN, E. J., III, and SMITH, L. H., JR.: The use of an artificial kidney. I. Technique. J. Clin. Invest. *29:* 412, 1950.

QUINTON, W., DILLARD, D., and SCRIBNER, B. H.: Cannulation of blood vessels for prolonged hemodialysis. Trans. Amer. Soc. Artif. Intern. Organs *6:* 104–113, 1960.

SCRIBNER, B. H., BURI, R., CANER, J.E.Z., HEGSTROM, R. and BURNELL, J. M.: The treatment of chronic uremia by means of intermittent hemodialysis:

a preliminary report. Trans. Amer. Soc. Artif. Intern. Organs 6: 114–122, 1960.

I. KIDNEY TRANSPLANTATION,
INCLUDING CLINICAL RESULTS AND PSYCHIATRIC
MANAGEMENT

CARPENTER, C. B., and AUSTEN, K. F.: The early diagnosis of renal allograft rejection, in Rapaport, F. T., and Dausset, J. (eds.), Human Transplantation. New York, Grune and Stratton, 1968, pp. 151–169.

CARPENTER, C. B., and MERRILL, J. P.: Modification of renal allograft rejection in man. Arch. Intern. Med. 123: 501–513, 1969.

DAMMIN, G. J.: The pathology of human renal transplantation, in Rapaport, F. T., and Dausset, J. (eds.), Human Transplantation. New York, Grune and Stratton, 1968, pp. 170–200.

EISENDRATH, R. M., GUTTMANN, R. D., and MURRAY, J. E.: Psychologic considerations in the selection of kidney transplant donors. Surg. Gynec. Obstet. 129: 243–248, 1969.

HAMBURGER, J., and DORMONT, J.: Functional and morphologic alterations in long-term kidney transplants, in Rapaport, F. T., and Dausset, J. (eds.), Human Transplantation. New York, Grune and Stratton, 1968, pp. 201–214.

HUME, D. M., MAGEE, J. H., KAUFFMAN, H. M., JR., RITTENBURY, M. S., and PROUT, G. R., JR.: Renal homotransplantation in man in modified recipients. Ann. Surg. 158: 608–641, 1963.

KINCAID-SMITH, P.: Histological diagnosis of rejection of renal homografts in man. Lancet 2: 849–852, 1967.

KÜSS, R., LEGRAIN, M., MATHE, G., NEDEY, R., and CAMEY, M.: Homotransplantation rénale chez l'homme hors de tout lien de parenté. Survie jusqu'au dix-septième mois. Rev. Franc. Etud. Clin. Biol. 7: 1048–1066, 1962.

KÜSS, R., LEGRAIN, M., MATHE, G., NEDEY, R., and CAMEY, M.: Nouvel essai de transplantation rénale hors de tout lien de parenté, Evolution favorable au quinzième mois. Bull. Soc. Méd. Hop. Paris 114: 231–239, 1963.

MERRILL, J. P.: Medical aspects of transplantation. Transplantation Proc. 1: 162–170, 1969.

MERRILL, J. P., MURRAY, J. E., HARRISON, J. H., and GUILD, W. R.: Successful homotransplantation of the human kidney between identical twins. J.A.M.A. 160: 277–282, 1956.

MERRILL, J. P., MURRAY, J. E., HARRISON, J. H., FRIEDMAN, E. A., DEALY, J. B., JR., and DAMMIN, G. J.: Successful homotransplantation of the kidney between nonidentical twins. New Eng. J. Med. *262:* 1251–1260, 1960.

MERRILL, J. P., MURRAY, J. E., TAKACS, F. J., HAGER, E. B., WILSON, R. E., and DAMMIN, G. J.: Successful transplantation of kidney from a human cadaver. J.A.M.A. *185:* 347–353, 1963.

MURRAY, J. E., MERRILL, J. P., and HARRISON, J. H.: Kidney transplantation between seven pairs of identical twins. Ann. Surg. *148:* 343–357, 1958.

MURRAY, J. E., MERRILL, J. P., HARRISON, J. H., WILSON, R. E., and DAMMIN, G. J.: Prolonged survival of human-kidney homografts by immuno-suppressive drug therapy. New Eng. J. Med. *268:* 1315–1323, 1963.

MURRAY, J. E., WILSON, R. E., TILNEY, N. L., MERRILL, J. P., COOPER, W. C., BIRTCH, A. G., CARPENTER, C. B., DAMMIN, G. J., and HARRISON, J. H.: Five years experience in renal transplantation with immunosuppressive drugs: survival, function, complications, and the role of lymphocyte depletion by thoracic duct fistula. Ann. Surg. *168:* 416–433, 1968.

SHACKMAN, R., DEMPSTER, W. J., and WRONG, O. M.: Kidney homotransplantation in the human. Brit. J. Urol. *35:* 222–255, 1963.

STARZL, T. E., MARCHIORO, T. L., and WADDELL, W. R.: The reversal of rejection in human renal homografts with subsequent development of homograft tolerance. Surg. Gynec. Obstet. *117:* 385–395, 1963.

STARZL, T. E., PORTER, K. A., HALGRIMSON, C. G., et al.: Long-term survival after renal transplantation in humans: with special reference to histo-compatibility matching, thymectomy, homograft glomerulonephritis, heterologous ALG, and recipient malignancy. Ann. Surg. *172:* September, 1970.

TRENTIN, J. J.: The arterial obliterative lesions of human renal homografts. Ann. N.Y. Acad. Sci. *129:* 654–656, 1966.

WOODRUFF, M.F.A., ROBSON, J. S., NOLAN, B., LAMBIE, A. T., WILSON, T. I., and CLARK, J. G.: Homotransplantation of kidney in patients treated by preoperative local irradiation and postoperative administration of an antimetabolite (Imuran). Report of six cases. Lancet *2:* 675–682, 1963.

J. EXPERIMENTAL AND CLINICAL LIVER
TRANSPLANTATION

ALPER, C. A., JOHNSON, A. M., BIRTCH, A. G., and MOORE, F. D.: Human C'3: evidence for the liver as the primary site of synthesis. Science *163:* 286–288, 1969.

BENGOECHEA-GONZOLES, E., AWANE, Y., AMMONO, Y., and REEMTSMA, K.: Experimental auxiliary liver homotransplantation. Arch. Surg. *94:* 1–7, 1967.

BIRTCH, A. G., and MOORE, F. D.: Experience in liver transplantation. Transplantation Rev. 2: 90–128, 1969.

CALNE, R. Y., WHITE, H. H. O., YOFFA, D. E., BINNS, R. M., MAGINN, R. R., HERBERTSON, R. M., MILLARD, P. R., MOLINA, V. P., and DAVIS, D. R.: Prolonged survival of liver transplants in the pig. Brit. Med. J. 4: 645–648, 1967.

CALNE, R. Y., and WILLIAMS, R.: Liver transplantation in man: I. Observations on technique and organization in five cases. Brit. Med. J. 4: 535–548, 1968.

FULGINITI, V. A., SCRIBNER, R., GROTH, C. G., PUTNAM, C. W., BRETTSCHNEIDER, L., GILBERT, S., PORTER, K. A., and STARZL, T. E.: Infections in recipients of liver homografts. New Eng. J. Med. 279: 619, 1968.

GOODRICH, E. O., JR., WELCH, H. F., NELSON, J. E., BEECHER, T. S., and WELCH, C. S.: Homotransplantation of the canine liver. Surgery 39: 244–251, 1956.

GROTH, C. G.: World Statistics of Liver Transplantation. Presented at the Cambridge Liver Transplantation Conference, April 10, 1969.

Liver Transplantations (ed.). Transplantation Rev. 2: 3–170, 1969.

MARCHIORO, T. L., PORTER, K. A., DICKINSON, T. C., FARIS, T. D., and STARZL, T. E.: Physiologic requirements for auxiliary liver homotransplantation. Surg. Gynec. Obstet. 121: 17–31, 1965.

McBRIDE, R. A., WHEELER, H. B., SMITH, L. L., MOORE, F. D., and DAMMIN, G. J.: Homotransplantation of the canine liver as an orthotopic vascularized graft. Histologic and functional correlations during residence in the new host. Amer. J. Path. 41: 501–519, 1962.

MOORE, F. D.: Orthotopic homotransplantation of the liver—looking ahead after the first decade, in Read, A. E. (ed.), The Liver, Proceedings of the 19th Symposium of the Colston Research Society, Volume 19 Colston Papers. London, Butterworths, 1967, pp. 299–305.

MOORE, F. D., BIRTCH, A. G., DAGHER, F., VEITH, F., DRISHER, J. A., ORDER, S. E., SHUCGART, W. A., DAMMIN, G. J., and COUCH, N. P.: Immunosuppression and vascular insufficiency in liver transplantation. Ann. N.Y. Acad. Sci. 120: 729–738, 1964.

MOORE, F. D., SMITH, L. L., SHOEMAKER, W. C., GRUBER, U., and DAMMIN, G. J.: One-stage homotransplantation of the canine liver after total hepatectomy. Soc. Int. de Chir. XVIII Congrès, Bruxelles: Imprimerie Médicale et Scientifique, 1959, pp. 337–341.

MOORE, F. D., SMITH, L. L., VURNAP, T. K., DALLENBACK, F. D., DAMMIN, G. J., GRUBER, U. F., SHOEMAKER, W. C., STEENBURG, R. W., BALL, M. R., and BELKO, J. S.: One-stage homotransplantation of the liver following total hepatectomy in dogs. Transplantation Bull. 6: 103–107, 1959.

MOORE, F. D., WHEELER, H. B., DEMISSIANOS, H. V., SMITH, L. L., BAL-ANDURA, O., ABEL, K., GREENBERG, J. B., and DAMMIN, G. J.: Experimental whole-organ transplantation of the liver and of the spleen. Ann. Surg. *152*: 374–385, 1960.

SCHALM, L., BAX, H. R., and MANSENS, B. J.: Atrophy of the liver after occlusion of the bile ducts or portal vein and its compensatory hypertrophy of the unoccluded portion and its clinical importance. Gastroenterology *31*: 131–155, 1956.

STARZL, T. E., and PUTNAM, C. W.: Experience in Hepatic Transplantation. Philadelphia, W. B. Saunders Company, 1969.

STARZL, T. E., MARCHIORO, T. L., HUNTLEY, R. T., RIFKIND, D., ROWLANDS, D. T., JR., DICKINSON, T. C., and WADDELL, W. R.: Experimental and clinical homotransplantation of the liver. Ann. N.Y. Acad. Sci. *120*: 739–765, 1964.

STARZL, T. E., PORTER, K. A., BRETTSCHNEIDER, L., PENN, I., BELL, P., PUTNAM, C. W., and McGUIRE, R. L.: Clinical and pathologic observations after orthotopic transplantation of the human liver. Surg. Gynec. Obstet. *128*: 327–339, 1969.

STUART, F. P., TORRES, E., HESTER, W. J., DAMMIN, G. J., and MOORE, F. D.: Orthotopic autotransplantation and allotransplantation of the liver: functional and structural patterns in the dog. Ann. Surg. *165*: 325–340, 1967.

VAN DER HEYDE, M. N., and SCHALM, L.: Auxiliary liver graft without portal blood: experimental autotransplantation of left liver lobes. Brit. J. Surg. *55*: 114–118, 1968.

VON KAULLA, K. N., KAYE, H., VON KAULLA, E., MARCHIORO, T. L., and STARZL, T. E.: Changes in blood coagulation: before and after hepatectomy or transplantation in dogs and man. Arch. Surg. *92*: 71–79, 1966.

WELCH, C. S.: A note on transplantation of the whole liver in dogs. Transplantation Bull. *2*: 54, 1955.

WHEELER, H. B., BALANKURA, O., PENDOWER, J. E. H., GREENBERG, J. B., DAMMIN, G. J., and MOORE, F. D.: The homograft response to whole-organ transplantation of the canine spleen. J. Surg. Res. *2*: 114–123, 1962.

WILLIAMS, R., et al. Liver transplantation in man: III. Studies of liver function histology and immunosuppressive therapy. Brit. Med. J. *3*: 12–19, 1969.

K. Experimental and Clinical Heart Transplantation; Cardiac Surgery

Ackerman, N.J.R.W., and Barnard, C. N.: The effect of direct infusions of cortisone into the renal artery of a transplanted kidney. South African Med. J. *40:* 83–87, 1966.

Barnard, C. N.: Human cardiac transplantation: an evaluation of the first two operations performed at the Groote Schuur Hospital, Cape Town. Amer. J. Cardiol. *22:* 584–596, 1968.

Barnard, C. N.: Human heart transplantation: the diagnosis of rejection. Amer. J. Cardiol. *22:* 811–819, 1968.

Barnard, M. S., and Barnard, C. N.: Thrombo-embolic complications following total mitral valve replacement with the UCT lenticular mitral prosthesis: an experimental study. South African Med. J. *40:* 263–264, 1966.

Beck, C. S.: The development of a new blood supply to the heart by operation. Ann. Surg. *102:* 801, 1935.

Campeau, L.: Hemodynamic studies following cardiac transplantation. Circulation *40* (Suppl. 3): 55, 1969.

Crane, D., and Matthews, D.: Heart transplant operations. Diffusion of a medical innovation. Presented at the 64th Annual Meeting of the American Sociological Assoc., San Francisco, California, September 4, 1969.

DeBakey, M. E., Diethrich, E. B., Glick, G., Noon, G. P., Butler, W. T., Rossen, R. D., Liddicoat, J. E., and Brooks, D. K.: Human cardiac transplantation: clinical experience. J. Thorac. Cardiovasc. Surg. *58:* 303–317, 1969.

Effler, D. B., Favaloro, R. G., and Groves, L. K.: Coronary artery surgery utilizing saphenous vein graft techniques. J. Thorac. Cardiovasc. Surg. *59:* 147–154, 1970.

Favaloro, R. G.: Saphenous vein graft in the surgical treatment of coronary artery disease; operative technique. J. Thorac. Cardiovasc. Surg. *58:* 178, 1969.

Gibbon, J. H., Miller, B. J., and Fineberg, C.: An improved mechanical heart-lung apparatus. Med. Clin. N. Amer. *37:* 1603, 1953.

Gorlin, R., and Taylor, W. J.: Myocardial revascularization with internal mammary artery implantation: current status. J.A.M.A. *207:* 907–913, 1969.

Hallman, G. L., Leatherman, L. L., Leachman, R. D., Rochelle, D. G., Bricker, D. L., Bloodwell, R. D., and Cooley, D. A.: Function of the transplanted human heart. J. Thorac. Cardiovasc. Surg. *58:* 318–325, 1969.

JOHNSON, W. D., and LEPLEY, JR.: An aggressive surgical approach to coronary disease. J. Thorac. Cardiovasc. Surg. 59: 128–138, 1970.

LOWER, R. R.: Prospects of heart transplantation, in Mitchison, N. A., Greep, J. M., and Verschure, J.C.M.H. (eds.), Organ Transplantation Today. Amsterdam, Excerpta Medica Foundation, 1969, pp. 238–247.

LOWER, R. R., DONG, E., JR., and GLAZENER, F. S.: Electrocardiograms of dogs with heart homografts. Circulation 33: 455–460, 1966.

LOWER, R. R., DONG, E., JR., and SHUMWAY, N. E.: Long-term survival of cardiac homografts. Surgery 58: 110–119, 1965.

LOWER, R. R., STOFER, R. C., HURLEY, E. J., DONG, E., JR., COHN, R. B., and SHUMWAY, N. E.: Successful homotransplantation of the canine heart after anoxic preservation for seven hours. Amer. J. Surg. 104: 302–306, 1962.

LOWER, R. R., STOFER, R. C., and SHUMWAY, N. E.: Homovital transplantation of the heart. J. Thorac. Cardiovasc. Surg. 41: 196–204, 1961.

MANN, F. C., PRIESTLEY, J. T., MARKOWITZ, J., and YATER, W. M.: Transplantation of the intact mammalian heart. Arch. Surg. 26: 219–224, 1933.

MARCUS, E., WONG, S.N.T., and LUSADA, A. A.: Homologous heart grafts: I. Technique of interim parabiotic perfusion. II. Transplantation of the heart in dogs. Arch. Surg. 66: 179–191, 1953.

MILAM, J. D., SHIPKEY, F. H., JR., LIND, C. J., JR., et al.: Morphological findings in human cardiac allografts. Circulation 41: 519–537, 1970.

SINITSYN, N. P.: A transplantation of the Heart. (In Russian). Klin. Med. Mosk. 31 (7): 5–14, 1953.

SPENCER, F. C.: A critique of implantation of a systemic artery for myocardial revascularization. Progr. Cardiovasc. Dis. 11: 351–370, 1969.

STINSON, E. B., DONG, E., JR., SCHROEDER, J. S., and SHUMWAY, N. E.: Cardiac transplantation in man. IV. Early results. Ann. Surg. 170: 588–592, 1969.

VINEBERG, A. M.: Development of anastomosis between coronary vessels and transplanted internal mammary artery. Canad. Med. Ass. J. 55: 117, 1964.

WILLIAMS, G. M., DEPLANQUE, B., GRAHAM, W. H., and LOWER, R. R.: Participation of antibodies in acute cardiac-allograft rejection in man. New Eng. J. Med. 281: 1145–1150, 1969.

ZERBINI, E. J., and DECOURT, L. V.: Experience on three cases of human heart transplantation. Laval Med. 41: 149–154, 1970.

L. EXPERIMENTAL AND CLINICAL TRANSPLANTATION
OF OTHER ORGANS: SPLEEN, LUNGS, PANCREAS,
INTESTINE, ENDOCRINE GLANDS;
XENOTRANSPLANTATION

ALLCAN, F., HARDY, J. D., CAYLRIL, M., VARNER, J. E., MOYNIHAN, P. C., TURNER, M. D., and ANOZ, P.: Laboratory experience with intestinal transplantation and a clinical case. Gastroenterology 39: 627, 1971.

BARNES, A. D. and CROSIER, C.: Effect of antilymphocyte serum on the survival of ovary allografts in the mouse. Nature 223: 1059–1060, 1969.

BARNES, B. A., and FLAX, M. H.: Experimental pulmonary homografts in the dog. II. Modification of the homograft response by BW 57–322. Transplantation 2: 343–356, 1963.

BARNES, B. A., FLAX, M. H., BURKE, J. F., and BARR, G.: Experimental pulmonary homografts in the dog. I. Morphological studies. Transplantation 1: 351–364, 1963.

BEALL, A. C.: Human lung allotransplantation. Report of two cases. Presented at the Twenty-First Annual Meeting of the Southwestern Surgical Congress, Stateline, Nevada, June 2–5, 1969. Amer. J. Surg. (In press.)

BLUMENSTOCK, D. A.: The lung and other organs. Transplantation of the lung. Transplantation 5: 917–928, 1967.

BLUMENSTOCK, D. A., COLLINS, J. A., THOMAS, E. D., and FERREBEE, J. W.: Homotransplants of the lung in dogs. Surgery 51: 541–545, 1962.

BLUMENSTOCK, D. A., COLLINS, J. A., HECHTMAN, H. B., THOMAS, E. D., and FERREBEE, J. W.: Functioning homografts of the lung in dogs. Ann. N.Y. Acad. Sci. 99: 882–890, 1962.

BROOKS, J. R., STURGIS, S. H., and HILL, G. J.: An evaluation of endocrine tissue homotransplantation in the millipore chamber with a note on tissue adaptation to the host. Ann. N.Y. Acad. Sci. 87: 482–500, 1960.

DAMMIN, G. J., WHEELER, H. B., MONTAGUE, A. C. W., DEALY, J. B., JR., GREENBERG, J. B., and MOORE, F. D.: The splenic homograft: its course in the unmodified and modified canine recipient. Ann. N.Y. Acad. Sci. 99: 861–869, 1962.

DEROM, F., BARBIER, F., RINGOIR, S., ROLLY, G., VERSIECK, J., BERZSENYI, G., RAEMDONCK, R., and PIRET, J.: A case of lung homotransplantation in man (preliminary report). Tijdschr. Geneesk 25: 109–114, 1969.

DIXIT, S. P., and COPPOLA, E. D.: A new technique of adrenal transplantation by vascular anastomosis. J. Surg. Res. 9: 42–48, 1969.

FILATOV, A. N., and ROMANOVA, A. M.: The results of transplantation of the parathyroid glands in the treatment of parathyroprivic tetany. (In Russian). Vestn. Khir. Grekova. *102:* 14–20, 1969.

HARDY, J. D., ERASLAN, S., DALTON, M. L., JR., ALICAN, F., and TURNER, M. D.: Re-implantation and homotransplantation of the lung: laboratory studies and clinical potential. Ann. Surg. *157:* 707–717, 1963.

HARDY, J. D., WEBB, W. R., DALTON, M. L., JR., and WALKER, G. R., JR.: Lung homotransplantation in man. Report of the initial case. J.A.M.A. *186:* 1065–1074, 1963.

HUQUET, C., DALOZE, P., ORCEL, L., and SUSSMAN, D. E.: Endocrine function of pancreatic homotransplants in dogs: the effect of immunosuppressive therapy. Arch. Surg. *98:* 375–380, 1969.

IDEZUKI, Y., GOETZ, F. C., MERKEL, F. K., NAJARIAN, J. S., KELLY, W. D., and LILLEHEI, R. C.: Experiences with pancreaticoduodenal allotransplantation. Rev. Franc. Etud. Clin. Biol. *1:* 996–999, 1968.

KOHLENBRENER, R. M., SHERIDAN, J. T., STEINER, M. M., and INOUYE, T.: Fetal adrenal transplantation attempt in juvenile Addison's disease. Pediatrics *31:* 936–945, 1963.

KORNBLUM, J., and SILVERS, W. K.: Modification of the homograft response following intrasplenic exposure to ovarian or testicular tissue. Transplantation *6:* 783–786, 1968.

LEMAIRE, R., LANCE, E.–M., and CASTERMANS, A.: Survie et valeur fonctionnelle à long terme de greffons thyro-parathyroïdiens autogéniques allogéniques. C. R. Soc. Biol. *162:* 1250–1254, 1968.

LILLEHEI, R. C., and IDEZUKI, Y.: Current Status of Pancreatic Transplantation. Experimental and Clinical, in Ex. Med. Mono. "Organ Transplantation Today," Amsterdam, 1969, p. 175.

LILLEHEI, R. C., IDEZUKI, Y., KELLY, W. D., NAJARIAN, J. S., MERKEL, F. K., and GOETZ, F. C.: Transplantation of the intestine and pancreas. Transplantation Proc. *1:* 230–238, 1969.

LILLEHEI, R. C., IDEZUKI, Y., UCHIDA, H., KELLY, W. D., NAJARIAN, J. S., MERKEL, F. K., and GOETZ, F. C.: Pancreatic allotransplantation in the dog and in man. Brit. J. Surg. *56:* 699, 1969.

LILLEHEI, R. C., SIMMONS, R. L., NAJARIAN, J. S., and GOETZ, F. C.: Pancreaticoduodenal and renal allotransplantation in juvenile onset, insulin-dependent diabetes mellitus with terminal nephropathy. Surgery, 1970. (In press.)

MAGOVERN, G. J., and YATES, A. J.: Human homotransplantation of left lung: report of a case. Ann. N.Y. Acad. Sci. *120:* 710–728, 1964.

NORMAN, J. C., COVELLI, V. H., and SISE, H. S.: Transplantation of the spleen: experimental cure of hemophilia, Surgery *64:* 1–14, 1968.

NORMAN, J. C., COVELLI, V. H., and SISE, H. S.: Spleen perfusion, preservation and transplantation: new relationships to hemophilia, *in* Norman,

J. C., Folkman, J., Hardison, W. G., Rudolf, L. E., and Veith, F. J. (eds.), Organ Perfusion and Preservation. New York, Appleton-Century-Crofts, 1968, pp. 831–856.

NORMAN, J. C., COVELLI, V. H., and SISE, H. S.: Experimental Transplantation of the Spleen for Classical Hemophilia A. Rationales and Long-term Results. The Hemophiliac and His World, Proc. 5th Congr. World Fed. Hemophilia (Basel–New York, Karger) 34: 187–199, 1970.

NORMAN, J. C., LAMBILLIOTTE, J., KOJIMA, Y., and SISE, H. S.: Antihemophilic factor release by perfused liver and spleen: relationship to hemophilia. Science 158: 1060–1061, 1967.

PARRA, H., LEVY, J., and BROOKS, J. R.: Pancreatic tissue homotransplantation in the dog. Surg. Forum 18: 383–385, 1967.

PRESTON, F. W., et al: Survival of homografts of the intestine with and without immunosuppression. Surgery 60: 1203–1210, 1966.

REEMSTMA, K., LUCAS, J. F., JR., ROGERS, R. E., SCHMIDT, F. E., and DAVIS, F. H., JR.: Islet cell function of the transplanted canine pancreas. Ann. Surg. 158: 645–653, 1963.

RUSSELL, P. S., and GITTES, R. F.: Parathyroid transplants in rats. A comparison of their survival time with that of skin grafts. J. Exp. Med. 109: 571–588, 1959.

SHAFFER, C. F., and HULKA, J. F.: Ovarian transplantation—graft-host interactions in corneal encapsulated homografts. Amer. J. Obstet. Gynec. 103: 78–85, 1969.

STURGIS, S. H., and CASTELLANOS, H.: Ovarian homografts in organic filter chambers. Ann. Surg. 156: 367–374, 1962.

WHEELER, H. B., BALANKURA, O., PENDOWER, J. E. H., GREENBERG, J. B., DAMMIN, G. J., and MOORE, F. D.: The homograft response to whole-organ transplantation of the canine spleen. J. Surg. Res. 2: 114–123, 1962.

WHITE, R. J.: Experimental transplantation of the brain, in Rapaport-Dausset, Human Transplantation, New York, Grune & Stratton, 1968, pp. 692–709.

WHITE, R. J., and ALBIN, M. S.: Mechanical circulatory support of the isolated brain, in Norman, J. C., Folkman, J., Hardison, W. G., Rudolf, L. E., Veith, F. J. (eds.), Organ Perfusion and Preservation. New York, Appleton-Century-Crofts, 1968, pp. 747–757.

WHITE, R. J., ALBIN, M. S., VERDURA, J. and LOCKE, G. E.: The isolated monkey brain: Operative preparation and design of support systems. J. Neurosurg. 27: 216–225, 1967.

YONEMOTO, R. H., DUSOLD, W. D., and DELIMAN, R. M.: Homotransplantation of uterus and ovaries in dogs—a preliminary report. Amer. J. Obstet. Gynec. 104: 1143–1151, 1969.

M. Tissue Typing, Tissue Preservation and Organ Banking

Belzer, F. O., Ashby, B. S., Huang, J. S., and Dunphy, J. E.: Etiology of rising perfusion pressure in isolated organ perfusion. Ann. Surg. *168:* 382–391, 1968.

Carpenter, C. B., Glassock, R. J., Gleason, R., Corson, J. M., and Merrill, J. P.: The application of the normal lymphocyte transfer reaction to histocompatibility testing in man. J. Clin. Invest. *45:* 1452–1466, 1966.

Couch, N. P., Maginn, R. R., Middleton, M. K., Appleton, D. R., Jr., and Dmochowski, J. R.: Effects of ischemic interval and temperature on renal surface hydrogen ion concentration. Surg. Gynec. Obstet. *125:* 521–528, 1967.

Couch, N. P., and Middleton, M. K.: Effect of storage temperature on the electrometric surface hydrogen ion activity of ischemic liver and heart. Surgery *64:* 1099–1105, 1968.

Kountz, S. L., Cochrum, K. C., Perkins, H. A., Douglas, K. S., and Belzer, F. O.: Selection of allograft recipients by leukocyte and kidney cell phonotyping. Surgery. (In press.)

Morris, P. J., Kincaid-Smith, P., and Marshall, V. C.: Leukocyte antigens in cadaver transplantation. Transplantation Proc. *1:* 376–379, 1969.

Patel, R.: Some logistics in the use of tissue typing for cadaver kidney transplantation. (In press.)

Patel, R., and Terasaki, P. I.: Significance of the positive crossmatch test in kidney transplantation. New Eng. J. Med. (In press.)

Patel, R., Mickey, M. R., and Terasaki, P. I.: Serotyping for homotransplantation. XVI. Analysis of kidney transplants from unrelated donors. New Eng. J. Med. *279:* 501–506, 1968.

Rapaport, F. T., and Dausset, J.: Ranks of donor-recipient histocompatibility for human transplantation. Science *167:* 1260–1262, 1970.

Reemtsma, K., McCracken, B. H., Schlegel, J. U., Pearl, M. A., DeWitt, C. W., and Creech, O., Jr.: Reversal of early graft rejection after renal heterotransplantation in man. J.A.M.A. *187:* 691–696, 1964.

Sicular, A., and Moore, F. D.: The postmortem survival of tissues. 1. A standardized glucose oxidation procedure for assessing tissue viability after death of the host. J. Surg. Res. *1:* 9–15, 1961.

Sicular, A., and Moore, F. D.: The postmortem survival of tissues. 2. The effect of time and temperature on the survival of liver as measured by glucose oxidation rate. J. Surg. Res. *1:* 16–22, 1961.

Stickel, D. L., Seigler, H. F., Amos, D. B., Ward, F. E., Gunnells, J. C., Price, A. R., and Anderson, E. E.: Correlation of renal allografting with HL-A genotyping. Ann. Surg. *172:* 160–179, 1970.

TERASAKI, P. I.: Antibody response to homografts. II. Preliminary studies of the time of appearance of lymphoagglutinins upon homografting. Amer. Surg. 25: 896–899, 1959.

TERASAKI, P. I., MARCHIORO, T. L., STARZL, T. E.: Sero-typing of human lymphocyte antigens: preliminary trials on long term kidney homograft survivors, in Histocompatibility Testing: Report of a Conference and Workshop, Publication No. 1229. Washington, D.C., National Academy of Sciences–National Research Council, 1965, pp. 83–95.

TERASAKI, P. I., MICKEY, M. R., SINGAL, D. P., MITTAL, K. K., and PATEL, R.: Serotyping for homotransplantation. XX. Selection of recipients for cadaver donor transplants. New Eng. J. Med. 279: 1101–1103, 1968.

WILSON, R. E., HENRY, L., and MERRILL, J. P.: A model system for the study of human skin genetics. Surg. Forum 13: 68–69, 1962.

WILSON, R. E., HENRY, L., and MERRILL, J. P.: A model system for determining histocompatibility in man. J. Clin. Invest. 42: 1497–1503, 1963.

N. CADAVER LAWS; DONOR PROCUREMENT; DONOR LEGALITY; SUPPLY OF TISSUES; DEFINITIONS OF DEATH; TRANSPLANTATION ETHICS

BEECHER, H. K., et al.: A definition of irreversible coma. Report of the Ad Hoc Committee of the Harvard Medical School to examine the definition of brain death. J.A.M.A. 205: 339–340, 1968.

CALNE, R. Y., in discussion of Murray, J. E.: Organ transplantations: the practical possibilities, in Wolstenholme, G.E.W., and O'Connor, M. (eds.), Ciba Foundation Symposium, Ethics in Medical Progress. Boston, Little, Brown & Company, 1966, pp. 54–77.

COUCH, N. P.: Supply and demand in kidney and liver transplantation: a statistical survey. Transplantation 4: 507–595, 1966.

COUCH, N. P., CURRAN, W. J., and MOORE, F. D.: The use of cadaver tissues in transplantation. New Eng. J. Med. 271: 691–695, 1964.

CURRAN, W. J.: A problem of consent: kidney transplantation in minors. N.Y. Univ. Law Rev. 14: 891–898, 1959.

DRINKER, P., and SHAW, L. A.: An apparatus with a prolonged administration of artificial respiration. I. A design for adults and children. J. Clin. Invest. 7: 229, 1929.

FOX, R. C.: A sociological perspective on organ transplantation and hemodialysis, in New Dimensions in Legal and Ethical Concepts for Human Research. Ann. N.Y. Acad. Sci. 169: 426–428, 1970.

JUUL-JENSEN, P.: Criteria of Brain Death: Selection of Donors for Transplantation. Aarhus, Denmark, Munksgaard, 1970.

KETY, S. S., quoted in Shelley, E. G.: Ethical guidelines for organ transplantation. J.A.M.A. *205:* 341–342, 1968.

MOORE, F. D.: Symposium on the study of drugs in man. Part II. Biologic and medical studies in human volunteer subjects: ethics and safeguards. Clin. Pharmacol. Ther. *1:* 149–155, 1960.

MOORE, F. D.: Medical responsibility for the prolongation of life. (Presented at 117th convention of the AMA, San Francisco, June 16, 1968.) J.A.M.A. *206:* 384–386, 1969.

MOORE, F. D.: Therapeutic innovation: ethical boundaries in the initial clinical trials of new drugs and surgical procedures. Daedalus *98:* 502–522, 1969.

MOORE, F. D.: Changing minds about brains (editorial). New Eng. J. Med. *282:* 47–48, 1970.

SADLER, A. M., JR., and SADLER, B. L.: Transplantation and the law: the need for organized sensitivity. Georgetown Law J. *57:* 5–54, 1968.

SADLER, A. M., JR., SADLER, B. L., STASON, E. B., and STICKEL, D. L.: Transplantation—a case for consent. New Eng. J. Med. *280:* 862–867, 1969.

SADLER, A. M., JR., SADLER, B. L., and STASON, E. B.: Transplantation and the law: progress toward uniformity. New Eng. J. Med. *282:* 717–723, 1970.

O. GENERAL LITERATURE OF SCIENCE AND HISTORY OF SCIENCE

HOWELL, W. H.: Heparin, an anticoagulant: preliminary communication. Amer. J. Physiol. *63:* 434–435, 1922.

HOWELL, W. H.: The purification of heparin and its chemical and physiological reactions. Bull. Johns Hopkins Hosp. *42:* 199–206, 1928.

HOWELL, W. H., and HOLT, E.: Two new factors in blood coagulation: heparin and pro-antithrombin. Amer. J. Physiol. *47:* 328–341, 1918.

MCLEAN, J.: The thromboblastic action of cephalin. Amer. J. Physiol. *41:* 250–257, 1916.

MCLEAN, J.: The discovery of heparin. Circulation *19:* 75–78, 1959.

MASON, H. L., MYERS, C. S., and KENDALL, E. C.: The chemistry of crystalline substances isolated from the suprarenal gland. J. Biol. Chem. *114:* 613–631, 1936.

MATSON, D. D.: A new operation for the treatment of communicating hydrocephalus: report of a case secondary to generalized meningitis. J. Neurosurg. *6:* 238–247, 1949.

MOORE, F. D.: New problems for surgery. Science *144:* 388–392, 1964.

SNOW, C. P.: The Two Cultures and the Scientific Revolution. Cambridge, Cambridge University Press, 1959 (The Rede Lecture, 1959).

SWAZEY, J. P., and Fox, R. C.: The clinical moratorium: a case study of mitral valve surgery, *in* Experimentation with Human Subjects, Freund P. (Ed.), New York, Braziller, 1970.

WATSON, J. D.: The Double Helix. A Personal Account of the Discovery of the Structure of DNA. New York, Atheneum, 1968.

P. GENERAL TEXTS OR REVIEW ARTICLES ON TRANSPLANTATION

CALNE, R.: A Gift of Life. Aylesbury, M.T.P. Publishing Co., Ltd., 1970.

EWING, M.: The transplantation argument. J. Roy. Coll. Surg. Edin. *14:* 67–82, 1969.

MOORE, F. D.: Give and Take, the Biology of Tissue Transplantation. Garden City, New York. Doubleday and Company, Inc., 1965.

MOORE, F. D., BURCH, G. E., HARKEN, D. E., Swan, H. J. C., MURRAY, J. E., and LILLIHEI, C. W.: Cardiac and other organ transplantation in the setting of transplant science as a national effort (Amer. Coll. Cardiol. Conference in Bethesda, September, 1968). J.A.M.A. *206:* 2489–2500, 1968.

RAPAPORT, F. T., and DAUSSET, J. (eds.): Human Transplantation. New York, Grune and Stratton, 1968.

SCHWARTZ, R. S.: Therapeutic strategy in clinical immunology. New Eng. J. Med. *280:* 367–374, 1969.

STARZL, T. E.: Experience in Renal Transplantation. Philadelphia, W. B. Saunders Company, 1964.

STARZL, T. E., BRETTSCHNEIDER, L., MARTIN, A. J., JR., GROTH, C. G., BLANCHARD, H., SMITH, G. V., and PENN, I.: Organ transplantation, past and present. Surg. Clin. N. Amer. *48:* 817–838, 1968.

WOODRUFF, M.F.A.: The transplantation of Tissues and Organs. Springfield, Ill., Charles C Thomas, 1960.

Index

About the Author

Dr. Francis D. Moore is Surgeon-in-Chief at Peter Bent Brigham Hospital, Boston, and Moseley Professor of Surgery at the Harvard Medical School. A native of Evanston, Illinois, he received his undergraduate and medical degrees at Harvard.

In assuming the Moseley Professorship in 1948, Dr. Moore succeeded the late Harvey Cushing and Elliott Cutler. Dr. Moore's department at Harvard has actively pursued several subjects in surgical research, particularly the application of radioactive isotopes, metabolic care of critically ill surgical patients, the study and treatment of cancer, and pioneering developments in transplantation. It was in Dr. Moore's department that Dr. Hume carried out the first homotransplants between unrelated individuals described in this book; and Dr. Murray did the first identical twin transplant; and eight years later (with Dr. Calne), the first kidney transplant in man under drug immunosuppression.

Dr. Moore has been Chairman of the Surgery Study Section, United States Public Health Service (1956–59); Chairman, Committee on Pre- and Post-operative Care, American College of Surgeons (1954–60); Chairman, Advisory Committee on Metabolism of Trauma, Office of the Surgeon General of the United States Army; President, Society of University Surgeons

(1958); President, American Surgical Association (1971); Lecturer, Harvey Society (1956); Biosciences Review Board for NASA (1970); and Visiting Professor of Surgery at universities in the United States and abroad. He has been the recipient of honorary degrees from the Universities of Glasgow and of Ireland, and Suffolk University.

He has published numerous articles in medical journals, and the following books:

Carcinoma of the Breast. The Study and Treatment of the Patient. Boston, Little, Brown & Co., 1956 (with Andrew G. Jessiman).

Metabolic Care of the Surgical Patient. Philadelphia, W. B. Saunders Co., 1959.

The Body Cell Mass. Philadelphia, W. B. Saunders Co., 1963.

Give and Take. New York, Doubleday, 1965.

Post-Traumatic Pulmonary Insufficiency. Philadelphia, W. B. Saunders Co., 1969.